One boy
and his Kop

Peter Etherington

signature

ACKNOWLEDGEMENTS

To get round to thanking everybody involved in the publication of this book would be an impossible task but I'll try anyway. My sincere apologies go to anybody I leave out. First of all Alan Edge: Edgey's support, advice and encouragement has been invaluable. He is my mentor, my guru, my Svengali, my inspiration but most of all a great mate. I'm nearly crying now! I thank Tim Kelly for the artwork and the many hours he has spent on my behalf: nice one Tim. I thank my three wonderful children, Steven, Evelyn and Angela for putting up with this contumelious, cranky, crotchety, cantankerous (and other words beginning with C) old get! Sorry kids, you know I love you all really! Brian Pead's "A Complete History of Liverpool Football Club" was an invaluable source of reference when the old memory cells were getting a bit befuddled. Thanks Brian. Thanks also to the editors of the various LFC websites and fanzines who have supported me for the past eighteen months. To the good people of the Red All Over The Land website Forum: Your support and encouragement gave me the boot up the bum to finally get round to actually writing the book that had been in my head for many years. Those same good people were also the catalyst for me at last being able to come to terms with and talk about the terrible events at Hillsborough. Finally there is one person without whom none of this, not just the book, everything, would have been impossible - my dear, beautiful Mam. God bless you Lily.

First published 2001 by the author, Peter Etherington, in association with Countyvise Limited.

Copyright © 2001 Peter Etherington

The right of Peter Etherington to be identified as the author of this work has been asserted by him in accordance with the Copyright, Design and Patents Act 1988.

British Library Cataloguing in Publication Data.
A Catalogue record for this book is available from the British Library.

ISBN 1 901231 27 5

Countyvise Limited, 14 Appin Road, Birkenhead CH41 9HH
Printed by Birkenhead Press Limited, 14 Appin Road, Birkenhead CH41 9HH

This book is dedicated to the memory of all those who ever went to play in or watch a football match and never came back.
God bless you all.
You'll never walk alone.

CONTENTS

FOREWORD

By Alan Edge (author of "Faith of our Fathers").

It was just another run-of-the-mill Saturday evening in April 1958. Yet it would come to represent a pivotal moment in my footballing development. I was fast approaching 7 years of age, that stage of life when most of my mates had already perfected the art of transforming dog-ends salvaged from the pavements into immaculate Peter Stuyvesent Kingsize. I meantime stuck – literally at times – to more innocent pursuits. Penny Arrowbars were my bag. Less addictive perhaps, but with infinitely higher tar content. As I sauntered into our back-kitchen chewing like there was no tomorrow, I spied that night's Footy Echo on the table. Back then it boasted a magnificent pink broadsheet format, later to be mimicked by the Financial Times, though they, of course, were never to have Ric George writing for them. I fingered my way voraciously through the results page to glean how the boys had fared; my heroes in red and white.

Disaster.

A nightmare by our goalkeeper; a 5-1 drubbing by our local Merseyside rivals. It was a result that would be scorched for eternity into my psyche. I gritted what was left of my toffee-welded teeth and hurled my remaining Arrowbars to the linoed floor in a fit of pique that only seven year olds or manic Evertonians can carry off. The time had arrived to question everything about the team I adored. The attack, the defence, the goalie, the reserve team kit man. Above all, to question the very management of the team itself. I mean what on earth was Mr Bugler playing at? What type of Footy teacher was he - sticking Wacker Williams in goal against St Lizzies? I ask you – Wacker Williams!?! Christ, Wacker had enough problems trying to catch a cold let alone a muddy ball on Orrell Pleasure Fields. I was livid. Angry even! Enough, indeed, to make me change my allegiances forever. That night Our Lady's Queen of the Mersey was ditched from my affections for a slightly more established local side in red and white. Suffice to say from that day on I have never looked back or so much as even glanced at another penny Arrowbar.

5

As chance would have it an avid supporter of St Lizzies that afternoon was none other than the author of the book you are about to read. Peter Etherington was just four years old at the time. A tiny, beady-eyed, beaming figure in the watching crowd who, between swigs of lager, would lead the St Lizzies army in song. Deafening choruses of *'Two, four, six, eight, who do we appreciate? LIZZIES!" "One, two, three and a quarter, who d'you think we're gonna slaughter? OUR LADY'S!'* and other memorable ditties were said to have rang around the Pleasure's vast acres in those days with the young Evo their source. Forty odd years later and little has changed. The same guy still beams, swigs lager and sings ditties, though Orrell Pleasures has long been replaced as the scene of his infectiousness by his beloved shrine of Anfield. And, of course, he's not quite so tiny any more.

There are footy fans and there are footy fans. Then there are the Peter Evos of this world. In an age of ever-mounting plasticity it is reassuring to know there is still room left on the mantelpiece for the likes of Peter Evo. His is a breed to be savoured by those who truly hold dear the game of the people. If anyone who has met him were ever asked to nominate a single fan who epitomised the spirit of football and our great club then Evo would be near the head of the list. Loyal, loud and true; steeped in redness from Shanks through to Houllier, this is a fellow who could look the Almighty himself in the eye and proclaim his loyalty to the Reds – if only he could keep those beady eyes of his open for long enough that is. Cut down on the Stella Pete lad.

For Peter, following his beloved Reds is not the result of any conscious decision. With Peter, there is no element of fashionability or posturing - no selection process. Quite simply, he IS – as expressed so fittingly by the sentiment of the song we all know and love – A LIVERPUDLIAN. Always was and always will be.

As some of you will already know, Peter Evo is a product of the Red All Over The Land website forum/fanzine school of writing. Along with the likes of Peter Carter, Allan Duggan, Dave Kirby, Chris Murphy, and others, he has been responsible for a truly outstanding body of writing and poetry that has emerged these past few years. In most if not all instances they are simply ordinary football fans who, hitherto, had scarcely written a postcard between them. It has been the privilege of many of us to be exposed to such burgeoning writing talent and it is to be hoped that Peter's book signifies just the start of the publication of their collective work. Certainly, there is no doubt all of it merits such exposure.

For the time being, however, we shall just have to content ourselves with Evo. And how fortunate we must count ourselves that this is the case. For, with *One Boy and his Kop*, Peter has penned a truly delightful tale. Poignant in parts yet often hilariously funny; impassioned yet chirpy, Peter's disarming and quite remarkable frankness allows us to share – warts and all – in his early life as a Liverpudlian. From his childhood in Bootle to his emigration to Skem we are invited to be there with him throughout it all. Reading it, I was reminded at times of *Distant Voices, Still Lives,* that beautiful Terence Davies's film of a young working class boy growing up in Liverpool. The vividness of Peter's writing offers us *that* sort of cinematic presence. Indeed, on occasions it can make us feel almost intrusive as we tune in on family conversations some thirty or forty years old, yet frozen in time for our digestion by Peter's crafting. Sometimes grave, yet never mawkish or lacking the writer's humorous knack of lifting the spirits, *One Boy and his Kop* is Peter's labour of love. I would like to say the book is a hoot from start to finish. And so it is. But it is so much more than that. Above anything else it is the tale of somebody who *is* what he writes about. And these days that is something rare indeed. A thing to be cherished by every football fan. Read and enjoy.

PREFACE

29th August 1953: Bootle Hospital Maternity Ward: 7:30 p.m.

"Yer late! Where've yer been?"

"Sorry Lily. The train got delayed comin' back from Bolton."

"Yer a lyin' get John! Yer've been in the Toll Bar 'avin' a bevy with Jimmy Boyle 'aven' yer?"

"Just a couple Lil."

"'Ow'd they get on anyway?"

"We got beat two nil. Rubbish we were. I think we'll go down this season."

"Wasn't worth goin' then was it?"

"Course it was worth goin'. Don't be stupid Lil."

"Anyway, yer can get back on the ale now. I won't be 'avin the baby tonight. I'm in slow labour. They reckon I'll 'ave it tomorrow mornin'."

"Slow? I don't think the little sod wants to come out!"

"Yeah, it's all right for you. You 'aven' been the one lyin' 'ere for two bloody days!"

"Well you were the one who said yer waters had broke."

"I thought they 'ad if yer know what I mean. Go on then. Get back to yer mates in the Toll Bar."

"Okay Lil, if you insist."

"Don't be bloody funny. Just make sure yer 'ere first thing tomorrow. If yer see Cissy Mulhall in there ask 'er to lend us five bob 'til next week."

"Sod that! I'm not going anywhere near that owld cow! I'll ask Charlie Clarke. I'll gerrit for nothin' off 'im. I'll just wait 'til 'e's pissed then tap 'im. 'E never remembers a thing once 'e's 'ad a few Mackies."

"In that case then ask 'im for ten bob."

"Okay Lil. See ya."

The following day:

Johnny Evo sat outside the delivery room and heard his newly born baby's first cry at ten past seven in the evening, the new addition to the family keeping up the great Evo tradition of unpunctuality. He hoped for a boy. The real dilemma though was whether to call him Billy or Bob. If he went for Billy he'd feel tight on Bob Paisley. Similarly if he went for Bob he would be showing disloyalty to Billy Liddell. He came up with the solution; he'd call his son (because surely it was a boy, he and Lily already had a girl) William Robert, or should he call him Robert William? Toss a coin Evo! The coin came down in Liddell's favour. William Robert Etherington it was to be then. A name that would surely strike fear into the hearts of defenders the length and breadth of the country in twenty years time. Yes, Billy Evo was going to be one of Liverpool's greatest ever players!

John's reverie was rudely interrupted by the crude bark of Nurse Hatchetface, Bootle's hardest midwife.

"You've got a son Mr. Etherington! Come in and see to your wife."

"John, John, it's a boy!" Lily managed to cry through her exhaustion.

"Yeah, I can see that Lily. A very well built boy too I see. Just like 'is owld fella! William Robert Etherington. Gorra great ring to it don't yer think Lil?"

"Er...no! Why William Robert?"

"Yer know, after Liddell and Paisley."

"Who?"

"Oh never mind."

"No chance John. You 'ad the choice with our Pauline. I'm 'avin' the choice with this little one."

"Well what are we gonna call 'im?"

"Peter."

"But there's nobody called Peter plays for Liverpool!"

"Does it matter?"

"Yeah!"

"Why?"

"Forget it. Peter it is then. 'E's gonna play for Liverpool though."

"Not if 'e takes after you! Remember when I came and watched yer playin' for that Navy team? You were rubbish. Jimmy Greenlea said yer were the worst player 'e'd ever seen."

"Oh aye yeah! What does 'e know about football? 'E's a bloody Evertonian! Anyway, who does 'e think 'e is - Stanley Matthews?"

"Who?"

"Yer really 'aven't gorra clue 'ave yer Lily?"

"No."

"Well even if 'e doesn't play for Liverpool 'e's definitely gonna be a Red. No mixes in our family Lil. We're all Red through and through. No blues in the Evo's! Me great-granddad stood on the Kop at our first ever match yer know."

"Oh did 'e? I'd be interested if I knew what the Kop was. Is it where all the Bobbies stand?" Lily's barely stifled yawn revealed the extent of her exhaustion. She just wanted to be alone now with her new son and get some sleep.

"Okay Lil, I'm goin' now."

"Go straight 'ome. Me Ma'll get a cob on if she's lookin' after our Pauline too long. She's goin' to Harland's tonight."

"Okay Lily. Will do. Ta ra luv."

Lily was asleep with little Peter in her arms before John got his last word out.

John thought about it for all of two seconds. Martha would be okay looking after Pauline. The Toll Bar was just a cock stride from the hospital. All his mates would be in there. He'd get some stick from the Evertonians, especially Jimmy Greenlea, after yesterday's results. Everton had beaten Oldham 3-1 but they were only in the Second Division. Liverpool were in the First Division and were not only the best team on Merseyside but also in the world! Anyway, he'd have Jimmy Boyle to back him up. The Toll Bar it was then. Gorra wet the baby's 'ead 'aven' yer? Nice choice Evo!

"Yer goin' down this season Evo!" Jimmy Greenlea's "welcome" was all that John could have expected from his blue brother-in-law.

"No we're not. We're gonna win the League."

"I'll show me arse from the top of Bootle Town 'All if yer do!"

"Yeah, who'd wanna look at your big fat arse?"

"We're gonna come up too Evo. It'll be nice passin' yer!"

John couldn't see Everton getting promotion but in his heart of hearts he knew it was a distinct possibility that his beloved Reds would go down. They stared the relegation trap door firmly in the face last season, eventually escaping by finishing just four places above the drop slot.

"We're gonna win the Cup too!"

"Piss off Johnny. The friggin' Liver Birds'll fly away from the Liver Buildings if youse ever win the Cup!"

John had no answer to this, as after sixty-one years of trying Liverpool had failed to lift the FA Cup. Arsenal had broken John's heart at Wembley three years earlier and it still hurt.

"Come on Johnny. Take no notice of the Evertonian shitehawk," Jimmy Boyle interjected, "'Ee arr, 'ave a bevy to wet the baby's 'ead. What're yer 'avin'?"

"Rum and black Jimmy. Friggin' Twinkletoes gets on me nerves!" It was a cause of great consternation to John that his sister Eileen had married an Evertonian. Jimmy Greenlea was not his favourite person for that fact alone! On the other hand it filled him with deep joy that another sister, Rosie, had married Jimmy Boyle, a staunch Red.

Ten rum and blacks and half-a-dozen bottles of Manns Brown later and John was well and truly bladdered! Derby Road resounded to John's considerably loud voice celebrating the birth of another Red. The fact this little one was also his son was a bonus.

"Look Jimmy look! My Lily's in there," shouted John pointing at the massive building that was Bootle Hospital.

"I know John, I know. Come on mate, let's get yer 'ome. Martha's gonna friggin' kill yer."

"Ah, I'm not arsed Jimmy. I love Lily yer know Jimmy. I do yer know, I love 'er. I love the friggin' bones of 'er. I just wish they were buried underground. Ha ha ha! Nah, I'm only messin'. I do, I love 'er. I love you too Jimmy. Yer my favourite brother-in-law yer know an' I friggin' love yer! What the bloody 'ell was our Eileen doin' marryin' a friggin' Evertonian? I mean Jimmy's all right an' all that but 'e's a friggin' Evertonian for Christ's sake!"

"Yeah, come on John, 'urry up will yer lad. I wanna get 'ome before the milk."

"Why, d'yer think the milkman's knockin' a slice off our Rosie? Eh, d'yer think she's gettin' a bit more than the cream? Ha ha ha!"

"Come on Johnny will yer. Yer a friggin' nuisance when yer drunk!"

"Look Jimmy, look. My little Peter's in there as well! Me lovely little son. Another Red in the family Jimmy."

"'Ow come yer called 'im Peter? There's nobody called Peter plays for us."

"I know Jimmy. That's what I told my Lily but she wasn't 'avin' any of it. I chose Pauline's name so lovely Lily wanted to pick this one. I mean, I love 'er an' all that Jimmy but she's friggin' thick yer know! She doesn't even know who Stanley Matthews is! If she 'ad a friggin' brain she'd still be a 'alf wit!"

"Yeah, I know John. Rosie's the same. If brains were dynamite she wouldn't 'ave enough to blow her friggin' 'at off!"

"Ha ha ha! You're funny you Jimmy. I love you. Come on Jimmy let's 'ave a song."

John and Jimmy stood arm in arm as their raucous tones echoed offBootle Hospital's walls and reverberated all round Derby Road.

"After the ball was centred, after the whistle blew
Liddell got excited and up the wing he flew.
He crossed the ball to Stubbins. Stubbins scored a goal
And left the poor old goalie lyin' on 'is 'ole.
They laid 'im on a stretcher. They laid 'im on a bed.
They rubbed 'is belly with cast-iron jelly and this is what they
said.
Liverpool's at the top of the League, 'oldin' up the Cup.
Everton's at the bottom shoutin', "Leg us up!"

"Ah, great that Jimmy. I love singin' with you!"
"Yeah, well Perry Como and Donald Peers 'ave got nothin' to worry about with us two 'ave they?"
"Ah bollocks to them Jimmy. I've got a son. 'E's a Red. Once a Red, always a Red!"

CHAPTER ONE

THE MATCH

1964 was a boom era for Merseyside. Work was plentiful with a thriving dock and car industry. If the music of The Beatles, Gerry and the Pacemakers, The Merseybeats and The Fourmost could be said to be the lifeblood of Liverpool, then football was surely it's beating heart.

"Evo, d'yer wanna come the match with us," Smudge said.
Of course I wanted to go the match with them, they had talked about nothing else for weeks. *They* were: Smudge, Timmy and Pilch.
I'd heard all the stories from them about the Kop: the singing, the noise and the atmosphere. The problem would be getting the money off my Mam.
"Yeah, 'ow much do I need," I replied.
" A shillin' to get in, fourpence on the bus there, fourpence on the bus back and fourpence for a programme. So two bob altogether."
"Right, I'll ask me Mam. What time are we goin'?"
"Twelve o'clock, we'll 'ave to get there early, there's always loads of queues." Smudge had done this before.

Two shillings was a king's ransom to my Mam. I had two brothers and two sisters, so Mam didn't have a lot of money to spare, even though she did have two jobs; one in Chung's restaurant, the other in Reid's tin works, and Dad worked every hour he could in Mersey Cables. I was going to have to earn the money. My ten-year old brain was ticking over with thoughts of how to get the Holy Grail *without* having to earn it.

"Mam, can I have two bob to go the match," I screeched in my boyish excitement.
"Shush, your Dad's in bed, 'e's been on nights."
"Oh please Mam, go on, if Liverpool win today they win the league."
I might as well have been telling my Mam that I needed the money to get a rocket to the Moon.
"Yer'll have to earn it," she said.
What a surprise!
"What d'yer want me to do?"

"Go to 'Arry Wilson's pawnshop on Marsh Lane and get yer Dad's suit out, before 'e realises it was in there in the first place."
Harry Wilson's pawnshop was a dark, dank place. I hated going into there, the smell was awful and Harry used to frighten me rigid. I was going to have to try to get out of this one.
"Ah eh Mam, I 'ate goin' there, can't I do something else."
"No, 'e needs the suit for tonight. We're goin' out. He won on the 'orses yesterday, so we're going to the Corry first, *in the best side*, and then to Harland's."
Nothing else for it; the pawnshop it was going to have to be.
"Okay, give me the bus fare."
"Eh, less of your cheek, yer getting' two bob. Yer getting' too 'ardfaced getting' you. Yer'll have to walk there and back."
This was getting worse. A twenty-minute walk into the toughest area of Bootle, where gangs would take money off kids and beat them up for not having enough money on them! Then, encounter the most frightening, bad-tempered man in the world, a twenty-minute walk back, with just one hour to spare.

Mam gave me the two shillings, plus a pound to get the suit out of hock. One pound and two shillings; what I could have done with all that money. If Mam had given that money to my brother, John, he would have been off with it, and away for a week.

I put the money in my sock. I hoped this would foil the thieving vagabonds of Marsh Lane. I would still have got beaten up, but at least I would have my match money.

Surprisingly, for a Saturday morning, Marsh Lane was strangely quiet. No gangs; the Bootle Bucks were nowhere in sight! This was going too well. I prayed it would stay that way!

It was a clear, bright, sunny April day, but not a shaft of natural light entered the dark portals of Harry Wilson's pawnshop. I entered the pawnshop with all the trepidation of a man going to the electric chair. Harry was behind the counter, with a smile on his face! No it couldn't have been a smile; he must have had wind. Either that or a funeral procession had just passed.
"'Ello lad, 'ow's your Mam?"

"Err-err f-fine Mister Wilson," I stammered, more frightened than I had ever been when he was bad-tempered.
"'Ow about yer Dad?"
"Er, yeah, s-smashing Mister Wilson."
"Big day today lad, Liverpool are gonna win the League."
"Er, yeah I know Mister Wilson, I'm goin' with me mates," I said with growing confidence in my new friend.
"Yeah, so am I."
My heart sank. The prospect of meeting Harry at the match was too awful to contemplate, even in his newfound good mood. The pawn ticket and a pound were exchanged for Dad's suit: if only he knew.
I was out of the shop quicker than a scared rabbit, with Harry's voice trailing behind me, "Ta ra lad, tell yer Mam and Dad I was asking about them. I might see you at the match."
"Not if I see you first," I muttered under my breath.

A quick glance around to make sure there were no gangs. The Bootle Bucks must have been at the Odeon getting easy pickings from the Saturday morning picture goers. Then up Marsh Lane, still in scared rabbit mode. The twenty-minute walk became a ten-minute run. My little legs couldn't carry me fast enough as I legged it all the way home.

I arrived home in one piece, physically if not mentally, deposited the suit on the couch and was halfway out of the door before my Mam grabbed me back by the shirt.
"What time will you be 'ome?" Mam asked.
"I dunno, about six o'clock I think Mam."
"Well make sure you are. Me and your Dad are goin' out at six o'clock. Yer lookin' after John, Mark and Collette. Our Pauline's gone to yer Granny Martha's."
"Okay Mam. Harry Wilson said to tell yer he was asking about you and Dad."
"What, that miserable old sod?"

Getting off the bus at Spellow Lane and walking up to Anfield I couldn't believe what I was seeing. There were people everywhere!
"Fab, isn't it?" Smudge said, "Wait 'til we get in the ground, it's even better."

17

We queued for two hours, but I didn't mind. The sight of people going in and out of the Albert pub, the smell of onions, the sound of people in the ground singing Beatles songs, the size of the big police horses, all left me completely enthralled.
Finally I got to the front of the queue. A shilling handed over, a push and a click of the turnstile. I had entered the Promised Land. It was a world I had heard about but not yet seen.

My first sighting of fifty thousand people all gathered together: twenty eight thousand of them on a swaying, singing, bouncing Spion Kop, is something I will remember forever.
"You'll never walk alone," sang the masses in a moving, colourful display of togetherness.

I was in the Boy's Pen, which was a steel cage structure built high into a corner of the Kop. It afforded a marvellous view of the people below and also of the football on the pitch. It would have been easier to escape from Colditz than to climb the fence that separated us from the Kop, where the admission price was three shillings and sixpence, but there were streams of foolhardy lads attempting it.
"Come on Timmy, let's bunk in the Kop," Pilch said.
"Alright Pilch, let's go." Timmy had been waiting for somebody else to suggest it.
"They do that every match and always end up gettin' thrown out by the coppers," sighed Smudge, who knew what he was talking about.

Pilch and Timmy were the same age as myself. Smudge was two years older than we were. He was twelve and in big school. I looked up to him, as, even at my tender age, I realised he had to grow up very quickly. His Dad had died in a gas explosion at Harland and Wolff shipyard a year earlier.

"Liverpool, Liverpool, Liverpool." "She loves you, yeah, yeah, yeah." How could twenty eight thousand people all sing in unison? Liverpool won the match five-nil and Arsenal were lucky to get nil!
"Ee-aye-addio, we've won the league." "Shankly, Shankly, Shankly," sang my fifty thousand comrades.

I arrived home just before the appointed hour of six o'clock.
"Alright son, I believe yer've been to the match," said Dad.

"Yeah Dad, it was brilliant."
"Good lad, yer a Red now. Once a Red always a Red."
My Dad and Harry Wilson both in a good mood on the same day!
Something must have been drifting in the air from the Mersey.
"'Ere's two bob. Get yerself some lemonade and sweets.Yer mates
can come in as long as yer behave yourselves."
Definitely something in the air!

Smudge came around at about seven o'clock, followed an hour or so
later by Pilch and Timmy.
"Fantastic game wasn't it?" I said to Pilch.
"Don't know, the coppers threw us out," said Pilch.
"Yeah, before the kick-off," moaned Timmy.
Smudge smiled.

What a perfect day! Liverpool had won the League, money off my
Dad and I'd managed to avoid Harry at the match! Life couldn't get
any better.

My mates left at about eleven o'clock. Pilch and Timmy were still
moaning. I fell asleep shortly after; my belly full of crisps, cream
soda and sweets.

Harry threw a big red flag over a police horse. Pilch and Timmy
jumped on it and rode off along Walton Breck Road. Smudge and me
went in to the Albert where we met my Mam and Dad. Along with
about two hundred other people we sang, laughed, danced and drank
copious amounts of beer until we all fell down in a drunken heap.

I was woken from this most lucid of dreams by the sound of Mam and
Dad crashing up the garden path. The strains of "Ee-aye-addio, we've
won the league" filled the cool, clear, spring night air.
"Lily, next time yer pawn me suit make sure yer take the ticket off
before puttin' it back in me wardrobe," laughed Dad.
"Come on John, let's go to bed," chuckled Mam.

CHAPTER TWO

SEASON OF FIRSTS

"Evo, look, the fixtures are out," shouted Smudge excitedly, clutching the Liverpool Echo. It was a blazing hot July day and the furthest thoughts from our minds should have been football. But this was us! "We play Arsenal at 'ome first game, Leeds away then Blackburn away. Are yer comin' to Blackburn with us?"

Blackburn? Blackburn was miles away!

"I don't know. 'Ow long will it take us to get there?"

"Only abarr an hour. We'll go on the Ribble coach."

"'Ow much will I need?

"About ten bob."

That was a lot of trips to Harry Wilson's!

"Yeah, okay. I'll start savin' up now. What date is it on?"

"August the twenty-ninth. That's the day before yer birthday isn't Evo?"

"Yeah, so I should be all right. I might get some birthday money early."

I wouldn't get much off my Mam, I knew that. She'd do her best but she was nearly always skint anyway. My Aunts, Ann and Maureen, and my Grannies, Martha and Rose Ann would probably see me all right though.

I worked tirelessly throughout that Summer, doing all manner of odd jobs: running errands for neighbours, cutting privet hedges, washing cars, anything to get a few bob. There were also the inevitable trips to Harry Wilson's, which were still frequent but far less daunting. I was even beginning to like the old goat! I was growing up you see; I'd been to the match and I was starting big school in September!

The match against Arsenal was the first to be shown on Match of the Day on the new BBC 2 channel, watched by an audience of thirty thousand. We were winning two-nil with goals from Hunt and Wallace before Arsenal scored two themselves. Time was running out for a victory when a black cat ran across the pitch in front of the Kop. Shortly after, Wallace netted the winner. Very superstitious!

Came the big day and my efforts had paid off; I had easily enough money! I had also done very well for birthday money; even my Mam had given me more than I thought she would, probably more than she could afford.

The Ribble "coach" turned out to be a double-decker bus.
As well as Smudge, Timmy, Pilch and me there was Tommy Hardacre and his brother Davie and an assortment of men and young scallies. Most of the singing though came from "the four musketeers."

Once inside Ewood Park, there seemed more red-and-white than blue-and-white around. There were thousands of Liverpudlians on a terrace at one side of the ground. Phil Ferns and Tommy Smith gave us a two-nil half-time lead, but Blackburn, roared on by their own vociferous supporters and with good players such as Mike Ferguson, Ronnie Clayton, Brian Douglas and Fred Pickering in their team, made a great second-half comeback to win three-two.

The coach journey home was subdued until I asked the driver if he would stop so I could have a pee. He refused, so the only alternative was to go in the alcove under the stairs and use the cream-soda bottle I'd just emptied to pee in! No pun intended, but I had the piss well taken out of me. It seemed everybody on the bus was singing, "Evo's got a little one!" I didn't mind though: I'd just been to my first away match!

We had made a very indifferent start to our defence of the League winning only two of the first seven matches when Everton came to Anfield on September 19th. Smudge had told me how the "derby" matches were different than the others. He was right too, the atmosphere was unbelievable. So much noise! Before the start of the game a lad ran out of the Kop and stuck a big purple heart in the centre circle, a reference to a drug scandal that was besetting Everton at the time. When the teams came out another lad ran on to the pitch and gave Gordon West a handbag! This was great! It didn't matter that we hadn't been playing very well before this match, Everton had a lot of their best players out because of injury so we would win easily. It didn't turn out that way. Everton deservedly stuffed us four-nil. I'd been to my first derby but I was inconsolable that night.

"Peter, are yer goin' to Blackpool tomorrow?" It was New Year's Day 1965 and I was a bit puzzled as to why my brother John wanted to know why I was going to the match; he'd never shown much interest before.

"Yeah, I wanna go but none of me mates are goin'."

"I'll come with yer."

"Okay. 'Ow much 'ave yer got?"

"Five bob. What about you?"

"Yeah, the same. We'll have to ask me Mam for another five bob each."

Well all I can say is, my Mam must have had a very good Christmas! We didn't get five shillings each, but we did get three, which with our own money was just about enough to get us on the bus and in the ground. Just before we left Mam gave us both a big slab of Christmas cake to eat on the coach. We were waved off by Mam all the way down Grogan Square. As soon as we were in Kirkby Road and out of sight the cake was well and truly walloped!

We went in the Kop at Bloomfield Road, which although a fair size was nowhere near as big as ours. It was like ours though in respect that it was full of Liverpudlians. Our John was only ten and Mam had trusted me to look after him, so it was a bit worrying when he kept disappearing for five minutes at a time. He said he had to keep going for a pee. I did tell him to do what everybody else did and pee on the steps, but he insisted on going to the toilets at the back of the terrace. We were losing two-nil at half time. I was absolutely starving as Mam had only given us the bare minimum we needed; no money for sweets or crisps. I was wishing I'd have saved the cake. All in all I was feeling pretty miserable. I was searching for John when I found him at the snack bar; with a meat pie!

" Where d'yer get the money for that?"

"Some fella bought me it 'cos I said I was starvin'"

Before I could ask him for a bite it was down his neck and gone!

The second half was much better. The Reds were attacking our Kop end and with us roaring them on we were level through two Roger Hunt goals when the hour mark was reached. Our John stayed with me throughout and was getting very excited. Our amazing comeback was completed when Ian St. John netted after seventy-five minutes.

When we got home Mam was waiting for us at the front door; with Lily eyes! Lily eyes were when Mam's eyes would nearly pop out of her head when she had a cob on; and boy, did she have a cob on! "There's five bob gone missin' out of me purse!" She didn't have to ask who took it. John legged it past her to try to make good his escape to his bedroom. Who was standing at the top of the stairs? Dad! John got a good hiding for that but it didn't stop him robbing. He broke into the local Co-op one night, robbed all the ciggies and evaded capture from the Bobbies by hiding in a cardboard box. On another occasion he had been watching the milkman doing his Friday collection. When said milkman was servicing one of the neighbours, John got on to his milk float and relieved him of all his takings!

I was getting right into this away game lark now and the following week went with a lad called John Jones to West Brom where we playing in the third round of the FA Cup.
Again there were thousands of Reds at the ground and it wasn't long before I'd lost John. We were cruising the match two-nil with goals from Hunt and St. John before a late penalty by Bobby Cram gave them some hope. I had made my way down to the front of the terrace to look for John. When the final whistle went I vaulted the wall and ran on to the pitch. I'll never forget touching Ian St. John's shirt! Yes! My first time on a football pitch!

My first time out of the Boy's Pen was for a game against Wolves on February 13th. I was allowed to go in the Anfield Road end but not the Kop: Dad said I was too young and too small to go in there. An exciting game saw Hugh McIlmoyle give Wolves a half-time lead. We were attacking the Kop goal in the second half. A goal from Roger Hunt levelled matters in the forty-ninth minute. Excitement was reaching fever pitch when Chris Lawler scored just after an hour. Chris was running back to our end to take up his position when an eleven-year-old boy ran on to the pitch and congratulated him. Yes: Me! I was escorted back to my place by a kindly copper! Fifteen years later I was refereeing a match between Skem United and a Norwegian second division team called Raufoss who were managed by Chris Lawler. I reminded Chris of the incident and he said that he remembered it. Whether he did remember it or whether he was just being kind I'm not sure but it made me very happy. The next time I was to set foot on the

Anfield pitch would be in tragic circumstances: Laying flowers three days after the Hillsborough disaster. It was the twenty-fifth anniversary of my first match and I can't begin to tell you how much it upset me. Our League season petered out into a seventh place finish, but we were going great guns in the Cup competitions.
The first week of May would be the most momentous in the seventy-three year history of Liverpool Football Club.

BACK IN NINETY-SIXTY-FIVE, WHEN THE GREAT BILL SHANKLY WAS ALIVE...

May 1st 1965 was one of the greatest days in the history of Liverpool Football Club; the day we won the FA Cup for the first time. For anyone, winning the FA Cup in those days was a really big thing, bigger even than winning the League. After all we had won the League eight times but in seventy-three years of trying we had never claimed the Holy Grail. Evertonians used to skit us by saying that if we ever won the Cup the Liverbirds would fly off the Liver Buildings.

There was never any chance of me going to Wembley, even if I could have got a ticket. For one thing, neither my parents nor me would have been able to afford it and also as I was only eleven years of age I was considered too young to be making such a trip. So watching it on the goggle box it was going to have to be.
Came the big day and the streets everywhere in Liverpool were bedecked in red and white. The pavements were painted; bunting was stretched between houses on opposite sides of the road, and even the exteriors of houses were completely re-painted for the occasion.
The media as usual had wanted the two "glamour" teams, Chelsea and Manchester United in the final; no change there then. They were determined to cry down the final and they duly did. It was described by them as the worst final ever; it wasn't a great game, but it wasn't that bad.

In those days each club was allocated just sixteen thousands tickets each. We had an average attendance of forty thousand and Leeds about thirty thousand, so you can imagine what the scramble for tickets was like. However, on the day, Scousers seemed to take over Wembley and the stadium was a sea of red and white, although you couldn't tell that on our black and white telly!

The Queen was there to present the Cup and as she was wearing a red coat became an immediate favourite with our fans. She was said not to be best pleased though when we started singing, "Ee-aye-addio the Queen's wearin' red." That might have something to do with the fact that she's never attended an FA Cup Final since.

Gerry Byrne had, it later transpired, broken his collarbone in the second minute of the game. This was in the days before substitutes, so Gerry (crunch, crunch) bravely played on for the best part of two hours. Can you imagine that happening now? No chance! If they break a bootlace now they want to come off.

It was brave Gerry's cross which was headed into the net by Roger Hunt in the third minute of extra time. The scenes of pandemonium at Wembley were as nothing compared to what was going on in the Etherington household! My Dad was throwing me round the room like a rag doll, my Mam was jumping all over the place and my two-year old sister Collette was running around screaming and obviously wondering why everybody had suddenly turned into lunatics! Things calmed down eight minutes later when Billy Bremner, in my opinion one of the greatest midfielders ever, scored the equaliser. However, normal service was resumed nine minutes from time when Ian Callaghan's right-wing cross was met by a thumping diving header from Ian St. John to give Gary Sprake in the Leeds goal no chance.

So, we'd won the Cup for the first time and how we all celebrated! The streets were choc-a-block with people singing and dancing. Parties were going on everywhere. Mam and Dad went out to the Corry, coming home at midnight very drunk indeed!

A song of the time said it was Leeds United's Labour Day and it certainly was! The next day an estimated quarter of a million people turned out to welcome our victorious lads home: Tommy Lawrence, Chris Lawler, Gerry Byrne, Geoff Strong, Ron Yeats, Willie Stevenson, Ian Callaghan, Roger Hunt, Ian St. John, Tommy Smith and Peter Thompson, they were heroes, every one of them.

"Mam, I'm goin' to watch the school team tonight. They're playing the Cenny at Marine's ground." I lied through my teeth. The said match was indeed taking place, but I wouldn't be there. I'd be at Anfield! I'd never been to a night match before as Mam and Dad wouldn't let me; said I was too young. I had to be at this one; this was Inter Milan!

"Okay, what time will you be 'ome?"

"Abarr seven o'clock."

"Well make sure yer are. I'm in work at 'alf-past seven."

"Okay Mam, see you tonight."

I knew I'd get a good hiding the next day but it would be worth it.

OH, INTER ONE TWO THREE...

One of the greatest ever European nights at Anfield. May 4 1965: Inter Milan came to Anfield for the European Cup semi-final first leg as reigning European and World Club Champions.

We had done well in our first season of European competition to reach this stage. We had some impressive victories on the way but facing the might of Inter was expected to be a different story.

54,000 people were packed in to the ground; a sea of red and white to greet the team who had won the FA Cup for the first time in our history three days earlier. The two injured players, Gerry Byrne and Gordon Milne, paraded the famous trophy round the ground before the game. The crowd was whipped in to such a frenzy that the Inter coach, Helenio Herrera, later accused Bill Shankly of bad sportsmanship and called our fans animals.

Herrera was famous for his "cattenacio" tactics; defending in numbers with a sweeper and hitting on the break. These tactics were undone after just four minutes when Ian Callaghan crossed for Roger Hunt to score. The rejoicing was short-lived as Sandro Mazzola, probably the world's best player at the time, equalised shortly after. Liverpool were rocking Inter with their attacking play and passion with the crowd playing their part, roaring on every attack. After thirty-four minutes a marvellous free-kick routine by Callaghan, Willie Stevenson and Hunt finished with Cally giving Sarti in the Inter goal no chance. Pandemonium broke out all around Anfield and as Liverpool continued to charge Chris Lawler had the ball in the net only for it be controversially ruled offside against another player.

Liverpool continued their incessant battering of the Inter defence in the second half and went close to scoring on several occasions before Ian St. John clinched the game in the seventy fifth minute. Herrera couldn't stand this any longer and spent the last fifteen minutes of the game staring at the wall behind him (according to Shanks that is). Some of the world's best players, Burgnich, Facchetti, Jair, Mazzola and Suarez had been shaken to the core. The crowd were going wild and the Italian song "Santa Lucia" was adapted by the Kop as "Oh Inter, one, two, three. Go back to Italy." Tommy Lawrence, Chris Lawler, Ron Moran, Geoff Strong, Ron Yeats, Willie Stevenson, Ian Callaghan, Roger Hunt, Ian St. John, Tommy Smith and Peter Thompson were magnificent; every one of them.

The Italian media, public and supporters were determined that we wouldn't win the tie and all kinds of trickery, including keeping our players awake all night, was employed before and during the return game.

We lost the second leg 0-3 in front of ninety thousand screaming Milanese. The great man reckoned we were cheated out of it, especially the manner in which the third goal was scored, but TV replays showed that to be not really the case.

We had given the best team in the world the fright of their lives and showed that we were now a European force to be reckoned with.

I'M GONNA GET MY F.... N' 'EAD KICKED IN!

"Your Mother's gonna murder you tomorrow!"
Oh yeah, tell me somethin' I don't know yer owld bat!
"I'm sorry Mrs. Reid," I said, crocodile tears running down my cheeks.
"Yer will be when yer Mother gets hold of yer."
Shut up you interferin' owld witch!
"The other kids 'ave been carryin' on unmercifully! Pauline's been up bakin' cakes, John and Mark 'ave been 'aving pillow fights and poor little Collette's been screamin' 'er 'ead off all night. I 'ad to bang on the bedroom window with me clothes prop."
Yer mean yer broomstick don't yer, Witchypoo!

"It's a bloody disgrace the way you kids carry on. Yer getting' worse than the wild kids."
I had to put up with another ten minutes of her wittering on about nothingness before I was able to make good my escape to bed.

Mam got in from her shift at Chung's at half-past two.
I pretended to be asleep. No chance of getting away with that!
"Mrs. Reid said yer didn't get in 'til after eleven o'clock. Where'd yer been?"
The lyin' owld bag!
"It was 'alf-ten Mam, honest. I went the match."
"We'll see what your Dad 'as to say when 'e gets in."
Oh no! I'd got away with it off my Mam, but there was no chance with my owld fella.
Dad was just getting in from his night shift when I got up for school at eight o'clock.
"What time did yer get in last night? Yer weren't in when I left at seven o'clock."
"'E got in just after you left John."
Mam had saved my bacon. Good old Ma!
"'Ow d'yer team get on?"
"We won three-one Dad."
"Was it a good game?"
"Yeah it was a great game Dad, the best I've ever seen."
"'Ow come you don't get a game?"
"Oh I might do one day Dad, maybe one day."
Mam looked across at me and smiled that lovely smile I remember so well.

The following Saturday Dad came in drunk from the Corry.
"Peter," he slurred, "D'yer know Mister Fitzpatrick who lives in number six?"
"Yeah Dad, he does the St. John Ambulance at the match. I see 'im there sometimes."
"Yeah well I've been 'aving a pint with him tonight…and 'e said… 'e saw yer there the other night…but you didn't…."
Dad fell asleep before he got to finish the sentence and the subject was never mentioned again!
Three-one to Liverpool: One-nil to Evo!

CHAPTER THREE

DRAGONS AND DEVILS

The first game of the 1965-66 season saw us playing Manchester United at Old Trafford in the FA Charity Shield. We drew 2-2 with goals from Willie Stevenson and Ron Yeats but the "highlight" of the match was when George Best knocked "Rowdy" out with a beaut of a left hook. Whether the big man was feigning injury or not I'm not sure but Besty certainly did hit him with a cracker!
George Best was my favourite non-Liverpool player even though he did play for them! George was truly a great player who would have put some of today's so called "greats" to shame. The only British player who came anywhere near to him was our own Kenny Dalglish.

That same day Mam was in hospital after having her seventh miscarriage. Everybody I knew came from a family of four, five, six or even seven kids. Mam would have had thirteen children all told if she had have carried full term. If nothing else Dad was certainly prolific!

Mam was still fighting the unequal struggle trying to make ends meet. There were still regular trips to Harry Wilson's although Mam was now also using Addicott's pawnshop. I preferred going to Harry's though as he was now a firm friend of mine. We used to always have the crack about going to the match and the dread I used to hold him in was now well and truly gone. I was also no longer scared of the Bootle Bucks: I was twelve now and felt I could handle myself. Taking Harry's place as the most frightening person on Earth was Cissy Mulhall. Cissy Mulhall was a local moneylender who would call at our house every Friday night. Christ, she was ugly! She was it seemed, about seventy, although she could have been younger; it was hard to tell with a kipper like that.

"Eh, you lad, make me a cup of tea," she boomed at me.
Piss off yer owld witch!
"Okay Mrs. Mulhall. 'Ow many sugars?"
"Three, an' 'urry up! I'm bloody freezin' 'ere!"

Well you 'urry up and freeze to friggin' death, yer 'orrible owld trout!
"Yeah, I'll make sure it's 'ot Mrs. Mulhall."
I closed the door leading from the living room to the kitchen and made
sure the harridan's tea was hot by pissing in it!
"There yer are Mrs. Mulhall, nice and 'ot for yer."
"Argh, that's bleedin' 'orrible! It tastes like dishwater."
Well it's not dishwater, it's piss, yer stupid owld mare!
"Sorry Mrs. Mulhall. D'yer want me to make it a bit stronger for
yer?"
"No, just sit there and shut up yer stupid little get!"
I sat silently as ordered and watched with barely restrained joy as her
face contorted when she swallowed the vile mixture of tea and piss!
"Mrs. Mulhall, I can only pay yer ten bob off what I owe yer this
week. I'll pay yer the rest next week. Is that okay?" whispered Mam
meekly.

"No it friggin' isn't!" roared the monster, "I'm gonna charge yer double
interest. Make sure it's paid next week."
I truly hated her! The most horrible sight in the world was seeing
Cissy sitting open-legged with her piss-stained bloomers on show. I
still bear the mental scars! She would carry a shopping bag stuffed
full of money; there must have been thousands of pounds in it. One
day she had dropped a big wad of money under the chair she was
sitting on and left without it. Mam ran off down the street after her to
give it back. Mam would have got away with it but Auntie Maureen
snitched to Dad. Dad went off his head! There must have been
hundreds of pounds in that wad and would have solved many of my
parents' money problems but Mam was so scared of the old dragon
she had to give it back.

We had started the season well, winning four and drawing two of our
first eight matches. Roger Hunt was in particularly good form scoring
seven goals; three of them in a memorable 5-1win at West Ham.
Everton came to Anfield for the derby match on September 25th looking
to repeat their great win of twelve months earlier. I was in the Boys
Pen with two Evertonian mates of mine: John Shaw and Brian Walker.
Once again the atmosphere was electric; the noise at derby matches
seemed to be twice as loud as it was at other games. Gordon West
received his annual "present" of a handbag before the game started. I
met Gordon at a football presentation many years later and had the

great privilege of shaking his hand. He was a huge man and I for one would certainly not have liked a dig off him, so for him to have taken the ribbing in such good part was a massive credit to him.

We were well on top in the first half-hour with Hunt, Yeats and St. John all going close. We took the lead after thirty-four minutes when Tommy Smith scored with a stooping header. Kicking towards the Kop in the second half we proceeded to completely overwhelm them. Hunt netted our second in the 49th minute. Willie Stevenson then scored a cracker of a lob three minutes later. By now John and Brian were looking very distraught, especially as I was taking the piss out of them something rotten! Hunt scored his second in the seventy-third minute to reverse the score of the year before. The Kop though wouldn't settle for this and were chanting, "We want five! We want five!" The fifth duly arrived with a minute to go when Ian St. John scored with a bullet header. Sweet revenge for "the Saint" as the Evertonians had been calling him a monkey and throwing bananas at him throughout the game.

"One two, one two three, one two three four, five nil!" chanted the Kop. I loved every minute of it! Taking the piss out of my blue mates on the way home was brilliant.
"What time is it Evo?" asked John.
"Five past West," I answered, quick as a flash.
"I suppose yer think yer funny," snarled Brian.
"'Arry Catterick's in hospital yer know. 'E's got a bad side!" I laughed uproariously.
And we've played the toffees for a laugh and we've left them feeling blue, five-nil!

Our John and me were always fighting with each other and after one particularly violent ruck it was decided that I should stay the weekend at my Auntie Maureen's. I did my usual Saturday morning chores and went to Auntie Maureen's to do her errands. It was nearly two-thirty when I finished and so consequently it was approaching half time when I got to Anfield. The Boys Pen was closed but the half time gate to the Kop was open. The admission price was two shillings, half the full price. Two bob was all I had so there was nothing else for it but to hand my money over and face a long walk back to Auntie Maureen's in Waterloo.

It was a cold December day but as I pushed, shoved and jostled my way to the middle of the Kop I was warmed, not only physically but also emotionally, by the thousands of bodies around me. This was my first time in the Kop and I was determined to enjoy it. The score was already one-all, Peter Thompson having scored our goal, so everything was set up for a great second half.

I was a good Catholic boy so the sacrilegious plagiarising of the hymn, "Adeste Fidelis" should have appalled me, but I was in the Kop, supporting my beloved Liverpool and so I bellowed it out loud and proud.
"Oh come all ye faithful, joyful and triumphant,

Oh come ye, oh come ye to Anfield,
Come and behold them, we're the cream of Europe,
Oh come let us adore them, oh come let us adore them,
Oh come let us adore them, Liverpool."

We were soon in to our stride in the second half and it wasn't long before Ian St. John gave us the lead. Geoff Strong scored a whopper after seventy minutes to give us a three-one lead. There was a battle at the time between Geoff and Gordon Milne for the number four shirt, but as Geoff was one of my favourite players I joined in when half the people in the Kop chanted, "Geoff Strong."
The other half retorted by chanting, "Gordon Milne." Everybody then joined in with the Geoff Strong song.

"Geoff Strong was made for scorin', and that's just what 'e'll do.
One of these days Geoff Strong is gonna score a goal or two.
Are you ready Geoff? Start scorin'!"

By now we were taking the piss out of poor old Arsenal so it was no surprise when Roger Hunt added the fourth with ten minutes to go. England had beaten Spain 2-0 in Madrid three days earlier and such was their dominance that the Spanish crowd shouted, "OLE!" every time an English player touched the ball. So of course we had to do it, although Tommy Lawrence did look slightly bemused by it all! About as quick as a 44 up the Valley was our Tommy!
A young lad called John Radford scored a late consolation goal for the Gunners but it had been a great second half display by the mighty

Reds. We all walked down the exit steps of the Kop singing a nice
little ditty about our Cockney friends!.

"London Bridge is fallin' down, fallin' down, fallin' down.
London Bridge is fallin' down, poor old Arsenal!
Build it up in red and white, red and white, red and white.
Build it up in red and white, poor old Arsenal!"

My state of euphoria, brought on by Liverpool winning and my Kop
debut, was quickly deflated by the realisation that I had a good two-
hour walk ahead of me. I was walking along the side of Stanley Park
feeling very sorry for myself when I kicked, what I thought was, an
empty wage packet. I picked it up. Hallelujah! There were two pound
notes in it! I said a quick prayer, repenting for having blasphemed,
and scuttled off to the nearest sweet shop. I had a ball that weekend
guzzling sweets like there was no tomorrow. During my school lunch
break on the Monday I went to the sports shop on Litherland Road and
bought a Wembley football (size 5, regulation weight) and a red and
white scarf - one of those new ones with the stripes running horizontally
that looked like a tube of Colgate toothpaste.
Of course I hadn't told Auntie Maureen of my good fortune; she would
have been right on to my Mam and my new found wealth would have
been taken off me. I also had to bribe our John with a shilling not to
grass me up.

I got home from school on Monday night to be met by Lily eyes.
Oh no!
"Where d'yer get the money for that scarf and the ball?"
"I washed some cars for the teachers," I lied unconvincingly.
Slap!
"No yer didn't."
Well why ask then?
"I did Mam, honest!"
Slap!
"Yer found two pound on Saturday. Why didn't yer give it to me?"
Oh, that's fair isn't it? I find two pound, but I've gotta give it to you.
Oh yeah, that's dead fair!
"I'm sorry Mam," I sobbed, "I 'ad no bus fare, then I just spent the rest
on sweets and stuff."
Slap!

35

I ran in to the living room. Dad was standing there. Double whammy! "Why didn't yer give that money to yer Mother? Yer know she needs it with Christmas comin' up."
Slap!
As I continued to be pummelled for my heinous crime, our John sat in an armchair smiling that sweet smile of revenge.
Why do you whisper green grass?

New Year's Day 1966: We were playing the League Champions: The famous Man. United: Best, Charlton, Law and all! I was in the Kop nice and early; good job as the gates closed at two o'clock. The noise surpassed even that at derby matches. I was right into the singing now and I wasn't afraid to swear any more.

"Man. United, Man. United, you're not fit to wipe my arse, you're not fit to wipe my arse!"

I liked that one!
We went a goal down but equalised through Tommy Smith just before half time. It was Gordon Milne's turn to play, ahead of Geoff Strong and it was the little man who scored the winner two minutes from time to send fifty-odd thousand Liverpudlians home happy.
"Ee-aye-addio, we're gonna win the League!"
The couple of thousand United fans left with the sentiment that they were not fit to wipe the bottoms of their superior Scouse neighbours ringing in their ears!
Our defence of the FA Cup ended at the first hurdle when we were beaten 1-2 at home by Chelsea.
Roger Hunt had given us an early lead before goals from Bobby Tambling and the emerging Peter Osgood gave Chelsea a deserved victory.

Our European Cup-Winners Cup campaign on the other hand was going great guns. Fine successes against crack teams: Juventus, Standard Liege and Honved took us to the semi-final where we would face Scotland's finest: Glasgow Celtic.
We lost the first leg at Celtic Park to a goal from Jimmy Johnstone. Jimmy was the George Best of Scotland, if not in looks then certainly in ability. He was a fast, jinky, little winger who could cause havoc in any defence. The rest of the players around him formed the basis of

team that would win the European Cup the following year. Players of the calibre of Billy McNeill, Bertie Auld, Bobby Lennox and Steve Chalmers would not give up their lead easily. The return leg at Anfield was going to be a mighty hard game, especially as Roger Hunt was out injured; the versatile Geoff Strong taking his place up front.

The Jocks came in their thousands! In town the night before the game they were bowing to Corporation buses and putting two fingers up at the Ribble ones. Why? Corporation buses were green; Ribble were red!

For the first time ever the whole of the Anfield Road end was allocated to the visitors. It was quite a sight to see the whole of that end covered in green and white.

Us in the Kop for our part were giving it our usual deafening noise. The banter between the fans was, for the most part, good-humoured. "Yer can stick your fuckin' 'aggis up your arse," was retorted with, "Yer can stick your fuckin' scouse up your arse."

Our: You'll Never Walk Alone, was countered with that great Celtic song:

"Hail, hail, the Celts are here, what the hell do we care, what the hell do we care.
Hail, hail, the Celts are here, what the hell do we care now.
Oh it's a grand old team to play for; oh it's a grand old team to see.
And if you know their history it's enough to make your heart go wooaaah.
We don't care what the Rangers say, what the hell do we care.
For we only know that there's gonna be a show and that Glasgow Celtic will be there."

Celtic's brilliant defence stood firm against all our efforts in the first half. The pressure on their goal in the second half was unrelenting and they finally gave way when Tommy Smith scored with half-an-hour left to play. Urged on by the mighty roars from the Kop we kept hitting Celtic with wave after wave of attacks.

Geoff Strong had sustained an injury, but as substitutes were not yet allowed in European competitions he had to soldier bravely on. Geoff

37

was hobbling round, playing on virtually one leg. He was no more than a passenger, left on the pitch only for nuisance value. After sixty-seven minutes a cross came in from the right wing. Geoff used his one good leg to lever himself into a prodigious leap and headed the ball firmly in to the Celtic net.

The Kop went wild! The Anfield Road end fell silent for the first time that night. Celtic then started their own wave of attacks, but if we could hold out we would be in our first ever European final. Bobby Lennox had the ball in the net late in the game. Extra time loomed. But no, the referee had disallowed the goal for offside. The previous good humour of the Bhoys fans turned to ugliness as they rained hundreds of bottles on to the pitch. Tommy Lawrence was forced to flee upfield from his goal. For a while it looked as if the match would have to be abandoned, but once order was restored and the pitch was cleared of bottles the game once more got under way. The final whistle was a blessed relief to all concerned except the Jocks. After the game Shanks saw the funny side and said to the Celtic manager Jock Stein, "Do you want your share of the gate receipts or do you just want to take back the empties?"

The final home game of the season eleven days later against Chelsea saw us needing just a point to win the League. Chelsea were a good young side managed by the dynamic Tommy Docherty. Docherty was a good friend of Shanks and had taken over Bill's number four jersey at Preston when the great man ended his playing career there. Shanks had said to Tommy at the time, "You won't need to run son, the shirt knows where to go."

This was an ideal opportunity to avenge our cup defeat earlier in the season. It was a red-hot day on the last day of April and I had decided to go in the Anfield Road end for this game. The Chelsea players formed a guard of honour to applaud the Champions-elect on to the pitch. This was a nice gesture but once the action started the Londoners were in no mood to give anything away. The first half was a tense affair with chances being few and far between. The second half however was a different story and we were soon in to our stride. Roger Hunt, back after missing the previous six games through injury, scored after forty-eight minutes and added the second twenty minutes later. Great film footage just after that goal was scored shows Gordon Milne swinging monkey style in the Kop net, fans in the Kop going mad and a policeman laughing his head off at it all! Barry Bridges pulled a goal back for Chelsea, but we were not to be denied our seventh Football League Championship. The last five minutes of the game was a cacophony of noise as the chant of, "Champions, Champions" rang out from an exultant Kop.

The end of the game saw the Chelsea players once again applauding as Rowdy and co did their lap of honour. Rowdy called Shanks on to the pitch to take the adulation of his adoring people. Once the chants of, "Shankly, Shankly" had died down the next name to be boomed out by the crowd was that of Geoff Strong. A huge roar greeted the arrival on the pitch of the great hero of the Celtic game. The poor man, dressed in his best suit, could hardly walk but he did every step of that lap of honour. What a guy!

I was right at the front of the Anfield Road end so I got a brilliant view of the players as they came round to us. At such close quarters they all looked like giants and I'll never forget Rowdy smiling at me, yes me, as I threw him my red and white bobble hat. Auntie Ann had bought me it for Christmas but I'm sure she wouldn't have minded. I somehow think it wouldn't have fitted the big man's head though! The celebrations were long and loud and it was a good job we savoured them as it would be another seven years before we would experience the like again.

CHAPTER FOUR

GETTING AN EDUCATION

I sagged school for most of the summer term. Why? Because Alan McCluskey would beat me up for not paying three bob which I owed him and the World Cup was being played in England. I went up to Goodison Park every day to watch some of the best players in the world training. I saw, in the flesh, players such as: Pele, Garrincha, Eusebio, Torres, Asparoukhov, Albert, Bene, Farkas, Yashin, Seeler, Beckenbauer, Pak Doo Ik and Lee Dong Woon. Pak Doo who? Who what Woon? You might well ask. They were two of the North Korean team who gave Portugal the fright of their lives in the quarter-final, going three-nil in front before eventually losing five-three. Security was very low at Goodison and kids were actually welcomed in to watch the players training.

I knew I'd receive a terrible hiding when Mam found out I was sagging, especially as I was spending my five bob weekly school dinner money every Friday, but I reckoned it was worth it. Our John had found out about my indiscretion and insisted on joining me or he would snitch to Dad. I'd seen some of the hidings Dad had given him for sagging; I didn't want any of that thank you very much, so I let him tag along.

Our John had at least been in school for his exams, so he might get away with it. I, on the other hand, had no chance. John brought his school report home; shite as usual, he wasn't the brightest kid in the world. Great things, however, were expected from me.

My report came through the post. Right, this was it, time for some serious lying. Mam opened the envelope. Lily eyes! "What's this? Yer were absent from every exam!"
"I wasn't Mam, honest. There must be a mistake. Somebody must be messin' about. I did okay in my exams. I think it might 'ave been Gerrard Byrne, 'e's always messin' about."
"If I find out yer've been saggin' school, there'll be murder," Mam glowered at me.
Christ, it looked as if I was going to get away with it!
"All right Mam, I'll sort it out when we go back to school." I was

becoming a very accomplished liar!
"Yeah, well make sure yer do and tell that Gerrard Byrne if it was 'im
I'm coming up there to sort 'im out."
Phew!

Our John meantime had been grassed up and received said good hiding
off Dad. All credit to our kid though, it would have been easy enough
for him to snitch on me but he didn't. The fact that I'd bribed him
with twenty Woodbines I'd nicked from our next door neighbour's,
Sophie Stevens, house helped! Sophie used to send me on the most
weirdest of messages: Two ounces of Blackcurrant and Liquorice
sweets, three mushrooms, a shilling's worth of faded fruit (faded? The
bloody things were maggot-ridden!), two potatoes and a nice stick of
celery for eating! What else would you do with celery? Stick it up
your arse? I liked going for Sophie's messages though. I would always
get away with eating a couple of her sweets, there would be a couple
of bob lying around waiting for me to take, the dim old bat would
never know where she'd left her ciggies so I'd have them off for our
John and she gave me threepence for going. Happy days!

The 1966 FA Charity Shield was a great occasion, one I'll never forget.
Over sixty-three thousand people were at Goodison Park. Before the
game Ron Yeats and the Everton captain, Brian Labone did a lap of
honour with the Football League Championship trophy and the FA
Cup, which Everton had won in a marvellous final against Sheffield
Wednesday. The World Cup winners, Roger Hunt and Everton's Ramon
Wilson, parading the Jules Rimet trophy followed them. Wilson was
a brilliant left back: fast, tough in the tackle, a decent header of the
ball and one of the hardest shots in football. I was in the Boy's Pen
with John Shaw and Brian Walker. Everton's Pen was in the top left-
hand corner of the Gwladys Street. That terrace was nowhere near as
highly banked as The Kop, so I had a brilliant view of the proceedings.

The only goal in a match we totally dominated was scored after just
nine minutes when Roger sent a thirty- yard screamer into the roof of
"Pansy" West's net at the Gwladys Street end. The thing I remember
most from this day though is a song. The Beatles were at number one
in the charts at the time with *Yellow Submarine*. Our fans adapted this
to:

"On a Saturday afternoon, support a team called Liverpool.
And we'll cheer them to the top, from the mighty Spion Kop.
Two, three, four.
We all live in a red and white Kop, a red and white Kop, a red and
white Kop."

When I returned to school in September I was faced with the awesome
prospect of explaining away my two months absence. I was called in
to the Headmaster's office. Tom Diggle was a bit of a "Mister Chips"
figure, but was ferocious when it came to giving "six of the best" on
the hand with a leather strap. I was therefore shitting myself as I
entered his office.

"Etherington, where were you for the last two months of term?"
"I was in 'ospital sir. I 'ad a bug in me stomach an' I kept being sick
and pooin' all the time sir."
"Why didn't your parents inform me?"
"I don't know sir. I think they must 'ave forgot because they were
dead worried about me sir."
"They were *very* worried about you Etherington, *very* worried."
"Yeah sir they were, *dead* worried."
"Are you all right now son."
Yer believe this don't yer? Yer daft owld get!
"Yes sir, I'm fine now. Thank you for askin' sir."
"Well, you look after yourself properly from now on and be careful
what you eat."
"Yes sir. D'yer want me to wash yer car this week sir?"
Creep, creep!
"Yes. Friday lunchtime please Etherington."
"Yes sir. I'll make sure I do a good job on it sir."
"Yes, yes. Go to your class now boy and make sure you close the door
behind you," he said a little exasperated by now.
Jesus Christ, I'd fluked it! I must have been the jammiest thirteen-
year old in the world. Even Alan McCluskey had forgotten about his
three bob! Life was sweet again.
When I got home from school Mam was waiting.
"Did yer sort out yer school report?
"Yeah Mam, no problem. They got my report mixed up with Mark
Smith's. It was 'im who'd been off school. 'E'd been in 'ospital 'cos
'e had a germ in 'is stomach."

"Where's yer report then?"
"They're gonna post it to yer this week Mam."
"Where'd'yer come in class anyway?"
"Where'd'yer think Mam? Top of course!"
"Oh I'm made up!"
"Yeah, so am I Mam."
"I'll give yer the money to go in the Anfield Road end this week instead of the Pen."
"Ah, thanks Mam. I 'ate goin' in the monkey cage."
I tell you, Billy Liar had nothing on me! In the end, Mam just forgot all about the report and nothing more was said about it.

After a fairly inconsistent start to our defence of the title, we hit peak form in November. Nottingham Forest, who were second in the League at the time, were stunned by a "firework" display which saw us beat them 4-0 at Anfield on the 5TH. I was still getting my education in the Boy's Pen but I was learning quickly. **"You can stick your bows and arrows up your arse,"** was a Kop favourite whenever we played Forest. Our song in the Pen was better though:

"Robin Hood saw a nude riding through the glen.
Friar Tuck ran like fuck to tell his merry men.
When they got there, Robin was bare.
Being rude, with a nude, Robin Hood."
We had to pronounce Hood in such a way that it rhymed with nude, but it was great stuff anyway.

The next two games against Burnley at home and Newcastle away were both won by a 2-0 scoreline. We were therefore in rampant form for the next game; the visit of Leeds United, always a tough game. Chris "Silent Knight" Lawler gave us the lead just before half time. We tore them apart in the second half. In one of the greatest displays I've ever seen from a Liverpool side, further goals from Thompson, St. John and Strong saw us establish a 4-0 lead. Leeds were well and truly demoralised. The Kop cheekily used their own *Ilkley Moor* tune to sing to them, "What's it like to be outclassed." The Leeds fans response to this was to sing, strangely enough, *You'll Never Walk Alone.* "Oh you got your education from the Kop," boomed the Kopites. They were in pleats laughing when us "Penites" starting singing to them, "Oh, you got your education from the Pen." Five hundred squeaky-voiced kids were taking the piss out of the most famous fans in the world. It seemed somehow sacrilegious, but it was fun! Geoff Strong wrapped it all up with a cracking goal in the last minute. 5-0 against Leeds! Go 'ead! We were going to win the League again; I was convinced of it.

An unknown Rumanian team, Petrolul Ploesti, had given us a tough time in the preliminary round of the European Cup. The tie was settled by a third game in Brussels, which we won 2-0. Our opponents in the first round proper would be a little-known team from Holland called Ajax. Little known to most people maybe, but not to me. I was well into my football and collected programmes from all over the world. I had pen pals in Holland, Denmark, Switzerland and America as well as those in this country: Manchester, Leeds, Glasgow and Southend. The Everton programme shop in Goodison Road also had great programmes from everywhere you could think of. Indeed all of my spare cash used to go on football. My mates were beginning to get girlfriends, but I couldn't be arsed with all that! I was in love with football!

"Evo, who's this Ajax we're playin'?" Timmy's knowledge of football didn't extend beyond Anfield.
"They're supposed to be a very good team."
"'Ow do you know?"
"I've got some of their programmes. They've got a player called Johann Cruyff. World Soccer says he's gonna be one of the best players in the world one day." I wasn't trying to show off or anything but I was very proud of my football knowledge.
"Fuckin' 'ell Evo! Is there anythin' you don't know? All I know about Ajax is me Ma cleans the sink with it!" chuckled Timmy.
"Come on Timmy, let's 'ave a game of two gates. I'll be Liverpool, you be Ajax."
"Yeah, up to ten. *I'll* be Liverpool and *you* can be Ajax, 'cos you're shit and I'm gonna batter yer!"
I couldn't argue with that. My footballing knowledge was not matched by my playing ability. I was, and still am, quite comfortably the worst footballer in the world! Timmy won 10-1. My goal was the result of an extravagant overhead volley by Timmy ending up in his own goal, or more correctly, his own gate!

"'Ow d'yer think we'll get on against them anyway Evo?"
"I think we'll beat them over the two legs. Probably draw in Amsterdam and beat them at Anfield."
"Fuckin' 'ell Evo, you sound like Kenneth Wolstenholme!"
"Well, yer did ask. Anyway, where've yer been lately? I haven't seen yer for ages. Aren't yer goin' the match anymore?"
"Yeah, I go with me Dad now in the Anny Road end."
I was jealous as fuck! I'd always wanted to go the match with my Dad. He would spend hours regaling me with stories of going to away matches: Wolverhampton, Portsmouth, Huddersfield, Bristol, Plymouth and other such far flung places. He would also tell me of great Liverpool players: Billy Liddell, Albert Stubbins, Bob Paisley, Cyril Done, Cyril Sidlow, Nivvy, and John Evans.
He told me of the great players in other teams: Stanley Matthews, Tom Finney, Nat Lofthouse, Stan Cullis, Jimmy Dickinson and the like. He would tell me how players now were nowhere near as good and how they were all paid too much money. He wasn't always in the best of health; due probably to him working twelve-hour night shifts, and so consequently didn't feel he cut put up with all the crushing.
"Ah, fuck that Timmy! I wouldn't be seen dead in the match with me owld fella!" I told you I was a good liar!
"Nah, it's dead good Evo, honest. 'E buys me loads of sweets an' let's me stand in the doorway when 'e's in the Albert."

You bastard Timmy!

The first leg in Amsterdam should never have been played. Thick fog enveloped the pitch, so much so that Bill Shankly was able to go on to the pitch and deliver a team-talk as the match was going on! Not that it did much good however as we were completely overwhelmed, losing 1-5. "No problem," insisted Shanks, "We'll win 5-0 at Anfield." Do you know what? We believed him!

We were going to have to change our kit for the home leg as Ajax had changed in Amsterdam. Shanks had said that Ploesti's kit of yellow shirts and socks with black shorts had looked good under floodlights at Anfield, so that was indeed the kit we would wear. The atmosphere that night was unbelievable! Fifty-three thousand of us believed that we were going to turn the tie round on a rainy December evening. Plenty of Kopites had swapped scarves with the few hundred Dutchmen that were there. Their scarves were thick woolen white ones with red chevrons and very nice they looked too! Looking down at the Kop from the Boy's Pen was an incredible sight as great clouds of steam came billowing up. It was thought at first that the Kop was on fire, but it was just that the crowd was packed so tightly and everybody was so wet that condensation was caused. It was a strange sight though. We never had any real chance of turning the tie around as Ajax proved what a good team they were. We did well in the end to gain a creditable 2-2 draw with the magnificent Cruyff scoring both of their goals, his feat being matched for us by Roger Hunt.

Our next game was a 2-1 win at Chelsea on Christmas Eve. I was in the Kop for the return game two days later. We were right back on track and a marvellous game saw us repeat the scoreline. Willie Stevenson scored with a fabulous thirty-yard shot and Roger gave us the winner after Chelsea's brilliant Scottish winger, Charlie Cooke had equalised.

The scoreless derby game at Anfield on New Year's Eve was memorable only for a knighthood being conferred by the Kop on Roger Hunt. It had been announced that Alf Ramsey would receive a knighthood in the Queen's New Year's Honours list and that Bobby Moore, captain of the World Cup winners would be awarded the OBE. The Kop though decided that Roger Hunt was worthy of a knighthood. **"Sir Roger Hunt, Sir Roger Hunt, Ee-aye-addio, Sir Roger Hunt."** Roger was my favourite ever player. He was fast, could head a ball, worked his socks off and had a kick like a mule. I absolutely adored him! My bedroom wall was quite literally plastered with pictures of Liverpool players, but there were more of Roger than all of the other players put together.

Seven days later Bobby Moore had the misfortune to come to Anfield with West Ham. Bobby was a great player and was considered for years to be the best defender in the world, but he did look like a bit of a ponce! He advertised Brylcreem on television and he must have worn it during matches, as he never had a hair on his head out of place. **"Bobby Moore, OBE. Other Bugger's Energy,"** was the irreverent chant from the Kopites. We also lost no time in letting him know that Roger was worthier of a knighthood than he was, **"Ee-aye-addio, Sir Roger Hunt."** Poor Bobby must have been well pissed off!

Scenes for an episode of *Till Death Us Do Part* were being filmed at Anfield that day. The storyline was that Alf Garnett had won a couple of tickets to watch his beloved Hammers at Anfield. His son-in-law Mike, who was a rabid Red, naturally wanted to go with him. As they were walking around the perimeter of the pitch to take up their places in the Kemlyn Road stand they were serenaded by the Kop, "If you all hate Cockneys clap your hands!" "Oh, where's your silly moo?" Peter Thompson won the game for us with two smashing goals. Thommo, on his day, was every bit as good as George Best. It was just that he didn't very often have his day; brilliant, but inconsistent. Where Besty would beat a couple of men and then deliver a telling cross or shot, Thommo would beat a couple of men, go back and beat them again, then invariably lose the ball!

We were drawn to play Everton at Goodison in the fifth round of the FA Cup. It was to be an historic occasion. Such was the demand for tickets that it was decided to broadcast the game live, on giant screens, at Anfield via closed circuit TV. Dad decided that he would come to this match with me, but we weren't going to the "churchyard" as he called Goodison; we would watch the match at Anfield. Yes!

In the weeks building up to the match my Mam, Aunts and Grannies kitted me out with all kinds of Liverpool paraphernalia: new scarf, new bobble hat, rosettes and a bright new red coat. This was the magic of the FA Cup you see, especially as it was a derby match. I think only on Merseyside, at the time, could such fervour have been generated for one match.

Came the big night, Dad and me took our places at the front of the Anfield Road end so we could get a good view of the screens. There were over 40,000 people at Anfield, added to the crowd of nearly 65,000 at Goodison gave a combined attendance of exactly 105,000. Great stuff! The match, for us, however wasn't so great. We were watching the action on one screen when it ripped in the high wind. The crowd watching that screen just shuffled over to watch it on the next screen. Alan Ball scored the only goal of the game. I was absolutely gutted. Walking down Commercial Road after the game we were being taunted by Evertonians. "What's our name, Everton," imitating the taunt Muhammad Ali had used against Ernie Terrell a few days earlier in a World Heavyweight Title fight when Terrell refused to call Ali by his adopted name, calling him, instead, his old name; Cassius Clay. All of this was too much for Dad who left me to make my own way home while he went to the Melrose for a pint.

Dad had got the taste again of going to the match, so a few weeks later we took our places again at the front of the Anny Road for the visit of Newcastle. We won the match 3-1 but not before goalkeeper John Ogston, playing his first and last game for Liverpool in place of the injured Tommy Lawrence had put the shits up everybody with a totally inept display. Dad, who stood every inch of five-foot-three, summed him up superbly, "If 'e's a goalkeeper, so am I!" Dad had to go to work after the match, so I still didn't get the chance to go anywhere near a pub with him. Still; never mind, maybe one day.

"Peter, d'yer wanna to come to Wembley with me tomorrow." Uncle John McKeown said.
Skem United were playing Enfield in the FA Amateur Cup Final and Ian St. John coached them. Interest on Merseyside was pretty high. Skelmersdale was a new town that was just beginning to take off.
"No thanks Uncle John. We're playin' West Brom at 'ome tomorrow.
"Yeah, but wouldn't yer rather go to Wembley. We're goin' on a coach. There'll be loads of ale and butties. Go on, I'll let yer 'ave a couple of bottles of brown as long as you don't tell Mister Piper." Uncle John had nicknamed Dad Mister Piper after a very small character on telly.
"Uncle John, there's no place in the world I'd rather be than at Anfield when Liverpool are playing at 'ome."
"You're fuckin' mad."
Yeah, well I'd rather be mad than an Evertonian twat like you!
"Thanks for the offer Uncle John. It's very kind of yer, but I 'aven't missed a 'ome match for two years an' I don't wanna miss this one."
"Fuck yer then! I'll ask our Joey to go."
Yeah, you do that. Take the other blue prick with yer. Good fuckin' riddance to the pair of yer!
"Yeah, I'm sure 'e'll enjoy that Uncle John."

The match against West Brom was a dire affair. It pissed down all day. We lost when Ron Yeats took the worst throw-in in the memory of man. The ball landed straight at the feet of Jeff Astle who promptly lashed it into the net.

I was baby-sitting for Auntie Maureen that night. She was out with Mam and Dad while soft arse was at Wembley. Uncle John rolled in at eleven o'clock, totally arseholed as usual.

"Ah yer got beat didn't yer. I told yer to come with me."

Fuck off, prick!

"Yeah, I should 'ave done Uncle John. I'm sorry I didn't now."

My arse!

"What was the game like Uncle John? I 'eard Skem should 'ave won. They missed a penalty didn't they?"

"I don't know. I got thrown out before the kick-off for fightin' with some woolyback bastard from Skem!"

Knob'ead!

The season ended ignominiously with a 1-3 defeat at home to already relegated Blackpool. The crowd of 28,000 was disappointingly low, but we showed our loyalty when thousands of us gathered outside the main entrance chanting for Shankly. Our song of, "We're not goin' 'ome 'til 'e comes," was finally heeded when Shanks appeared at an upstairs window and waved to his multitude below. That was enough for us. The Messiah had blessed us and we could all go home and endure another football-less summer.

CHAPTER FIVE

HORMONES AND HOLIDAYS

The history books say that the summer of 1967 was momentous. You know, flower power and all that. Me? I just wanted the footy season to start. I'd made some new mates: Cainy, Benno and Ragger, through staying a lot at my Auntie Maureen's. They, of course, were all Reds. Cainy was a very good footballer who had already been for trials at a number of clubs including Liverpool. He was also a bit of a boxer as I found out to my cost when I thought I could fight him, as I was a bit older than he was. A short, sharp right jab and one bloody nose later soon put paid to that notion!

"It's just been on the wireless lads, we've signed Tony Hateley!" I shouted excitedly to my three compadres.
"Tony who?" came the reply from Benno.
"Chelsea's centre-forward, 'e's dead good, brilliant in the air. We've just paid ninety-six thousand pounds for 'im."
I had indeed been impressed with him during his spells at Aston Villa and Chelsea. He was big, strong and deadly in the air. Shankly had seen we needed a new centre-forward and was prepared to pay lots of money, but had stopped just short of making big Tone our first £100,000 player.
"Never 'eard of 'im," said Ragger.
This was doing my head in. Okay, Hateley was no Jimmy Greaves or Denis Law, but they should have heard of him.
"Oh go 'way, 'aven't yer? I thought yer might 'ave done; you having yer finger on the pulse of British football and all that."
"Fuck off Evo. Who do you think you are, David Coleman?"
"Oh nice one Ragger, yer know who David Coleman is, but not our record signin'."
"'E played in last season's Cup Final didn't 'e?" Cainy interjected.
Hallelujah! A kindred spirit!
"Yeah, that's right. Come on; let's watch 'im in 'is first game. We play Man. City away first game of the season."
I was going to have to work hard throughout the summer to save the money to go, but it would be worth it to watch my beloved Reds and especially our new centre forward.

I scrounged a pair of shears off Mrs. Mabbs, Auntie Maureen's next door neighbour, and set about the task of becoming Bootle's top topiarist; well cutting privets for a few bob anyway. This was to supplement my blossoming career as Bootle's best errand-boy. I was still ripping Sophie off for a few bob and Mam's best mate, Jane, was easy pickings. She would send me to the launderette, or bagwash as she called it, with two bags of washing. Each bag was to be put in a separate washing machine. I was to buy one packet of soap-powder for each machine. Each lot of washing was to be put in separate spin-dryers. The washing was to be taken from the spin-dryers and put in separate tumble-dryers so that Jane would receive her washing back sparkling clean and completely bone dry. I did all this didn't I? Not bloody likely! One packet of soap-powder, one washing machine, one spin-dryer, one tumble-drier and pocket half the money! I shouldn't have done this really, as Jane was more than generous to me, but what the hell; I had to get the money for Manchester somehow! I also shouldn't have done it because I was deeply, madly in love with her. Or was it just a schoolboy crush? Whatever it was, my thirteen-year old hormones were running riot as this very attractive thirty-five year old woman gave me the most stinking horn every time I clapped eyes on her! I was bringing her washing back one day after ripping another five bob off her and let myself in through the back door as I usually did. There, before me, stood Jane, dressed only in black bra and knickers as she was putting her corset on.

"Oh, oh, s-sorry Jane," I stammered as my sex-goddess struggled to cover herself up, but not before I'd managed to get a very good eyeful.

"Yeah, yeah, tell yer Mam I'll see 'er later," she screamed.

Most of my fantasies about her were coming true before my very eyes, as this beautiful woman just didn't have enough hands to cover all her vital bits. I don't know who was more embarrassed, me or her, but I do know who got the biggest thrill out of it; I had a sore right wrist for weeks after that!

The fragrant and lovely Jane used to come to our house every day after work. She came one day looking more attractive than ever; tall, slim, her lovely long legs accentuated by a black mini-skirt, gorgeous dark-brown hair cascading down her shoulders. I truly was in love with her!

Even though it was a summer day, the fire was blazing in the hearth. Mam was sat directly in front of it; no wonder she had chilblains. I was sitting in Dad's armchair at the side of the fireplace - I loved claiming his chair when he was in bed! Jane was sat in an armchair directly opposite me. Her legs were crossed to reveal a vast expanse of milky white thighs. She crossed and uncrossed her legs as her skirt rode ever higher up her legs, bringing more and more of her lovely white knickers into view. I couldn't help the stirring in my young, adolescent loins. My imagination was running riot! The heat of the day and from the fire wasn't helping to alleviate my burgeoning erection; I felt as if I had Cleopatra's Needle in my trousers.

"Peter, get up an' make Jane a cup of tea."

Yer jokin' aren't yer Ma! I'm 'avin' a job to sit down, never mind stand up!

"I will in a minute Mam."

Just give me a chance to get rid of this hard on.

"Never mind in a minute, get it done now!"

Yer don't really want me to do it now Mam. I'm sure you an' Jane don't wanna to see my petrol pump sticking through my trousers.

"Okay Mam."

Shit! I had about ten seconds to think how I could get from the living room to the kitchen without my protruding trouser snake being eminently noticeable. I was frantically planning my campaign of action, but quickly realised there was no way round it; one of them was going to have to see Percy and it obviously couldn't be my Mam. I rose gingerly from my chair, trying to shuffle out sideways while I kept my crossed arms below my waist.

"Peter, are you all right?" Mam asked worriedly.

"Yeah Mam, I've just got a bit of belly ache."

I'd been on this planet nearly fourteen years and this was surely the most embarrassing moment I'd ever experienced.

I managed to keep my back to Mam, but there was no way I could hide my protuberance from Jane. As she looked at it, my tumescent member seemed as if it was going to burst, any minute, out of my trousers. Jane stared at me open-mouthed as my face lit up like the beginning of Bonanza.

I wanted the ground to open up and swallow me. No, death would have been better! I stumbled out to the kitchen to make the tea. How was I going to get rid of my throbbing storker before I returned with the tea? Got it! Why didn't I think of it before? Cissy Mulhall's bloomers! Thinking of them for two seconds was enough to bring my

53

blood-engorged dong back to its normal flaccid little state.

As I returned to the living room with the tea I'm sure a little smirk played across Jane's face.

"Peter, son, go to bed and 'ave a lie down, you don't look a bit well," said Mam, very concerned about the colour I'd turned, which was a sickly combination of green and red.

God Bless my Mam! If only she knew.

"Okay Mam. I'll see you later."

But not before I've given myself a sore wrist again!

I was making a good few bob out of cutting privets for people and was quite honoured when the local librarian and spinster of the parish Miss Duffy, asked me to cut hers. She was known to be quite well off, had never been married and lived on her own in a big house on Fernhill Road. I was looking forward to a big payday.

"Hello there young man, how long do you think it will take you to trim my privets?" she asked me in her plummy, posh voice.

"About two hours probably Miss Duffy."

It would only take an hour, but I wasn't going to tell her that. I'd probably get more money if I finished the job quickly, then I could get off and earn more money doing another job elsewhere.

"You've got an hour," she said stiffly, "I want you to cut the grass for me when you've finished."

No problem there thought I. The lawn was quite short anyway. I wouldn't be more than an hour-and-a-half.

I toiled away tirelessly under the boiling hot July sun, fortified by Miss Duffy's delicious home made lemonade.

I finished the privets right on the stroke of the allotted hour.

"I've finished Miss Duffy. Where's the lawnmower an' I'll get on with cuttin' the grass?"

"Lawnmower? Lawnmower?" she screeched incredulously.

What d'yer mean? Lawnmower? Lawnmower? What am I supposed to use? Surely not my shears?

"Sorry Miss Duffy, what d' yer want me to use?"

"These," she said, as a pair of scissors were handed to me.

Scissors? Scissors? You're 'avin' a laugh aren't yer!

"Oh, right, okay Miss Duffy."

"Make sure you do a good job young man; you'll be getting well paid."

I'd better 'ad do, yer owld bag!

"Yes Miss Duffy."

Another bloody hour I was under that sweltering sun...Mad dogs and

Englishmen and soft arse Evo. All the time I could hear the strains of flower power records: *If You're Goin' To San Francisco, Flowers In the Rain, Itchycoo Park, California Dreamin'* etc.

Yeah, try being here and cutting grass instead of smoking it; see if you preach love and peace then!

"I've finished Miss Duffy."

I'd been burning to a crisp as the witch was sitting in her nice, cool conservatory, sipping iced lemon tea, but never mind I was going to get well paid.

"Here you are young man. A fair day's pay for a fair day's work," she said sniffily as a shilling was pressed in to my hand.

A shillin'? You're fuckin' kiddin' me aren't you missus? I've been sweatin' me bollocks off 'ere for the last two bastard hours! It's worth at least five bob an' you wanna give me a lousy shillin'. I'm no poncey Boy Scout you know on Bob-a-Job week! I want payin' properly.

"Thank you Miss Duffy."

"Come inside and have a sandwich made with my own strawberry jam. I'll also give you a glass of my home made lemonade."

Stick yer fuckin' jam butty an yer lemonade up yer fuckin' arse yer fuckin' owld crow!

"No thank you Miss Duffy. Mam will be wonderin' where I am."

"Very well then young man. Tell your mother I was asking about her."

Like fuck I will! She fuckin' 'ates yer, yer fuckin' stuck-up old crone!

"Yes, Miss Duffy."

I swear, at that moment, compared to her she made Cissy Mulhall look like Jane. No wonder she'd never been married!

Us four young intrepid travellers placed our trust, not to say our lives, in the hands of Lawrenson's coaches for the trip to Manchester-brave boys that we were. To be fair to Lawrenson's most of their coaches were okay; it was just me that always seemed to get on the most rickety coach in the world. To say the coach ride was scary is to understate the fact. At one point on the East Lancs Road I really did think the old jalopy was going to explode. Where were the Ribble double-deckers when you needed them?

it was fast approaching kick off time and we were nowhere near the ground. The driver, a fat Jock called Tommy, didn't have a clue where we were.

"Right lads, get off now. I'll pick you up here a quarter of an hour after the game." Fat Tommy Jock spoke with no authority whatsoever.

"Where the fuck are we?" was the earnest question from forty-odd hot, frustrated people.

"Och, yer okay, the ground's only ten minutes away," lied Jumbo Jocko unconvincingly.

Oh great! Just dump us in the middle of Moss Side, we'll be all right. Bloody marvellous!

We got to Maine Road shortly after kick off and just about managed to get in. The match itself was fairly uneventful, except for Tommy Lawrence saving a penalty from the City captain, Tony Book. The real action was happening off the pitch. The big open terrace we were on was full of Reds. The City supporters in the Kippax Street terrace, nice people that they were, started throwing bricks at our contingent. These tokens of the Manchester people's affection for us Scousers were quite naturally returned with interest. Me, Cainy, Benno and Ragger were lucky that we were on the opposite corner of the terrace to where the bricks were flying. Ragger and Benno, like the knob'eads they were, wanted to go and join in the "fun".

"Come on Evo, let's go over there. They're throwin' bricks at each other." Ragger's powers of observation were razor sharp.

"Er, I can see that Ragger."

"Well come on then, let's get over there."

"Oh yeah its what I've always wanted, a brick in me 'ead."

"Ah yer just chicken." Superbrain Benno had spoken!

"Stay where yer are, yer pair of daft twats!" Cainy's voice of reason to the rescue. They weren't going to argue with Cainy!

We managed to negotiate leaving the ground safely enough and made our way along Princess Road in search of our coach. We were walking along when we heard this strange gurgling noise behind us. Cainy had heard it first, so it was he who got it: a big, horrible wodge of green spit and phlegm, right in his face! The guy who had spat this vile mixture rode off on his bike, laughing maniacally. It wasn't his fault. He didn't know this mad Scouser was going to run after him, much less how fit and how hard said mad Scouser was.

"Yer fuckin' 'orrible bastard!" Cainy shouted, before starting his sprint in pursuit of the Moss Side spitter.

The gurgling grotcher had foolishly decided to stick to the road rather than cycle on the pavement. He was stuck at red traffic lights and was totally unaware that Cainy was running along on the pavement, gaining on him with every stride. The lights changed to amber; Cainy was alongside him now. As the lights changed to green Cainy made a mad lunge and grabbed the gruesome gollier off his bike. Cainy then knocked seven kinds of shite out of him before the horrible prick managed to escape and ran off crying for his Mam. Drivers of cars that had screeched to a halt were watching the shenanigans in disbelief. The bike, which Cainy had used to wreak revenge on his cowardly assailant, was left, totally wrecked, right there in the middle of Princess Road. We eventually found our coach, but not before the sweet shops of Moss Side had been shoplifted of most of their chocolate. What a start to the season!

CHAPTER SIX

WITCHES AND WIZARDS

Big Tony's third game for the club was a spectacular affair. Newcastle United were the visitors in front of nearly 52,000 people. The crowd went wild when Tony scored his first goal for the club with a trademark header. There was a real excitement about our new signing and his name was booming out from the Kop. Further goals from Roger Hunt and Emlyn Hughes gave us a 3-0 interval lead. Tony achieved god-like status when a further two goals gave him a brilliant hat trick. Roger wrapped things up three minutes from time. This was great, a 6-0 win and a hat trick from our new hero; he was going to be a star for years to come!

Chelsea were the visitors to Anfield on September 9th. I'd been feeling terrible for a few days; difficulty with breathing and all the symptoms of flu'. Mam didn't want me to go to the match I was feeling so bad. It hadn't stopped her sending me on my usual Saturday morning pawnshop run though! I moaned that much to go that in the end Mam just gave in. My physical well being wasn't helped by the fact that the Boys Pen was absolutely chocker on a stifling hot September day. Tommy Smith had given us a first half lead from the penalty spot. Then it was Tony's turn to take centre stage. His first goal, a minute in to the second half was a marvellous effort, a low cross being turned in by the lightning-quick Tony, just before centre half Colin Waldron could reach it. Tony's second, a minute later, however was even better. Peter Thompson crossed another brilliant low ball which Tony met with a fantastically brave diving header no more than a foot from the floor with Waldron's boot only inches from his face. Tony had dived that low there was a worm attached to the end of his donga! Waldron was a big brute of a centre half, so for Tony to even attempt that header was bravery personified. The Kop went wild, as only the Kop could in those days. "Hateley for England," was the cry and indeed there couldn't have been many better English centre forwards than Tony around. He had scored six goals in his first seven games and was only just behind Sir Roger in my affections. A banner had appeared at the front of the Anfield Road end proclaiming, **"Tony Hateley King in the air"** and indeed he was. Another one alongside it read, **"Sir Roger Hunt"** I was definitely going to stand next to them the next time I had the money to go in the Anny. My Dad had long regaled me with the tale of Albert Stubbins' "goal in the snow" - a fabulous diving header against Birmingham. A goal, according to Dad that would never be equalled.

Dad had been to the match with his mates and was just getting ready to go to the Walnut pub with Mam when I got home.
"All right son, did yer see that header from Hateley?"
"Yeah Dad, brilliant wasn't it but I'll bet yer say it wasn't as good as the goal in the snow."
"No, it was better."
Christ, that was praise indeed coming from my Dad!
"You look the colour of boiled shite," was Mam's diagnosis of my rapidly deteriorating medical condition.
Well hang on Mam. How would you know what the colour of boiled shite looked like? Unless of course you have actually been to the trouble of putting shite in to a pan and boiling it. If you have, I would say this was a very strange thing indeed for you to have done. Strange occurrences in this house are plentiful I know, but this would indeed be the strangest!
"I know Mam. I feel as if I've been run over by a bus."
Not that I'd ever been run over by a bus.
"I'll ask Mrs. Reid to 'ave a look at yer."

Mrs. Reid, old bag though she was, had been in the Women's Royal Voluntary Service during the war, had been a nurse before she retired and knew her stuff. She had actually saved the life of my sister Collette when little Collie was only fourteen months old, on the day JFK was assassinated incidentally, so I know exactly where I was that day! Collie had electrocuted herself and Mrs. Reid had given her the kiss of life after Collette's heart had stopped beating. It was particularly brave of Mrs. Reid as she suffered severe heart problems herself. I suppose I should have been eternally grateful to her, but she was an old bag.
"'Ow are yer feelin' lad?"
Oh fuckin' wonderful, can't yer see? Yeah, I'm a picture of health. Yer wouldn't be in 'ere if I was feelin' all right would yer? Yer stupid old witch!
"Terrible Mrs. Reid. I can't breathe properly, I've got a headache, my back's killin' me, I feel dead faint and my chest is dead sore." I was actually crying now.
"It sounds to me like he's got pleurisy."

What the fuck's that!
"Does he need to go to 'ospital Maggie?" Mam asked.
Why did adults do that? Talk about you to each other as if you weren't there. Why didn't they just talk directly to me? One of the great mysteries of life!
"Yeah 'e does. I'll go an' phone an ambulance," said the wicked witch of Grogan Square.
Can't yer take me on yer broomstick?

I spent two nights under observation in Bootle hospital. The diagnosis of Maggie "Florence Nightingale" Reid had been spot on - pleurisy it was. I was sent home to complete my recovery under the care of the marvellous Doctor Owen from Rimrose Road. I was to take a course of antibiotics and stay in bed until I was better. Yippee! Much better than school! But shit! We were playing Bolton at home in the League Cup on Wednesday. Mam put her foot down with a firm hand and flatly refused to let me out of bed to go. To be honest I was too weak to protest very much, but I was pig-sick at having to miss my first home match for eighteen months.

I passed a late fitness test on the morning of the derby match ten days later to see us win 1-0 with a goal from Sir Roger. All the usual stuff went on: the ritual burning of a blue and white scarf on the Kop, Gordon West getting a handbag etc. Keith West was at number two in the charts with "*Excerpt from a Teenage Opera*". The chorus of the song - "Grocer Jack, Grocer Jack is it true what Mommy says you won't be back, oh Grocer Jack?" was adapted by the Kop to, "Alan Ball, Alan Ball, is it true what Shankly says you're worth fuck all, oh Alan Ball?" This wasn't strictly true, as Shanks had been desperate to sign Ball before Harry Catterick stepped in, but it was a good song to take the piss with. Shanks had the utmost admiration for Ball as a player, and quite rightly so. "*Mr. Perpetual Motion*" would run all day and allied to bags of skill it made him the complete midfielder. Suffice to say I would have loved him to play for us. This game though was most memorable for me as the first time I heard this famous song:

"Oh I am a Liverpudlian and I come from the Spion Kop.
I like to sing, I like to shout, I get thrown out quite a lot.
We support a team that's dressed in red; it's a team that you all

know.
It's a team that we call Liverpool and to glory we will go.
We've won the League, we've won the Cup and we've been to
Europe too.
And we've played the toffees for a laugh and we've left them feelin'
blue. Five nil!
One two, one two three, one two three four, five nil."

I went back to school on the Monday after my enforced holiday and hammered that song in to as many Evertonians as I possibly could.
"What are you singin' that for? You're supposed to be a Catholic, not a bloody Proddydog," was the reply from most of them.
"What's that got to do with anythin'?"
"It's to the tune of, "The Sash my father wore." It's an Orange song that."
"So fuckin' what. I don't give a fuck about religion. People kill each other in the name of religion. My religion is LFC."
"Yer don't wanna let Holy Joe hear yer sayin' that."
Holy Joe was our Religious Education teacher: Joe Fearon. He really was a great bloke, but he couldn't half bang on about religion. He had a bit of a soft spot for me; as to outside appearances I was a good Catholic boy. I knew all the colours of the vestments the priests would wear on any given Sunday and could recite the Catechism verbatim. This was only because I had a better memory than most people did though. I had memorised the vestments and Catechism at ten years of age. This was because Canon Wilcox from St. Elizabeth's would come to classes on Monday mornings and if you didn't know what colour vestments the priest had worn at Mass the day before he would hit you very hard with a blackboard duster. Either Sister Frances or Sister Agnes who would rap you across the knuckles with a ruler if you couldn't recite any given passage of the Catechism would closely follow him. Can you imagine that? We were nine, ten; eleven years of age and getting twatted by these people dressed all in black because we weren't religious freaks like them! Scary or what? Canon Wilcox died on September 25th 1965; the day we beat Everton 5-0. Maybe there is a God after all. Mam and Dad insisted that I go to Mass every Sunday even though the only time they saw the inside of a church was for weddings, christenings and funerals. The good side of it though was that Mam used to give me threepence to put on the collection plate. This would be spent in Grimley's sweet shop just before I went

to watch the Corry football team at Orrell Pleasure. The timing of it fitted in quite nicely though. Mass would last about ninety minutes, or so it seemed with all that Kyrie Eleison, Christe Eleison shite going on: very convenient!

"Who said Mass today Peter?"
Jimmy Brinkley; fuckin' blindin' goal.
"Father Kelly Mam."
"Is 'e the one yer Auntie Maureen fancies?"
"Yeah, I think so. She fancies Father Coakley as well."
"Did yer put yer threepence on the collection plate?"
Yeah, Mister Grimley said thanks very much. 'E gave me an Arrowbar, four Walker's Caramels an' two Flying Saucers in return.
"Yeah Mam."
"Was it a good service?"
Yeah, The Corry beat The Walnut 3-1. Fuckin go' 'ead!
"Yeah Mam. We said prayers for everyone who's sick an' Father Kelly gave a boss sermon."
"Who's that new priest Peter?"
John Scott. Brilliant winger 'e is. Signed 'im from The Linacre. Plays for Aintree Royal on a Saturday in the Bootle J.O.C. Could have been a professional 'im.
"Father Byrne Mam. I think Auntie Ann fancies 'im."
"Who did yer see in church?"
We all went: Smudge, Timmy, Pilch, Conk, Miggy, Mogsy and me!
"I saw loads of people Mam, but they didn't see me. I was sittin' right at the back of the church."
"Did yer see Mrs. Reid?"
"Yeah Mam."
That was safe enough. The old trout never missed.
"She's goin' to Mass tonight."
"Is she Mam? She's keen isn't she, twice in one day?"
"'Er son plays for the Cuckoo football team doesn't 'e?"
"Yeah Mam, they 'ad a big game today. They were playin' a team from Huyton at Orrell Pleasure."
"Yeah I know an' the reason Mrs. Reid's going to Mass tonight is because she went to watch 'im play this mornin'." Mam's eyes were widening on the way to... **LILY EYES.**
Oh shit!
"So yer didn't see 'er in church this mornin', did yer Peter? Because

63

yer didn't go to Mass this mornin', did you Peter? Because yer went to Orrell Pleasure this mornin', didn't yer Peter." Full-blown Lily eyes!
In that order: no, no, yes.
"I'm sorry Mam."
The fuckin' old twat had grassed me up again! I hated this woman with a passion! Why were adults, Maggie twattin' Reid in particular, so intent on making my life as difficult as possible? I wasn't bothered what they did; going around having affairs, beating their wives and fiddling the UAB. Why couldn't they just leave me alone and let me get on with my life? All I lived for was footy. Okay, I used to fiddle a few bob off them but it wasn't as if I was breaking in to their houses or knocking old ladies over the head and stealing their handbags. Leave me alone, you shower of bastards! I knew what was coming next. Mam had perfected this technique where she would get me in a headlock and then elbow me in the back; Ma elbow. It sounds cruel but it wasn't really. It didn't really hurt and it was much better than getting slapped.

Funnily enough I started going to Mass quite a bit after that (well when The Corry weren't playing anyway). Mam didn't pester me to go anymore, but I didn't get threepence to put on the collection plate either. Miggy had volunteered to be an altar boy, which was strange as he was a right little urchin. Even stranger still, the church accepted him.
"'Ow come yer an altar boy Miggy? I didn't think yer were really bothered about church."
"Because I can rob loads of money off the collection plate when the priest isn't around"
Go 'ead! We had a ball every Sunday night for about six weeks until Miggy got caught and was excommunicated or something.

Our Inter Cities Fairs Cup campaign had started with an easy 4-1 aggregate victory over Swedish side Malmo.
In the second round we were to face crack West German team: TSV Munich, with the first leg being at Anfield. This was going to be tricky. The goals had dried up for Big Tony; he hadn't scored for eight games. He soon put that right however when he scored three minutes after "*Saint*" had given us a sixth minute lead. Tommy Smith scored a penalty just before half time and we then riot in the second half. Two goals each from Sir Roger and Cally plus another from Thommo

gave us an 8-0 lead with twenty minutes still to go. I was pissin' myself laughing when the Kop chanted, "Nine, nine, nine," in German accents to make it sound like, "Nien, nien, nien." Twenty-odd thousands coats please! We were going to win our first European trophy: no problem!

That victory set us up nicely for the visit of Man. Utd. They had won the League the season before and were in second place, lying one point behind us, this time round. I was quite confident of a good win. This was our eighth home League game of the season only one of which had been played before a crowd of less than 50,000. A crowd of over 54,000 created a crackling atmosphere for this one.

George Best absolutely destroyed us. Besty had everything. He was primarily left-footed but could use his right to good effect also. He had unbelievable speed, was a great dribbler, could cross a ball like nobody else, tackled like a demon, headed a ball beautifully and could look after himself. I watched him on Match of the Day once when United were playing Chelsea. Ron "Chopper" Harris, one of the games real hard men was trying to kick lumps out of him. I say trying because he couldn't get anywhere near George. "Chopper" was flailing away madly as Besty went past him time after time, just taking the piss out of him in the end. United, with Best running our defence ragged, were two-nil up at half time. Sir Roger scored a late goal, which was no more than consolation as we were deservedly trounced. I was in the Boys Pen and had befriended two United fans who had gone in there thinking that it would be a nice safe place to be. They were getting cracked right, left and centre. I was trying to protect the two lads, as I felt sorry for them so I was getting quite a few belts myself. At the end of the game it was absolutely horrible as the three of us got a severe battering. I eventually managed to get them to a copper and escape the baying mob. I then escorted them to their coach which was parked in Priory Road where there was total mayhem going on. Coach windows were getting smashed all over the place. The two lads were shitting themselves, but managed to get back to their coach in one piece. I decided there and then that I had been in the Boys Pen for the last time. No matter what it took to get the money to go in to the Kop or the Anny there was no chance that I would ever go in the "monkey cage" again. I had enjoyed my time in the Pen, it was at once scary, exciting, wonderful and atmospheric but I'd had enough of it. It had been fun though!

CHAPTER SEVEN

MYTHS AND MAGIC

"What the bloody 'ell 'appened to you?" Mam politely enquired when I got home.

I couldn't tell her I'd been defending a couple of United supporters.

"Some big lads beat me up in the Pen an' took all my money off me Mam," pretend tears streaming down my face. Crocodiles had nothing on me!

"Yer not goin' in there any more. I'll give yer a bit more money so yer can go in the Anfield Road end."

Re-sult!

"Thanks Mam."

At that moment I loved my Mam more than I loved Roger Hunt. Of course I couldn't tell her that I loved her, could I? Your Mam was your Mam and your Dad was your Dad; you couldn't go round telling them you loved them! If I got a slap or Ma's elbow I could mutter under my breath, "I hate you." Of course I didn't mean it; I loved my parents very much but to actually say it - no chance!

"Well yer leavin' school in the summer and yer'll be able to pay for yerself when yer get a job."

I really wanted to stay on at school to take my CSE's, but there was no chance. Mam and Dad insisted that I leave school as soon as possible to help with the family finances. After all, my elder sister, Pauline, had left school and was now working, slaughtering chickens in County Produce on Bridle Road. She had no desire to stay on at school anyway as she was fuckin' thick! I'd also been earmarked for a "career" in the "chicken factory." Oh yeah, I really wanted a lifetime of being covered in chicken shit and blood! Go and fuck yourselves!

I became a bit of a hero in school as I told everybody who would listen how I had single-handedly fought off two United fans who were trying to give me a good hiding outside the ground after the game. Over the course of a week I had exaggerated that number to six. Boss bullshitter I was! Even the cock of St. Wilfred's, Jimmy Best, congratulated me.

Smudge had got himself a girlfriend and only went to the occasional match. Timmy was still going with his Dad. Pilch had stopped going altogether. I didn't mind going to the match on my own but I knew that Michael Kavanagh went in the Anny so I was going to ask him could I go with him.

"All right Kav. Can I go the match with yer on Saturday?"

"Yeah okay Evo. I go in the Anny."

"Yeah I know. Where d'yer stand?"

"At the front, by the Hateley and Hunt banners."

"Fuckin' go 'ead! That's where I wanna stand."

"Yeah it's boss. The girls who run all the Fan Clubs stand there an' everyone of them is dead fit!"

They couldn't have been as fit as Jane. It seemed as if there were only two thoughts that occupied my mind: Jane and football, but not necessarily in that order! I was sitting in Maths class one day while Matty Dolan was banging on about sines, cosines and tangents. My thoughts drifted to my beloved: thoughts of her svelte hips; the slender lines of her long lovely legs; the firm, curvaceous swell of her voluptuous breasts, her nipples sticking out erect and proud like two of Tommy Smith's footy studs; her beautiful face which had been sculpted in heaven; her wonderful bottom in that tight little mini-skirt like two peaches in a hanky; the sweet smell of her delicious perfume; dark brown tresses falling about her shoulders like a waterfall cascading down a mountain; glimpses of her skimpy knickers when she sat opposite me or bent over. That familiar warm feeling stirring in my loins had completely taken my mind off Matty's inane algebraic ramblings.

"Etherington," I heard somewhere in the background, probably about a million miles away.

Fuck off Matty, I'm thinkin' about Jane.

"Etherington, explain what a hypotenuse is."

Matty, shove your fuckin' hypotenuse up yer arse!

Thwack! A piece of chalk, which I swear Matty himself had carved out of some great cliff, hit me just above my left ear.

"What's wrong with you boy?" Matty barked in his gruff Glaswegian growl. The rumour went that Matty had been deported from the Gorbals to Liverpool because he was too hard!

I'll tell yer what's wrong yer Glaswegian gorilla! Yer've just interrupted one of the most beautiful moments of my life. Fuckin' adults again. Leave me alone!

"I've got stomach cramps sir."

"Then go to the toilet and get rid of them!"

Why did adults do that; think that by having a shit you'd get rid of bellyache? Another great mystery!

"Yes sir, thank you sir."

I returned five minutes later, much relieved.

"Are you feeling all right now boy?"

"Yes sir, much better sir."

My right wrist is a bit sore like, but I can get over that.

Kav introduced me to the girls who ran the fan clubs. They were indeed, as Kav had said, all dead fit. I took a shine in particular to the Roger Hunt Fan Club secretary; a very nice girl called Irene. She wasn't the best looking girl of the group, but there was some thing about her I really liked. She lived in Crosby and was posh without being stuck-up. I might have been biased by the fact that Sir Roger was my favourite player, but I did strike up an immediate rapport with her.

We kicked-off the game against Wolves with our usual kick-off routine: Hateley to Hunt, back to Smith who plays it out to the left wing to Thompson. This usually resulted in a throw-in to the opposition. Miraculously, this day, we won a corner out of it. No problem for the Wolves defence though; we were crap at corners! Thommo ambled out towards the Kemlyn Road corner flag with that "do I really have to do this" attitude he very often displayed. The corner came over. Next thing the ball was in the Kop net - off Hateley. What had he scored it with? It certainly hadn't been with his head. The two girls who ran Big Tony's fan club, Sheila and Sue, were in paroxysms of delight. They didn't care what part of his body he scored it with. They wouldn't have been bothered if he'd have scored it with his knob; in fact they probably would have preferred it if he had have scored it with his donga! He had in fact scored it with his elbow! We went on to win the match 2-1. I had enjoyed my first match with my new friends. I did miss the atmosphere of the Pen though. I didn't want to two-time Jane or anything but I couldn't get Irene out of my mind that night. I had the solution at hand, so to speak. I used my left wrist instead of my right so that I wouldn't be cheating on Jane.

At school on the Monday all the talk between Kav and me was of how fit the girls were.

"All right Kav. Irene's dead fit isn't she?"

"Yeah, I fancy 'er myself."

"I thought you were goin' out with that Christine?"

"I am but I'm gonna chuck 'er."

"Why? She's dead nice."

"She won't come across."

"What d'yer mean?"

"Fuckin' 'ell Evo are yer thick or what? Yer know, she won't shag."

"Oh that! Oh right, yeah. I thought yer said she won't come along."

"'Ave you ever 'ad a shag Evo?"

"Oh aye yeah!"

"What was 'er name then?"

"Er, Jane. Yeah, she's lovely as well. Dead fit like!"

"You're a lyin' bastard Evo."

"I'm not Kav, honest. 'Ow many have you shagged?"

"Four."

Bastard! I believed him as well, good-looking twat that he was. He also never tired of showing everybody how enormous his weapon was after PE.

"Are yer gonna go for Irene then?"

"Yeah, next game against Leeds."

Prick! Leave 'er alone, I want 'er!

The match against Leeds was played on a freezing cold December day with a covering of snow on the pitch. All the girls were there again. I was, by now, a member of all the players' fan clubs. The only one I can remember not having a fan club was Ron Yeats, perhaps Rowdy was just too hard for that sort of thing. All the fan clubs were run by girls with the exception of Tommy Smith. The Anfield Iron's fan club was quite rightly run by a lad: Gordon Rimmer. Irene was a sweet, shy, retiring girl and as I was painfully shy myself we didn't get much beyond polite conversation that day. We did have one thing in common though: A burning love for Liverpool Football Club and Sir Roger Hunt in particular.

The attendance of just under 40,000 was quite comfortably the smallest of the season. All I can say is that we must have all been mad as it was absolutely bloody freezing!

Sir Roger gave us the lead after eighteen minutes. I was standing next to Irene who promptly grabbed me in a big bear hug-well hardly a bear hug, she was too small for that, but you know what I mean. I liked this feeling of a girl in my arms; it was good! I nearly died when

she planted a kiss on my cheeks.
Go on kiss me on the lips. Go on, go on, please. Go on put yer tongue
in me mouth like Kav had told me girls did to 'im. Go on please!
Why did moments like these seem to last only about a millionth of a
second, yet when I was getting punished by my parents or teachers it
seemed to last forever. Bastard adults again!

"Sir Roger Hunt is wonderful, Sir Roger Hunt is wonderful.
Full of health, full of go, full of vigour.
Sir Roger Hunt is wonderful."

Fuckin' right he was wonderful, especially if I was going to get a kiss
every time he scored, even if it was only on the cheek. I loved the man
even more than ever now!

A minute before half time came an incident that was to go down in
Kop folklore, not to say myth. Gary Sprake, the Leeds goalkeeper
who was quite good and had won many international caps for Wales.
had the ball safely in his arms and was ready to throw the ball out to a
defender. The ball which had collected quite a bit of snow was now
very wet. Sprake was about to throw the ball when it squirmed out of
his grasp and went behind him in to an obviously unguarded net.
Everybody in the ground, except the small contingent of Leeds
supporters behind us, were pissing themselves laughing after the initial
stunned reaction. I was trying to blag Irene that our hero had scored
the goal in order to get another kiss, but she was having none of it.
Shortly after, the referee blew his whistle for half-time. The first record
to be played over the tannoy at half-time was the song which launched
Des O'Connor's singing career, "Careless Hands." After the laughter
of nearly 40,000 people had subsided the Kop starting singing along
with the song. The myth that the Kop started singing it as soon as the
ball went in the net is just that. It was still bloody funny all the same
though.

Roger scored in the next two games. Yes! Kisses each time, still on
the cheek, but a kiss all the same. By contrast Big Tony wasn't scoring
at all. Rumours were rife that he was to be dropped amidst Chinese
whispers of bust-ups, both verbal and physical with Shankly, Smith
and St. John.

Tony was indeed dropped for the first game of 1968. I was in the Kop for the visit of West Brom with a cousin of mine: John Johannson. Jojo gained a certain kind of fame in the Kop during the late sixties and early seventies. He was a bit of a nutter, but he was a good lad really. Sir Roger returned to the team after being injured for the previous match. Geoff Strong was chosen as his strike partner ahead of Tony. Shanks' decision was vindicated as early as the third minute when Geoff put us in to the lead. Jojo stood on a crush barrier, as I thought to celebrate the goal, but then collapsed in a heap on the people in front of him. As he was being passed over heads towards the front of the Kop from where we were in the middle, he turned to me and gave a maniacal smile. That's just what he was: a fuckin' maniac, good lad though. He returned to his spec next to me at half-time.

"What the fuckin' 'ell were you doin' there Jojo?"

"Just 'avin' a laugh Evo."

"Yer fuckin' mad!"

"Yeah I know"

How could I argue with that?

Guess who scored a brilliant hat-trick in the second half? Yes, Roger. I missed out there big time didn't I?

Three kisses I would have got. Who knows what that would have led to? Yeah, absolutely fuck all!

CHAPTER EIGHT

GIRLS, GOALS AND GREATS

Zoltan Varga: If you think that name doesn't sit comfortably with past European greats such as Cruyff, Seeler, Beckenbauer, Albert, Muller, Eusebio, Riva, Rivera et al then you weren't at Anfield on January 9th 1968. Ferencvaros came to Anfield holding a one goal advantage from the first leg in Budapest. Florian Albert, who had taken Goodison Park by storm in Hungary's famous World Cup victory over Brazil eighteen months earlier, was celebrating his thirtieth birthday. "Happy Birthday dear Albert," sang the Kop but it was Varga who must have thought all his birthdays had come at once that night.

The pitch was very hard under a covering of snow and Varga quite literally skated effortlessly through our defence. Zoltan's display was the best I have ever seen by a visiting European player at Anfield. He had the balance and poise of Blondin, the grace and elegance of Nureyev and the speed and athleticism of Viren. Rather than defend their lead Ferencvaros, with Varga of course at the centre of everything, chose to attack and won the game 1-0. Branikovits scored the goal but it was the display by Zoltan Varga that will stay forever in the memory of those who were at the game. Zoltan defected from Hungary shortly after and went to play for Aberdeen but he never really hit it off in Scotland and was last seen with his underpnats on his head on top of an oil rig doing the mazurka.

"Mam can I 'ave me match money?"
"Don't be stupid, they're not gonna play in this."
What d'yer mean they're not gonna play in this? It's only bloody fog. It's an FA Cup match against Walsall yer know, not a friggin' girls match! Of course they're gonna play. Just give me the money will yer.
"Mam, they will play, honest. We played against Ajax in worse than this."
"Who's Ajax? That's what I use to clean the oilcloth with."
Oh only one of the best teams in Europe. Does it matter who they are anyway? Just give me the money.
"Mam can I 'ave the money please? If we don't play I'll give yer the money back."

"Yeah but you'll 'ave got the bus there and back, so that money will be wasted."

Mam, look it's six o'clock. If I don't go soon I'm gonna miss the kick off. Please, please, just give me the money.

"Well I'll walk there and back Mam, just give me enough to get in the Anny Road end."

"You're not walkin' in this. It's not fit to send a dog out."

You are fuckin' kiddin' me aren't yer Ma? You've sent me to Mrs. Roberts to borrow money when the snow's been a fuckin' foot thick an' no bastard bus fare to get there.

"Please Mam, come on I don't mind. Please just give me the money." I was nearly crying by now.

"No."

Ah, yer doin' me 'ead in! Just give me the fuckin' money!

"Ah Mam, please, please. Come on, I don't wanna miss the match." I was crying bucketloads of real tears now. I wasn't always a crocodile. Strange how I could put up with a good hiding and not so much as even moisten my lachrymal glands, yet the thought of missing a match could reduce me to a blubbering, quivering wreck crying rivers of tears. Help however was at hand in the unlikely shape of my beloved. Jane had just walked through the back door as my torrent of tears threatened to engulf Bootle in a great tidal wave.

"What's the matter with you Peter?" asked Jane with real concern in her voice.

"Me m-Mam w-won't let m-me g-go the m-match," I sobbed in a great wailing welter. Not a crocodile in sight!

"Oh Lily let 'im go. Our George 'as gone. 'E said it was on the wireless that the match is definitely on."

"Oh, 'ere go on then, go the bloody match. I suppose it's worth it just to get rid of yer. Don't blame me though if they don't play."

Halle-fuckin'-lujah!

I was out the back door like shit off a shovel.

My thoughts for Jane at that moment were, for once, not lewd ones. They were thoughts of genuine fondness and affection. She'd pulled me right out of the shit there, good and proper! How could I ever thank her? I know! I won't rip her off for any money when I go to the launderette on Friday. I also mentally promised the beautiful one not to investigate her underwear before I put it in the washing machine.

I'd been waiting ten minutes on Hawthorne Road for the 52 bus to take me to Spellow Lane when a Corporation bus inspector appeared. "All right lad. What are you waitin' there for."
For a fuckin' spaceship! What do you think yer silly old prick?
"For the bus to the match mister."
"Well you'll 'ave a long wait son, the buses came off the road an hour ago. The drivers won't go out in this. Anyway the match'll be off."
Don't you fuckin' start as well!
"I suppose I'll 'ave to walk then mister."

I ran nearly all the way to Anfield arriving just on kick-off time. The usual gang were all there, well I think they were, as you could hardly see your hand in front of your face in the dense fog. Standing at the front of the Anny we could just about see as far as the edge of the penalty area. We were attacking the Kop goal in the first half and after twenty-four minutes a great roar went up from that end. The chant of, "Tony Hateley" told us that the big man had scored. Nine minutes later a similar roar followed by the same chant signalled that Big Tone was well and truly back on form. A minute later, another roar and the Geoff Strong song meant we were three-nil ahead. Tony's hat trick goal came in the sixty-fourth minute. The Kop sang, "We wanna know who scored."
We sang, "Tony Hateley."
The Kop's reply was, "Thank you very much for Tony Hateley."
The chants were repeated when Tony notched his fourth after seventy-one minutes. I was willing Roger to score so that I would get my customary kiss but it was not to be. We ended up 5-2 winners. The two girls, Sheila and Sue were all over Kav; the jammy bastard! The long, cold walk back home in the freezing fog was made bearable only by the thoughts of Big Tone's scoring feat. Surely the rumours of him being a troublemaker and that he would be leaving at the end of the season could not be true.

A coach was organised by the Fan Clubs for the away game at Wolverhampton. I was getting more and more attached to Irene, so was made up when she sat next to me on the way there. The match itself was crap and we were a goal down for most of the game. Time was running out for us when Roger netted the equaliser ten minutes from time. Yippee; a kiss coming up! I turned round to grab Irene. Oh no! There she was in the arms of Kav and it wasn't just a peck on the cheek, it was a full-blown mouth to mouth snog! . If I hadn't have been so happy at Roger scoring I would have cried right there on the spot. Never mind, I'd be sitting next to Irene on the way home, so that would be some consolation. Wrong! As soon as we got back on the coach Kav made a beeline for Irene and I ended up sitting next to a lad I didn't know. Kav and Irene were in the seats opposite me so I had to put up with the sight of them swapping spit all the way home. Pair of bastards!

When we got off the coach and Kav had managed to extricate himself from the intertwining with Irene we made our way to the bus stop.
"Did yer see me gettin'' into Irene," preened the tall, dark handsome twat.
Yeah, I fuckin' did yer gobshite!
"Yeah go 'ead Kav. Get in there mate!"
"I'm takin' 'er the pictures next Friday."
Are yer, yer fuckin' prick? Oh deep fuckin' joy!
"Nice one Kav. 'Ope she er comes er across for yer like."
"Yeah, so do I."
Well if she does I'm gonna slit yer throat, yer big 'orrible bastard!

"'Ow d'yer get on son?" Mam asked.
"We drew one all Mam."
"Did yer 'ave a good time?"
"Yeah Mam, great."
"Well why do yer look so sad? Yer look as if yer've been cryin'."
"Nah Mam, it's just that my eyes are sore and they've been waterin'."
"Take an aspirin then."
Ma's answer to every ailment was, "Take an aspirin."
"Mam, I've got a bit of a cold."
"Take an aspirin."
"Mam, I've got a broken leg."
"Take an aspirin."
"Mam, some mad bastard 'as just 'it me with a machete. There's blood spurtin' all over the place. Me 'ead's 'angin' on by the merest thread, in fact it's just about to fall off and I think I'm probably gonna die."
"Take an aspirin."
I had no trouble falling asleep that night; tears were better than any sleeping pills.
Kav never did get it on with Irene. He was much too busy flirting with

all the other girls. I didn't get any more kisses when Roger scored though. My chance had well and truly disappeared.

We drew 1-1 at Tottenham in the FA Cup fifth round, our goal coming from another massive header by Hateley. There was a picture of the goal in the following Monday's Echo and I swear the big fella was two feet above the crossbar when he headed the ball.

The replay three days later stands out in the memory because of one very peculiar incident. The game was all square at 1-1 and looked to be heading for extra-time until we were awarded a penalty twelve minutes from time. As the penalty was about to be taken Spurs were making a substitution. Tommy Smith took the penalty, which was saved by Pat Jennings. However, the referee ordered the kick to be retaken as the Spurs player about to be substituted was still on the pitch along with the player who had come on as substitute. The Spurs Manager, Bill Nicholson, was going mental but really it was his fault that they had twelve men on the pitch when the kick was taken. The Anfield Iron however made no mistake from the retaken kick, which put us through to the next round where we would face West Bromwich Albion.

Our luck had deserted us in this round though. Alf Arrowsmith, replacing Tony Hateley, missed a glorious chance, which would have won us the tie at The Hawthorns. Tony was back in for the replay and scored our goal in a 1-1 draw. We lost the third game played at Spit City (Maine Road) by two goals to one with our goal once again being scored by "The King in the Air." The combined attendance for the three games was an astonishing 163,338. This was a very bad time for my family as my brother Mark, who was only eight years old, was critically ill in hospital after receiving massive head injuries when he was run over by a car on Scotland Road. Mark was transferred to a specialist unit at Heswall hospital. Mam and Dad made the long journey over there every day. I felt really sorry for them, as money was very tight and they had to fit these visits in with their work. They were promised help by a Catholic organisation called, I think, St. Vincent de Paul's. They never did get that financial help though and had to soldier on under the heavy burden themselves.

The Fan Clubs were running one of their social nights at Blair Hall and it was here I met my Number One and Number Two heroes of the time: Sir Roger Hunt and Tony Hateley. Roger and Tony were both perfect gentlemen and when told by Irene and Sue of Mark's condition both of them promised to visit him, which they did the next day. This social night was a joint affair with the Alan Ball and Colin Harvey Fan Clubs. Both the Everton players sent cards to Mark, good people that they were.

Roger and Tony were scoring freely in the run-in to the end of the season but defeats at home to Sheffield United and away to West Ham more or less put paid to our chances of the Championship. With two games left, at home to Nottingham Forest and away to Stoke, we needed maximum points. Manchester City on the other hand needed just one point from their last game at Newcastle.

The 6-1 win against Forest was too little too late. Another hat-trick from Tony, two from Roger and an Ian St. John goal somewhat eased the blow of City clinching the League with a 4-3 win at St. James's Park.

Another Fan Club outing to Stoke resulted in more heartache for me. We lost the game 1-2 and Kav was up to his slippery tricks again. That lad could have wore a top hat and still crawled under a snake's belly!

Irene's fifteenth birthday party was held at her parent's big posh house in Crosby. For me it was like walking in to Paradise. Irene's Dad had a bookcase full of books about Liverpool and every one of them got the Evo seal of approval: "Hunt For Goals" by Sir Roger and "Boom at the Kop" by Ian St. John got special attention from me. All the girls from the Fan Clubs were there, most of them with boyfriends, apart from Irene. Would this be my big chance?
Kav had somebody else on his arm, so I should be okay.
We were all in celebratory mood, especially as Everton had lost the FA Cup Final 1-0 to West Bromwich Albion, the goal being scored by Jeff Astle. W.B.A - Won By Astle.
Irene, as usual, looked lovely. I really was very fond of her - not in the same way as I felt for Jane but still very fond of her anyway. Maybe I'd spent too much time reading the Liverpool books but the night just

seemed to go in a flash. After we had watched the highlights of the Cup Final it was time to go home and I had hardly even spoken to Irene. The fact that I was painfully shy didn't help either. Evo's big chance had gone. I'd put football before a woman; it wouldn't be the last time that would happen. Well, you've got to get your priorities right, haven't you?

CHAPTER NINE

THE FLYING DUTCHMAN AND THE PSEUDO WELSHMAN

The three months between the end of the season and me leaving school were whiled away doing not much at all.

I left St. Wilfred's six weeks before my fifteenth birthday. The last day was taken up by promising to keep in touch with each other; we even did that blood brothers thing. I was going to miss the likes of John Durnin, Jed Coyne, Brian McIlroy, Paul Lloyd, Paul Flusk, Harry Wildman, John Shaw, Dennis Scowen, Mark Smith and Brian Walker. I would even miss most of the teachers: Dennis Costigan, Gus Swift, Matty Dolan, Tom Diggle, Bernard Forshaw, Tom Ditchburn, Tom "Pansy" Potter, Dan Brady, Paul Toole, Brian Cooper and of course dear old Joe Fearon. I would not, however, miss our PE teacher, Arthur Stevens. He was a right crotchety old git who would think nothing of humiliating a boy in front of the whole class for forgetting his kit. The fact that my Mam couldn't afford much kit for me meant that I was humiliated more than most. Funnily enough I met him about ten years after I left school when I was refereeing a schoolboys match in Crosby. He was scouting for Everton and was nice as pie to me. I suppose the old demon he had to be in school was replaced by a normal, decent person outside the classroom or the gym.

Most of the lads had jobs to go to when they left school, the majority of them in Litherland Tannery. I was going to have to wait a while though until I was at least fifteen, so it was going to have to be another summer of doing odd jobs. My first away match of the season was planned for Leeds the day after my birthday. The first match of the season would be at home to Manchester City.

"Peter, Mrs. Reid wants yer to go an' see 'er", Mam said.
Oh for fuck sake! What 'ave I done now?
"Okay Mam, I'll go and see her now."
I couldn't think what I'd done wrong. I hadn't given cheek to the old cow. I'd even done some messages for her yesterday and didn't get a single penny for going. Must be something bad though; you didn't get summoned to the inner sanctum for nothing. I will say this for the old

boot - she always used to call us in at Christmas and give us a selection box, nuts, oranges etc.
To be called in at the height of summer though was unheard of.

The front door was ajar; a bad sign, she was ready for me.
"Hello Mrs. Reid. Mam said yer wanted me."
"Yes, come in my son."
I'm not yer fuckin' son, yer owld witch.
I don't suppose she meant anything by it. After all, Auntie Eileen used to call me "My son" and I was her nephew! Very confusing! Perhaps there was something I wasn't being told.

Mrs. Reid's living room was a very confusing mixture of Catholic and Protestant. Predominantly Protestant I suppose seeing as Mrs. Reid was a staunch Orange Lodge member. She used to march every July 12th along Stanley Road. I threw a stone at her one year as the march reached the corner of Marsh Lane. I shouldn't have done that should I? After all, she wasn't doing me any harm. The picture of King Billy in all his regalia on one wall just didn't sit right when staring at him directly opposite was a picture of Jesus Christ. You know that one where he's holding his heart in his hand? Used to scare the shit out of me that one! On the other two walls the Pope and the Archbishop of Canterbury were competing in the final of the World Stare-Out Championship. I think the old Archbishop won it when the Pope couldn't take it any longer and broke down crying before offering Archie out!

"Peter, this is Keret, a friend of mine from Holland."
Oh aye yer dirty owld mare
"Hello Peter. How are you? Mrs. Reid has told me much about you."
Get to fuck! You're never Dutch; yer speak perfect fuckin' English. I 'eard Johann Cruyff being interviewed after Ajax beat us an' 'e didn't speak like you.
"Pleased to meet you sir. All good things Mrs. Reid's told you I hope!"
Yeah, like fuck! She'd probably been slagging me off rotten to him.
"Yes, many good things. You are supporting Liverpool Mrs. Reid says. Please, call me Keret."
Sounded too much like carrot to me. I was definitely gonna end up calling him carrot!
"Yes Keret, I'm going the match today; Man City at home. First game

of the season. Should be a great game. Man City are the Champions, they're a great side; Bell, Lee, Summerbee, Oakes, Pardoe, Book."
"Yes I know."
Do yer fuck! 'Ow the fuck do you know? You're from Holland!
"I follow English football very closely. Liverpool is my favourite team."
Fuckin' go 'ead! I was beginning to like this fella.
"Yeah, we're great Liverpool. The best team in the country we are. We've won everythin' yer know. The League, the Cup and all that! Do you support Ajax Keret?"
With that carrot's, sorry Keret's, face turned the colour of Sir Roger's shorts.
"No I am not supporting Ajax. I am supporting the greatest team in the whole of the Netherlands: FEYENOORD!" thundered the mad Dutchman.
Fuckin' 'ell, all right yeah, calm down will yer!
"Oh yeah, I've 'eard of them. From Rotterdam aren't they?"
It was all very nice this, but what was the point?
"I would like you to take me to the match at Anfield today Peter."
Fuck that! I'm going with me mates.
"Yes, no problem Keret. I'll call for you about half-twelve after I've done my Mam's messages."
For fuck sake! How was I gonna get out of this.
"Ah yes, you're Mother is Lily. Lily is a very nice lady."
Keep yer fuckin' eyes off, you dirty Dutch twat. That's me Ma yer talkin' about! I'll tell me owld fella on yer.
"I would like you to take me in to the Kop Peter. I have heard so much about it."
Well yer've got no fuckin' chance there mate! Even if I do take yer I'm goin' in the Anny with me mates. I've got unfinished business with Irene.
" I prefer to go in the Anfield Road end Keret, opposite the Kop. I'll show you where the Kop is though."
Right, I had about two-and-a-half hours to think of a way of getting out of this. Keret seemed a nice enough old fella but I didn't really wanna be lumbered with him all day.
"I will pay for you to go in to the stadium and also for the taxis."
Well that's fuckin' different then isn't it. Now you're talkin'!
Fuckin' 'ell, taxis to and from the match. Circle Cabs would be fuckin' made up. Cost an arm and a leg in a taxi from Bootle to Anfield; at

least three bob! This guy must be a millionaire!
"Thank you Keret. I'll see you later. Ta ra. Ta ra Mrs. Reid."
"Goodbye Peter."
"Ta ra Peter. Tell your Mam I'll call in later."

"Mam, is that fella in Mrs. Reid's a millionaire?"
"Don't think so son. Why?"
Fuck, nearly slipped up there! If she knew Keret was paying for me I wouldn't get any money off her.
Quick! Think on my feet.
"Oh, 'e was just tellin' me about 'e's got a big 'ouse in Holland."
"That's funny. Mrs. Reid told me 'e lives on a boat."
"Oh yeah Mam, that's right yeah, er a big er yacht or somethin' isn't it? That's right yeah, a big yacht."
"No, a barge on a canal."
I was losing this one so decided to quit while I was behind.
"Can I have me match money Mam?"
"No yer can't yer cheeky get. Keret's payin' for yer."
Ma was always one step ahead.

I felt like a king stepping into that taxi. Keret couldn't understand what the fuss was about as all the little kids stood open-mouthed in wonderment at Evo getting in to a fast black. All the kids were treated to my "royal" wave. Why doesn't the Queen wave with this hand? Because it's mine. Never mind, it's an old joke. I'll get my coat.

During the journey to Anfield I asked Keret how he knew Mrs. Reid. He told me he had fought in the Dutch resistance or something during the war. Mrs. Reid had been a nurse there and had saved many lives he told me. I truly was enthralled by all of this and started to see Mrs. Reid in a different light. I even began to feel sorry that I'd thought such nasty things about her.

"Would you like some candy Peter?" asked Keret as we stepped out of the taxi outside the Kop.
What do I want Cough Candy for? I thought. It wasn't winter and I didn't have a cough. Still, never look a gift Dutchman in the mouth. I'd take anything that was going free.
"Yes please Keret." I was such a well-mannered boy.
Keret then proceeded to buy half the sweet shop! Mars Bars, Milky

Way's, Everybody's Mixture, Licquorice Allsorts, Bon-Bon's and every other sweet you could possibly think of was thrust into my eager grasp. Strange though: no Cough Candy. It was only when watching a programme on the telly some years later that I learned "Candy" was an Americanisation of what we, quite correctly, called sweets. Thirty-odd years on Keret's "behaviour" would have raised not only eyebrows but suspicion and left him open to ridicule. Back in the innocence of the sixties though Keret was exactly as he appeared: a very kind man. This says more about the attitudes of today's society and the mistrust that has been engendered by some of the rubbish that now infests our planet than any other analogy I could make.

I put Keret in the queue for the Kop which was already snaking down Back Rockfield Road. I was certain he would get in though so I didn't feel too bad when I left him to join the queue for the Anfield Road End. I actually very nearly changed my mind and went in the Kop with him but another crack at Irene awaited!

The big pre-match news was that Tony Hateley would not start the season in the first team; his place being taken by Bobby Graham. Big Tone had fell out of favour with Shanks and, so rumour had it, would soon be on his way. Shanks was said to be changing the style of play to suit a more nippy type of centre-forward rather than using Tony's aerial prowess. To this end the transfer market was being scoured and one of the names in the frame was that of Chelsea's Peter Osgood.

 All the usual group were there. Everybody who had left school was fixed up with jobs. The ones who were staying on at school were all from fairly well off families. I felt like a bit of an outcast to be honest being an inbetweeny: no school, no job and, worst of all, no money!

"Hiya Kav. There's this millionaire stayin' with the woman next door to us. 'E lives in Holland in a big mansion. I've brought 'im today. 'E's gone in the Kop. 'E bought me loads of sweets an' 'e 'ired this chauffeur-driven car to bring us 'ere. I'm meetin' 'im outside the Albert after the match an' the car's gonna pick us up again."
Christ, I couldn't half lie! Well some of it was true.
"Yer a lyin' bastard Evo!
"I'm not Kav, honest. 'E flew a bomber plane during the war an' 'e's a Director of Feyenoord."

"Who the fuck are Feyenoord? Never 'eard of them!"
"Oh yeah, they're a boss team honest. They're better than Ajax!"
"They can't be better than Ajax. Ajax beat us!"
"Well Ajax are from Amsterdam an' Feyenoord are from Rotterdam. That's the capital of Holland so they must be good."
"Oh yeah, an' you'd know all about geography wouldn't you, *school-leaver!*"
Why was I being made to feel like a second-class citizen or worse just because me Ma and Da insisted I left school as soon as possible to get a job?
"Well anyway, Keret used to play for Feyenoord. An' Holland!"
By this time I had a nose the size of Mike Summerbee's!
"Where's all the sweets he bought yer?"
"Er, I ate them all." Telling the truth for once.
"Evo, not only are yer a lying bastard, yer a greedy bastard too!"
"Fuck off Kav!" The universal argument-ender.
Kav was a good mate of mine but I fuckin' hated him sometimes, especially as he was still joined at the hip to Irene!

It wasn't nice seeing one of my heroes displaced but Bobby Graham soon justified Shanks' selection by opening the scoring, with a header ironically enough, after 25 minutes. City weren't the Champions for nothing though and soon equalised. They were a great, very attractive, team to watch and really should have had a lot more success than they did. Mike Summerbee was doing great things for them on the wing. The Kop adapted the Small Faces song "Sha La La La Lee" to: "Sha la la la la Summerbee. Who the fuckin' 'ell is 'e? Bent-nosed cunt from Man City!"

Cruel? Maybe. Vulgar? Yes. Funny? Definitely!
He was a fine player though. Anything that Summerbee could do though Peter Thompson was more than capable of matching and it was Thommo who scored the winner with fifteen minutes to go. Great start to the season; beating the Champions. Sad about Big Tone though. Bobby Graham looked like he'd been in the team for years and he might yet save the club a fortune in the transfer market. Tony's days at Anfield were indeed numbered.

I managed to give Kav and the others the slip after the match and met Keret at the pre-arranged meeting point outside the Albert.

"Great wasn't it Keret?"

"I don't know", Keret cried mournfully, "I left ten minutes before the kick-off. The crush was too much for me. In Holland I sit to watch the football match."

I felt so sorry for him. For years he'd been looking forward to standing on the Kop and yet when it happened the realisation was too much for him. I felt sad that I hadn't gone in to the Kop with him to make sure he was okay. All right I was only nearly fifteen but by now I was seasoned in the art of crush-barrier evading and making space for myself by knowing exactly where to stand when the crush reached it's zenith.

The journey home in the fast black was quiet. I felt distinctly guilty about leaving Keret in the lurch. My natural cynicism for all things adult was, at the moment, being replaced by a sympathetic understanding of how Keret was feeling right now. Perhaps I was growing up. I still felt guilty, although not so much to refuse, when my Dutch benefactor thrust two half-crowns into my hand as we stepped out of the cab. Five bob! That would go towards my trip to Leeds. Go 'ead!

Bobby stayed in the team for the next two matches, a defeat at Southampton and a draw at Arsenal, before getting injured. The expected signing of a new centre-forward had not materialised so Big Tone was back in for a midweek match at home to Stoke. His reception was mixed to say the least. Half the Kop were chanting "Tony Hateley" while the other half followed this with "Not worth an 'alfpenny."

We won the match 2-1 and with Bobby still being injured Tony stayed in the side for the next match at home to Sunderland. We quickly established a 3-0 half-time lead with goals from Smith, Lawler and Cally. The best moment was yet to come! In the 66th minute Tony proved just what he was, "King in the Air" as a towering header flew into the net. A tumultuous reception was afforded him by the massed throngs, especially by the girls from the Tony Hateley Fan Club. I did my best to sneak a kiss off them but to no avail as Kav and Geoff Meehan were all over them like a rash. Fuck it though, I just went completely bananas on my own! Where were the "'Alfpenny Brigade" now? Twats, the lot of them! Tony was back!

The 99th Merseyside League derby played at Goodison was a stultefyingly boring affair; the highlight being when Big Tone hit the crossbar with a shot from about twenty yards. A crowd of nearly 64,000 was assembled for that one. I shudder to think what Goodison Park must have been capable of holding in those days, as I was in the Goodison Road terrace and had loads of room. By the way, this didn't count as an away match; it was only Goodison!

The fact I had survived fifteen years on this planet was no mean achievement when I think of the way adults tried to blight my life at every opportunity. I was still doing the regular runs to pawnshops and moneylenders for Mam. I was still going the bagwash for Jane. Still fiddling her rotten. Still fantasising about having her in my crusty bed.

Uncle Michael sent me a letter, a card and a load of money to mark my fifteenth birthday. I can't remember exactly how much but it was a lot. He was in the Army you see so was well paid and consequently had loads of money to spare. He talked about me joining the Army. Fuck that! He'd told me all about getting shot at in Cyprus, Kenya and Aden. Why the fuck did I wanna get shot? Fuck me, I cried if I cut my little finger never mind get a bullet in me! No thanks Uncle Michael. Thank you for your very kind offer and for thinking of my long-term future welfare but if it's a choice of being factory fodder or getting shot to fuck in some remote corner of the globe then it's the grindstone for me mate! Anyway, you only joined up yourself 'cos you had to do your National Service. Okay, you stayed in for a good few years after that but only because getting shot by an Arab was preferrable to Granny Martha twattin' you in the head with her stiletto heels at two o'clock in the morning after you came home having had a particularly raucous night out with one of the local Netherton floozies!

So it was armed with gangs of money that I boarded the coach to Leeds which was a jointly run venture once again by the Roger and Tony Fan Clubs. We got to the ground in plenty of time and headed for the Gelderd End where the Liverpool fans had congregated last year apparently. Things had changed though. In the summer a roof had been put on to the old open terrace at that end. They called it a Spion Kop but it was nothing like ours. The Leeds fans however had decided that this would now be their popular end rather than the old

Cowshed they had previously inhabited. Don't get me wrong, plenty of Liverpool supporters knew about this but it was seen as a "taking" of their end in much the same way that the North Bank at Highbury had been taken a fortnight earlier. Similar "takings" had occurred at Old Trafford, Chelsea and Newcastle.

The mood was ugly and frightening as we queued up to get in the ground. After all, our little bunch were only young teenagers totally innocent of what we had let ourselves in for. All the older Liverpudlians were stood outside one set of turnstiles while at the other set the Leeds mob were hurling all kinds at us: bricks, coins, bits of wood and anything else they could lay their hands on. The battle continued unabated inside the ground. Leeds at one side, Liverpool the other. There was absolute mayhem going on. Fans from both sides were either being thrown out or carried out with blood streaming from open wounds. This was my first real experience of football hooliganism inside a ground and I didn't like it. I'm not sure and don't really care who won the violent war that was going on but the Reds certainly won the "Battle of the Banter".

Leeds' "Send St. John to Vietnam, hallelujah" was countered by our, "Oh, 'e'd win the fuckin' war on 'is own!"

"Tommy Lawrence for Mothercare, hallelujah" was pissed all over by, "Youse are bouncers in Mothercare hallelujah."

We lost the match 0-1. The most memorable thing for me about the actual match was when Peter Lorimer (he of the million miles an hour shot) caught the ball as sweet as you like on the volley. The ball thundered into Tony Hateley's face with such force that it knocked the big man clean off his feet and into instant unconsciousness. The sight of Big Tone being led off on a stretcher was a sad one. That was to be his last ever appearance as a Liverpool player. An ignominious end to what could have been a glittering Anfield career.

Bobby came back into the team and scored in both 2-0 wins against QPR at home and Ipswich away. The hunt for a centre-forward looked to have been put on the back burner. Liverpool's transfer policy at the time seemed to be to tell the world who we wanted to sign, then let some other club come in and steal the player from under our noses. The most glaring example of this was when Howard Kendall's transfer to us from Preston was as good as signed, sealed and delivered; he even had his blue car re-sprayed red. Harry Catterick then crept in on the blind side and prised Kendall from Bill's grasp. Kendall would have been a great signing for us at that time. Make no mistake Kendall was a truly great player. The fact he never won an England cap was the biggest crime ever perpetrated in football. Still, instead of getting Kendall, Shanks went out and bought Emlyn Hughes. I wouldn't have swapped Emlyn for Kendall. Imagine the surprise then when it was announced without any preamble that we had actually signed a young lad from Wolves called Alun Evans. Alun had played just twenty-one games in Wolves' first team and scored four goals but was said to be one of the brightest young prospects for years. To secure this potential great Shanks had made Alun British football's first £100,000 teenager.

"What about this young Welsh lad that Liverpool 'ave signed?" said Dad

"'E's not Welsh Dad, 'e's English."

"'E's not. 'E's Welsh. Look at 'is name, ALOOIN Evans."

What?!

"It's not pronounced ALOOIN Dad. It's just plain Alun, as in Alan A'Court."

"I'm tellin' yer 'e's Welsh. 'Is Dad's name was Alun an' 'e was Welsh. I saw 'im play."

Oh, for fuck sake! So fuckin' what! You were in the fuckin' Navy. I've got no fuckin' intention of gettin' blasted to fuck by some big fuck off torpedo in the middle of the Atlantic bastard Ocean!

"I know Dad. 'Is Dad played for West Brom, that's 'ow come Alun was born in the Midlands an' played for Wolves."

"Look, for the last time, 'e's Welsh. You'll see when the Taffies pick 'im for an international."

Get it through yer fuckin' 'ead will yer, 'e's fuckin' English!

"Dad, please believe me, 'e's English. 'E's already played for England youth an' England Under-23's. There's no chance 'e can play for Wales now."

"Well we'll see when Wales pick 'im."

Fuck off!

"Do yer know what Dad, I think yer right. I think 'e is Welsh."

"I know 'e's fuckin' Welsh! See I told yer. Yer don't know everything about football, do yer?"

Piss off Dad, you're doin' me 'ead in!

Adults again! Why the fuck did they all do me 'ead in? Why the fuck didn't they just leave me alone? Why the fuck did they think they knew it all? Why the fuck could you never win an argument against them, even when you knew you were 100%, cast-iron, certainly, without a shadow of a doubt right? Moreover, why the fuck didn't they even *listen* to your side of the argument, even if it was your Ma and Da, *especially* if it was your Ma and Da? I hoped I'd never grow up like that.

Alun the Taffy, Evans the Goal made his debut in the home game against Leicester. Bobby Graham must have felt he'd been shit upon from a great height, as it was he who made way for our new superstar. There was no way on earth though that Shanks was going to pay all that money and not play Alun.

The ground, especially the Kop, was buzzing with excitement and expectation. Everybody was dying to see the blond, floppy-haired Alun in the flesh. Taking her place with us in the Anny Road end was the secretary of the new Alun Evans Fan Club, Leslie. How did she get that off the ground so quickly? Still, never mind, she was as fit as fuck. I handed over my three bob to her faster than shit off a shovel and was given instant membership. No chance of copping for her though: The dark spectre of Kav was already looming large, waiting like a tiger to pounce!

"Me Dad thinks Alun's Welsh." I chuckled, hoping that Kav and the others would join me in a bit of light-hearted banter.
"Daft twat!" said Geoff Meehan.
"Eh, fuck off you! Don't you call my Dad that!" I was allowed to slag me owld fella off but I wasn't having any other fucker giving him stick!
"Well 'e is a daft twat. Everybody knows Alun's English."
"Call 'im that again an' I'll chin yer, yer cunt."
I really did hope that Geoff wouldn't say it again, as he was a lot bigger than me. I could well do without getting fucked sticking up for me Dad. I'd come second in every fight I'd ever had.
"Daft twat!"
Next thing I knew me and Geoff had each other in a headlock, right there by the railings at the front of the Anny Road end. The girls were screaming. Kav was trying to pull us apart. "Come on will youse. Fuckin' pack it in!"
My fears about Geoff were unfounded. He, like me, couldn't fight his

way out of a paper bag. Couldn't punch a hole in a wet Echo. Couldn't knock the skin off a rice pudding. There was a bit of scratching and hair-pulling, I think maybe even a little bite here and there but it looked like the two girliest fighters in Anfield were set for a dishonourable draw. That is until Kav had just about separated us. I threw a beauty of a right uppercut just as we were dragged apart. All right I stole it on him but what could I do? I wasn't having him or any other beaut calling me Da bad names! Geoff's nose instantly turned into the Japanese flag! Oh fuck, what had I done?

"Eh, what's goin' on 'ere?" A big fat copper stood right beside us. Oh shit! I was gonna get thrown out before the match had even started and miss Alun's debut

"Oh, we were just messin' mister. I banged me nose on the railin's." Geoff might have been a prick for what he said about me Dad but he wasn't about to grass me up.

"Well pack it in. If I see youse messin' again I'll throw the pair of youse out!"

"Okay, sorry", said Cassius Clay.

"Sorry", said the Japanese flag.

Apologies all round, a quick handshake and it was never mentioned again. Geoff never called me Da a daft twat again though. Come to think of it, neither did anybody else.

As the teams came out every neck in the ground was craned trying to catch the first glimpse of our boy wonder. The Kop, as ever, had a song to greet our new arrival. Leapy Lee was at number two in the charts with a song called *Little Arrows*. The Kop adapted this to:

"Alun Evans centre-forward. Alun Evans scores our goals.
We paid a hundred thousand and he said goodbye to Wolves.
He said we'll win the Football League and Billy Shankly knows
We'll win the Football League because of Alun Evans' goals."

A sensational start to the game saw Rowdy give us the lead after two minutes: this must be going to be a special day! Two minutes later and Tommy Smith had increased our lead from the penalty spot. We didn't have to wait long for what we'd all came to see. Ten minutes into the game and we were three-nil up courtesy of an absolute beauty from Alun Evans. We were kicking into the Kop and they just went totally mental. The whole ground was a sea of jumping, twisting, writhing bodies! "Alun Evans! Alun Evans!" Cally scored our fourth after twelve minutes (indeed a special day!) to complete our victory. The rest of the match was spent admiring Alun and laughing whenever Tommy Smith kicked their centre-forward from behind, which was often. The said centre-forward went crying and snivelling like the horrible long piece of paralysed piss he was to the referee who took no notice of the moaning cunt. He was a decent player; went on to become a very good player and could always sniff a goal chance out but he was a prick. Name? Alan Clarke!

All the talk on the Fan Clubs' coach to Wolves the following week was of our new God. Alun was going to have this one tough though as he returned to his old club. So it proved as Alun was booed relentlessly from the first whistle by the Wolves beauts. Didn't affect his or any other of our player's games very much though as we raced into a two-nil lead after twenty-five minutes with goals from Sir Roger and Thommo. Five minutes later Alun shut his verbal assailants up in the best way possible. He scored a beauty, right in front of the North Bank too! Go 'ead! Alun repeated the feat in front of us after sixty-three minutes. Further goals from Sir Roger and Thommo again gave us a marvellous 6-0 win.

I bought a Footy Echo when we got off the coach at Anfield. There before me in big headlines was the legend, "Evans celebrates England Under-23 call up with two goals." Hehehehehehehe!

Mam and Dad were both out when I got home. I laid the paper ever so carefully on Dad's chair so that my proof was staring straight at him. He couldn't fail to miss it when he came in.

Mam and Dad came in at about midnight; both pissed as arseholes of course. I was on the couch pretending to be asleep.

"Evans. England." I heard Dad slurring almost incoherently as he scanned the Footy Echo back page.

"The little get was right after all." I could just about make out him mumble.

"I'm goin' to bed John, come on. Peter wake up, come on, time for bed!" said Ma.

"W-w-w-hat. Yeah, okay Mam. I'm g-g-goin'."

"Six-nil today eh lad." Dad managed to mutter.

"Yeah, great Dad. Alun Evans scored two. Seen the back of the Echo? 'E's been called up for the England Under 23-s again."

"Yeah, yeah, yeah. Go on, go to bed now."

"Okay Dad, goodnight."

Daft twat!

CHAPTER TEN

GORILLAS IN OUR MIDST

I was getting ready to go up to Anfield to catch the Fan Clubs coach for the match at Burnley when I heard Ma shout, "Peter, yer've got an interview at TJ Hughes in The Strand."

I legged it downstairs as fast as me little legs could carry me. I'd been for a number of interviews for office jobs in town but because I had no qualifications was seen as thick so consequently didn't get any of them. I'd applied for the shop assistant's job at TJ's as you didn't exactly have to be a rocket scientist to pack shelves.

"'Ow d'yer know Mam, 'ow d'yer know?"

"'Cos it says 'ere in this letter."

I fuckin' hated the way me Ma and Da did that, opened *my* letters. It wasn't fuckin' fair! I was only a kid so my feelings or opinions didn't count! Course, couldn't tell them that!

"Oh great, when is it Mam, Monday?"

"No, today at two o'clock."

No fuckin' chance, I'm goin' to Burnley!

"I can't go today Mam. I'm goin' to Burnley."

"Yer bloody not goin' to Burnley!"

"Ah, please Mam. Kav an' Irene and Geoff an' all the others'll be waitin' for me. I've gorra go."

"Yer goin' for that interview. I'm coming with yer to make *sure* you go. It's about time yer got a job."

Oh deep fuckin' unconfined joy! That's all I need, me Ma taggin' along as me fuckin' minder. No chance of getting out of this one, especially as *Lily Eyes* were out. *Lily Eyes* were always the end of any argument! Ma did have a point though I suppose. Dad wasn't working, having been made redundant from Mersey Cables. Our Pauline was working in the chicken factory and Ma still had about three million jobs. I'd been left school for three months so it was only fair that I get my finger out. Ma still never had any money though. Mrs. Roberts, a very kindly old lady from Rimrose Road had been added to Ma's ever-growing list of moneylenders. Mrs. Roberts should never have been a moneylender; she was far too nice and far too kind for all that. I used to like going down to pay Ma's money to Mrs. Roberts; she always had a cup of tea and a cake ready for me. A proper cake too; not the stale as you like, penny each, rock hard jaw-breakers that Ma got from Marie Dooley's for Sunday tea. Not slagging me Ma off; that was all she could afford. Mrs. Roberts' cakes though were big fat cream cakes freshly baked from Sayers: French Horns, Vanilla Slices, Strawberry Tarts and best of all Chocolate Eclairs about four feet long with cream dripping out over the side of them. The tea was made with that shite sterry milk like but it was at least wet and hot, which was always appreciated, especially on cold winter Saturday mornings. I always got a few bob off Mrs. Roberts too.

"Seein' as yer not going to Burnley yer can go down to Mrs. Roberts an' pay 'er this ten bob."

Some consolation then.

I arrived at Mrs. Roberts' in eager anticipation of the cream-filled delights that awaited me. A big, long, black car was parked outside her door. Unusual that. Never normally there. Never mind, must be a rich relative visiting or something. I knocked on the door. The door was answered by a fella at least seven foot tall in a black overcoat and a black trilby. Christ, it was like looking at a negative of Blackpool Tower!

"Hiya mister. I've come to see Mrs. Roberts." I couldn't put my finger on why, but Tall Man was frightening me almost as much as Harry Wilson used to all those years ago.

"Mrs. Roberts is dead," said Lurch in a balefully droll voice. Harry Wilson was a fuckin' pussycat compared to this monstrosity!

"What d'yer mean, DEAD? She's not dead. She can't be dead!"

"I assure *you* young man, Mrs. Roberts is *very* dead!" growled Blackpool Tower.

I was absolutely, totally shit scared of this man. It was the first time I'd ever set eyes on him but it was certainly not to be the last. I was to meet him many more times in the future. His name and who he was? Charlie Tritton: the local undertaker.

Shortly after Herman Munster had finished scaring me shitless, four other members of the same species came walking out of the living-room door with a coffin on their shoulders. That tiny wooden box looked so incongruous stuck in between these huge men. I'm sure one of the Munsters could easily have tucked poor old Mrs. Roberts and the mahogany box which encased her under his arm and carried it to the waiting hearse. It was about a ten-minute walk from Mrs. Roberts' house to the 61 bus stop at Seaforth terminus. I cried every second of the way.

The five-minute bus journey home gave me time to compose myself. I couldn't let me Ma see I'd been crying.
"Mam, Mrs. Roberts is dead. When I got there all these big fellas were carryin' 'er coffin to a car."
"Is she? Oh, that's a shame. Must 'ave been Charlie Tritton and 'is unmerry men. Well give us the ten bob then."
In my grief I'd forgotten all about the ten bob. I fished in my sock and retrieved the crumpled bit of brown paper. Mrs. Roberts was dead and all me Ma could think about was her ten bob!
"Oh yeah, ee ar Mam."
"Well that's ten bob I've got away without payin'. If Cissy Mulhall drops dead next week I'll be laughin'!"
I'm sure Mam wasn't being callous. I suppose it was a bit of a bonus for her to have an extra ten bob that week. It didn't stop me being heartbroken over Mrs. Roberts. I did agree with her though about Cissy Mulhall!

Me and my minder arrived in good time for the interview at TJ's. Fuck me, if any of my mates saw me I'd be skitted for a year! Hang on though: all my mates were at Burnley weren't they? Where I should have fuckin' been!

We were shown to a door marked "SUPERVISOR". After tapping twice on the door a soft, ever so gentle voice from within said, "Come in."
God, she must be fit, I thought.
You know when a face just doesn't match a voice? You know, like Alan Ball, Emlyn Hughes, David Speedie? The face behind this voice was like The Creature from the Black Lagoon. God this woman was ugly!
"Hello, I'm Miss Rigby," said The Creature With The Dulcet Tones.
Fuckin' 'ell, no wonder yer a Miss! Who the fuck'd marry you?!
"Hello Miss Rigby. Very pleased to meet you. I'm Peter Etherington and this is me Ma, I mean my Mum."
And then she stood up from behind her desk! She was about thirty-five. Not far short of six feet tall. Lovely dark-blue suit; skirt about halfway between knees and waist. Height accentuated by a pair of

black stiletto-heeled shoes. Legs all the way up to her arse encased in those gorgeous light brown sheer stockings. They had to be stockings; couldn't be tights! They were definitely gonna be stockings tonight when I was thinking about her in bed!

"Yes, I'm very pleased to meet you too Peter, and you Mrs. Etherington. Please take a seat."

Fuckin' right I'm gonna take a seat! Right opposite you so I can feast my eyes on those gorgeous legs and maybe catch a glimpse of your lace-trimmed, silky underwear. Gorra be lace-trimmed and silky! Well they definitely will be tonight!

"Thank you Miss Rigby."

Every second of the fifteen-minute interview was conducted with me making a tent in my trousers. Evo's donga was at it's most rampant, obdurate best; it just refused to go down! I just could not take my eyes off Miss Rigby's legs. Mind you, she must have been well versed in interviewing young, hormonal lads, as not once was there any sign of her thundercrackers. Plenty of leg, upper thigh too, but no chance of seeing that lovely white "V" I was so used to seeing with Jane. I did however now have enough tugging material to keep me warm and happy in my bed during the long winter nights to come. How could a woman so ugly have such a beautiful voice and the most stunning legs in the world? God must have run out of heads when he made Miss Rigby. She had a voice an angel would murder his Mother for. Her body had been sculpted by El Sculptio - the best sculptor in heaven. Her kite? Christ, that kite! I still can't get over it! "'Ee ar lads. I've ran out of 'eads for this woman. Do us a favour: go down and see Lucifer in the warm place an' ask 'im if he's got any owld ones left. Yer know, an owld moose's head'll do or anythin'. What, 'e's got an owld gorilla's one 'e's doin' nothin' with? Yeah, that'll do fine. Throw it up."

Interview over. Yes, I'd got the job! Start Monday. Stand up now Evo. No, I can't, still got a hard on. Cissy Mulhall's bloomers. See ya donga! Works every time.

"Kav, I've got a job mate."
"Nice one. Where?"
"TJ Hughes' in The Strand. Yer should see the Supervisor. Fit as fuck she is an' gorgeous too. She's only about twenty. I might ask 'er for a date." Sha la la la Summerbee!

"Fuck off Evo. The only date you're ever gonna get is one in a box at Christmas."
He was right of course but a lad has to have his dreams, doesn't he?

The 100th Merseyside derby was an inestimably better affair than the 99th. We were doing brilliantly in the League having lost only two games out of twelve and had won our last five games. It was shaping up to be a battle for the title between us and Leeds. Everton stopped our winning sequence. Alan Ball gave Everton the lead. We equalised when Tommy Smith thundered in a free-kick after 75 minutes. This song was heard for the first time:
If you're feeling tired and weary and your heart just skips a beat
You'll get your fuckin' 'ead kicked in if you walk down Heyworth
Street.
If you walk into the Albert, you'll hear our famous noise
"Get out you Everton bastards, we're the Billy Shankly boys!"
We're the boys from the Kop. We're loyal and we're true
And when we play the Everton we're ready for a do.
To the cry of "No Surrender" you'll hear our famous noise
"Get out you Everton bastards we're the Billy Shankly boys!"

I was working every other Saturday at TJ's and it was falling quite nicely that I would be off when we were at home. It was of course ruling out my away trips on the Fan Clubs' coaches and the chance, however slim, of getting nearer Irene.

In a four-week period between November and December we went on another marvellous sequence of six straight League wins. In the middle of this run Sir Roger equalled Gordon Hodgson's League goal-scoring record for the club at Nottingham Forest.

The almost inevitable happened after we played two successive home fixtures over Christmas. The home matches were now clashing with the Saturdays I had to work. Consequently I missed both 1-0 wins over West Brom and Sheffield Wednesday. This was getting too much for me. I couldn't take much more of this. I didn't have too. The fickle finger of fate decided to point firmly at Evo.

I was on my Saturday off at TJ's. Our FA Cup game at Leicester had been called off because of the bad weather. It was Mam and Da·''·

17ᵗʰ Wedding Anniversary and they were having "jars out" in the house after the club. I was going into work to see my mate, Brian Watkins, who worked on the cheese and bacon counter. Mam had asked me while I was there to get her some bacon, ham, cheese, roast beef etc for the party. I also went in to see a lovely blonde girl who worked on the cosmetics counter, Kathy Sheilds. I'd had a couple of sort of dates with her in a "tag along with your mate" sort of sense. Brian was seeing Kathy's cousin, Glynis Hughes. I was brought along as part of the deal and had a couple of dry snogs with the blonde beauty (no chance of tongues)! Kathy wasn't interested anyway and to be honest neither was I really. I couldn't be arsed anymore. I'd virtually given up my fruitless quest to get the ungettable. If there had been Olympic medals for tugging I would have won the lot! Brian cut me a load of meat and cheese which I put in the staff room to be checked by security. I then went to chat up "less than chatty Kathy". Might have a chance today seeing as I've got me best Benny on. Cracking shirt that Ben Sherman! Yellow with blue stripes, front placket, breast pocket, back pleat and a hanging loop. Just come out the cleaners too. Starched to fuck and as stiff as me knob when I thought about Jane. Cost me four quid but it was money well spent. Had my black barrathea blazer on too. That had cost me £13 in Matthew Street; well, to be more precise - ten bob down, half-a-crown a week for four weeks to make it look good and a false address! Fourteen-inch parallels looked good too. Completing the Evo ensemble were a pair of black Como's - the square-toed variety. Cool as fuck I was - the coolest dude in Bootle! I was feeling good. Yeah, I was deffo gonna pull today - no doubt!

Miss Rigby tannoyed me to her office. Maybe she had given in to her animal urges and decided to seduce young Evo right there on the floor of her very own office. Once I'd finished giving her all she'd ever wanted from a man on the lush pile carpet of her office floor I would then take her on her desk until she screamed out "Peter, Peter, no more please. I just can't keep up with your insatiable sexual appetite you sex God."
"Not a problem Miss Rigby; just don't rip me Benny in your throes of passion."
Shit! Donga's the size and consistency of a scaffolding pole. Quick, Cissy's bloomers. Phew, that's better. Brian's name was also called on the tannoy. She surely didn't want us to spit-roast her? Come on, stop it!

"What's this all about Evo?"

"'Aven't got a clue Wocko. She was talkin' about givin' me some kind of promotion. Said I might 'ave to go to the C&A store in Coventry to train to be an Assistant Manager."

"Yeah, I 'eard that. Don't know what she wants me for though. Maybe she wants me to give 'er the pork sword!"

"Nah, no chance Wocko. She wants my mutton dagger."

"It'd 'ave to be a two paper-bag job though wouldn't it?"

"What d'yer mean Wocko?"

"Yer know, two paper bags. One to put over 'er 'ead and one to put over mine in case 'ers fell off!"

"Fuck off Wocko. Yer don't look at the mantlepiece when yer pokin' the fire! Anyway, you'd get into a broken window. Are yer still porkin' Glynis?"

"Yeah, and your Pauline's mate June."

"Fuck me, that is a two paper-bag job!"

"Get anywhere with miserable arse?"

"Nah. Could've done like. She was after me and that. Asked me for a date and stuff but fuck that! I'm too fuckin' cool for her anyway."

"Yeah, about as cool as the fuckin' Sahara desert!"

We were still pissing ourselves laughing when we entered the Ugly One's office. Mr. Stevens, the store security guard was there too. What the fuck was that all about?

"Mister Etherington and Mister Watkins, you are both instantly dismissed for misappropriating Company goods."

Miswhat?! What the fuck are you goin' on about yer owld bag? Fuck me, you grow uglier by the day. I'd shag yer though! Why are yer calling us "Mister" anyway? Yer normally call us by our first names.

"Sorry Miss Rigby, I don't know what you're talking about."

"Yes, I'm afraid you do Mister Etherington. So too do you Mister Watkins. The goods you paid ten shillings for were weighed and should have been priced at two pounds and ten shillings."

What, you're 'avin' a fuckin' laugh aren't yer?

"There must be some mistake Miss Rigby."

"Yes, Mister Etherington. The mistake was made by you and Mister Watkins in thinking you wouldn't get caught. Here is a refund of your ten shillings. Mister Stevens will escort you both off the premises. Do not ever set foot in this store again. The police have been informed and will be visiting you both in due course."

So that was that! Sacked on the spot! I waited 'til we got out of the store before ripping into Brian.

"What the fuckin' 'ell were yer doin' Wocko?"

"Well I thought I'd give yer a little bit extra."

"Yeah, a little bit! A little bit would 'ave been all right. Fuck me, you gave me five times the amount I should 'ave had! For fuck sake, what were yer thinkin' of?"

"Oh fuck off will yer Evo! Stop fuckin' moanin' will yer, yer little twat! It's only a fuckin' job, yer'll get another one!"

"Yeah, an' what the fuck am I gonna tell me Ma? She's gonna fuckin' kill me. Yer fuckin' knob'ead!"

Bang! Wocko twatted me right in the mouth! Blood spurted from my lip like the Trevi fountain gone mad. For fuck sake all over me Benny!

"Fuckin' 'ell Wocko! Look at that! Yer've fuckin' ruined me Benny!" The blazer too was spattered but as it was black it could be salvaged whereas Benny, my dear, sweet, beloved Benny was on it's way up to that great shirt heaven in the sky!

Oh fuckin' great! I had no job, no money, no mate, no fuckin' Benny, I was gonna get nicked by the bizzies, Ma was gonna fuckin' batter me (Dad probably too), and on top of all that I had a bust fuckin lip! Marvellous! Why did life hate me?

The expected good hiding from me Ma didn't materialise mainly, I think, because I told her the truth that it was soft arse Wocko's fault. Okay I was a shithouse, but I was an intact "all in one piece" shithouse. Me Da was okay about it too but that might have been because he'd once been sacked by British American Tobacco for robbin' ciggies. Even his double standards wouldn't allow him to kick off on that one! My bust lip also got me the sympathy vote. Ma made me promise that I wouldn't hang round with Wocko again; not a hard thing to do seeing as he'd made my lip into the size of an orange.

I'd also decided that my Anny Road days were over. I'd given up trying to get a bird. I also didn't fancy getting skitted to fuck at the next home game for being sacked. So from now on it was the Kop for me. "Evo is a Kopite!"

CHAPTER ELEVEN

DADS, LADS, BIRDS AND TURDS

So it was that I signed on at the Youth Careers Office on Fernhill Road on the Monday morning. Careers? What a misnomer that was! Like working in the tannery, the lead works, the chicken factory, running your arse off as an office junior or making tea for some hairy arse builders was a career! I'd had a lifetime of making fuckin' tea and pissing in Cissy Mulhall's! I was adept at making tea from the age of five; I didn't want any fuckin' more of it. Bank Manager, Accountant, Tax Consultant; now they were careers! If they had been truthful it would have been called the "Shitty Jobs For Young Ragarses Office." All the likes of me, Pilch and Smudge were ever going to be was factory fodder. The more enterprising ones like Timmy and his brother Danny joined the Merchant Navy but even then they were only scrubbing decks or washing the crew's sweaty skids. The exception to all this was Jimmy Colquit. Conk as he'd always been called had no fuckin' intention of ever working. He couldn't work, he used to tell me, 'cos he had to look after his pigeons! How the fuck he got away with it I'll never know! My Ma had nagged me non-stop since Saturday to get a job. He was told at the SJFYRAO that he would have his dole stopped if he didn't look for a job. His reply of, "Stop me dole and I'll stop yer breathing," had me rolling on the floor because if there was anybody less hard in Bootle than me it was Conk. It worked though 'cos he didn't get his dole stopped. The cheeky bastard produced a copy of a letter he sent to the Queen applying for the job of looking after the royal pigeons and a reply from Betty's office!

I went seeking a top management job every day for a week to the SJFYRAO. Ma made sure I went by following me over there. On the Friday I was called in to Mr. Harty's office. Another misnomer as old Farty Harty was a miserable bastard! A smelly bastard too. Farty's SBD's were the talk of Bootle's youth! "Peter, I've got a job for you to start on Monday. You don't need an interview. I've had a word with the manager Mr. Gibb and he's going to give you a chance. You are very lucky to get this chance in view of your misdemeanour. *All right, all right, yer fuckin' owld bastard. D'yer fuckin' 'ave to keep bringin' it up!*
"Oh, thank you Mister Harty. Where is it?"
Go on, please say Trainee Manager of Barclays Bank in the New Strand.

"Tesco's on Linacre Road. You will be stacking shelves and performing other retail duties."

Well stick it up yer fuckin' arse yer owld bastard. I'm not workin' in a fuckin' shop again. I wanna proper job! Mind you, not too bad as shops only open at nine o'clock so at least I'll be able to 'ave a lie in.

"Oh brilliant Mr. Harty!"

"Yes, I thought you would be pleased. Now here's a letter of introduction to Mr. Gibb. Report there at eight o'clock on Monday morning." "Why eight o'clock Mr. Harty? Shops only open at nine o'clock don't they?"

"There is staff training and getting the shop prepared for customers for one hour before opening. There is also an hour's cleaning at the end of the day, sometimes an hour and a half, so you will be finishing between six and half past. A stock check taking approximately three hours will be done after closing every Saturday. You will get one day off per week on a rota system - Monday one week, Tuesday the next etcetera unless you are needed to work that day in which case you will be paid at overtime rate of time and a half."

Fuckin' listen 'ere mate, yer fuckin' can't 'ave April Fools Day in February. Yer fuckin' 'avin' a laugh! You know it and I fuckin' know it. One fuckin' Saturday off in every six? I might not get to see a match all fuckin' season. Take yer job, yer shop, yer cleanin', yer stock check, yer ten-hour days, twelve on a Saturday, yer one Saturday in every six, yer shelves, yer fuckin' retail duties, yer fuckin' time-and-a-half and yer tins of peas and shove them all up yer smelly fuckin' arse!

"Oh, that's smashing Mr. Harty. My Mam will be made up. So am I. Thank you very much."

For fuck sake! I had to sit through another five minutes of his shite, literally - the man fuckin' stunk, before being allowed to escape to the comparative sanctuary of home.

Matters got even worse when I got home. A big fuck off bobby was waiting for me. He was accompanied by a right fuckin' creep you definitely wouldn't let mind your kids called Mr. Richards who was the Juvenile Liaison Officer for Bootle police. Dad called Richards Molly Perkins behind his back, which used to always crease me up with laughter. "That fuckin Molly Perkins. 'E's nothin' but a fuckin' big ta ta!" Dad would say. My Dad was the funniest man in the world when he wanted to be - when he was Johnny Jekyll that was. When he was Johnny Hyde it was quite a different matter! Bobby Big had come to inform me that I would be attending Bootle police station in Oriel Road the morning after to receive an official caution from no less than the Chief Constable of Bootle. He made it sound like a fuckin' honour!

"Don't worry Peter, I'll be accompanying you," Molly Perkins said.

Oh fuckin' marvellous. I'm really fuckin' made up about that. That's all I need, you pipin' me arse while some fucker's givin' me down the banks!

"Oh thank you Mr. Richards. That's very kind of you."

"Well, we've got to make sure you get back on the straight and narrow now haven't we Peter?"

Fuckin' 'ell, it was only a bit of shitty bacon and a block of cheese not the fuckin' Great Train Robbery!

"Yeah, I'll be there too Peter."

Oh will yer Ma? That fuckin' does surprise me. I can't go any fuckin' where without you wanting to 'old me fuckin' 'and! Fuckin' 'ell let me go from yer apron strings will yer. I'm fuckin' fifteen now yer know!

I duly received my "award" from Bootle's finest bobby. He promised me that should I ever commit such a heinous crime again I would be incarcerated in Walton Jail for the rest of my natural life and have the key thrown away. **FUCK OFF!** I promised the arsehole of course that I would never get into trouble again and that I would be a very good boy, especially for my Mam. **MY ARSE!** Which reminds me; Molly Perkins did pipe my arse!

I celebrated my "honour" by stopping at the New Strand on the way home and buying myself a pair of round toed Como's from Timpson's. They were the really boss ones made by Frank Wright. I also bought "Gentle On My Mind" by Dean Martin, the number one song of the time. Evo had some style you know! Ma was there to hold my hand while I bought them though.

My first match as a fully-fledged Kopite was that afternoon. A blanket of snow covered the pitch but that didn't stop a player who I consider to be the third greatest ever Scottish footballer, Jim Baxter, giving a virtuoso display. A performance reminiscent of that by Ferencvaros' Zoltan Varga was largely instrumental in Nottingham Forest's 2-0 victory. "Slim Jim" was a brilliant player with a left foot that could open a tin of peas! Okay, his right foot was strictly for standing on but with a left foot like his you didn't need a right one!

Dad came in from Harland's that night and entertained us royally with the most marvellous impression of Molly Perkins. He was Johnny Jekyll tonight. Thing was you never quite knew what mood he'd be in. I got a crack and sometimes a belt, literally, for the most innocuous "offences" while things I expected, and deserved, to get a hiding for where passed off with a laugh and a joke.

Will you be Jekyll or will you be Hyde?
Will you be on the left or the right-hand side?
Will you be a prick or will you be cool?
Will you be gentle or will you be cruel?
Will you make me laugh or will you make me cry?
Will I be an outcast or the apple of your eye?
Will you be sober or will you be drunk?
Will you be screaming or as quiet as a monk?
Will you be nasty or will you be nice?
Will you be horrible or all sugar and spice?
Will you tell us off or be full of charm?
Will you be angry or will you be calm?
Will you be heartless or will you be kind?
Will you make Mam go out of her mind?
Will you shout at Mam or give her a kiss?
Will it be hatred or heavenly bliss?
Will you have money or will you be skint?
Will you stink of ale or a garden of mint?
Will you use words or will you use force?
Will you have wages or did you lose them on a horse?
Will we have marge or will we have butter?
Will you be sane or a right bloody nutter?
Will you be good or will you be bad?
Will you be a tyrant or our loving Dad?

Monday February 17th 1969 was a momentous day for me: one that would change my life forever. Why? Because I became a high-powered executive in the Tesco company overseeing the whole of the British corporation? Like fuck! Because of a beautiful girl who worked in the shop. She was really, absolutely, stunningly beautiful with all her bits and bobs in the right places. She was assigned to teach me the skills of shelf packing. I fell absolutely, totally, head over heels in love as soon as I clapped eyes on her! Everything about her was right:

the way she walked; the way she talked; the way she moved; her beautiful eyes; her long dark-brown hair; the sweet smell of her delicious perfume; her bum; her legs (her stunning legs!) accentuated by the miniest of mini-skirts; her breasts (oh God her breasts!) there before me in all their glory just about staying under the tightest and lowest of tight, low tops; oh, and last but by no means least her Tommy Smith's Footy Studs! She also had the advantage no other of Evo's fantasy women had of being attainable. There was also the added attraction of her being nearly a year older than me: Evo's penchant for older women! Not that I held out much hope of copping for her. Why would she wanna go out with a jug-eared, spotty skinhead? Anyway she probably had half the lads in Litherland after her. A lad though must have his dreams! The name of this vision of great beauty? Evelyn Hughes. I made much mock of her name being so close to that of our very own Emlyn Hughes. In fact I christened her "Crazy Horse" for a while but it not only went over her head it winged its way to Morocco! Evelyn, at the time, wouldn't have known Emlyn Hughes from Elvis Presley, although I was to slowly convert her by the end of that life-changing week.

"Ev, I see "Half As Nice" by Amen Corner went to Number One yesterday."

I told Evelyn that not just to impress her or make small talk but also because I was bang into my music.

"Yeah?"

The beautiful one's disinterest was obvious.

"Yeah, it's the first ever computerised Number One. I think it's been rigged though 'cos it jumped from last week's number fifteen an' that doesn't normally 'appen. I think it'll only last a week though 'cos "I'm Gonna Make You Love Me" by Diana Ross and The Supremes and The Temptations is at number two an' should 'ave been Number One this week. I reckon it'll be Number One next week though."

"Yeah?"

Come on Ev, give us a break 'ere! I'm tryin'!

"What music are yer into Ev?"

"Anythin' really. Just what's in the charts mainly."

Ah, more than a one word answer - a spark of interest!

"Oh, much the same as meself then."

"I 'ad a request played on Radio One last year."

The ice-maiden was breaking!

"Oh aye, what one?"

107

"Everlasting Love by Love Affair."

"Oh yeah, sound record that!"

I thought it was shite really but I'd chipped away at the icy exterior so I wasn't about to blow everything by telling her exactly what I thought of both the record and Love Affair themselves. It had been proven that Love Affair hadn't actually performed on the record and that session musicians had provided them with a nice little earner. Steve Ellis, the lead singer, was the only one of the band who had actually done any work on the record. This was indicative of the "bubble gum pop" bands of the era. Singer Tony Burrows appeared on Top Of The Pops one night fronting three different bands; White Plains, Brotherhood Of Man and Edison Lighthouse.

"You've got a dead sexy voice, like a film star."

FUCKING HELL!

My donga very nearly demolished a shelf full of tinned spaghetti! 'Ang on. She was takin' the piss wasn't she? She was gonna say, "Yeah Lassie" wasn't she?

"Yeah, d'yer think so?"

"Yeah, honest. It's dead deep and sexy."

JESUS CHRIST!

Cissy Mulhall, Cissy Mulhall, Cissy Mulhall! Fuckin' 'urry up will yer! Go down for fuck sake, I've gotta stand up before five o'clock! No. No good, it was there and it was staying there for a long time unless I did something about it. It was the first time Cissy Mulhall's bloomers had ever failed me.

"Err...yeah Ev... err... all right yeah...err...okay. Just goin' the bog. I've gotta see that Arab."

"What Arab?"

"Mustaphapoopoo."

"Yer a case you!"

"Yeah I know. When we go on 'oliday me Ma puts all the clothes in me mouth!"

I returned five minutes later, my donga back to its normal, flaccid little self. I had a grin on my grid cheesier than the big block of Cheddar I walked out with under my coat that night. I did a lot of that during that week (tuggin' and robbin' that is).

"Conk, I'm in love with the girl works on the checkout at Tesco's."

"Fuck off Evo, yer've only worked there two days! Even *you* can't fall in love after two days!"

"I am Conk, honest. Yer wanna see 'er, she's gorgeous!"

"What's 'er name?"

"Evelyn Hughes."

"Oh aye yeah. I
'aven't seen '
'er but I've 'eard she's a looker."

"A looker? I've told yer Conk, she's fuckin' gorgeous!"

"'Ang on, what d'yer say 'er name was? Evelyn Hughes? She gorra brother called John?"

"Yeah, that's 'er."

"Fuckin' 'ell Evo, yer wanna be careful there mate. 'E's a fuckin' loon ball. Knocks fuck outa anybody goes out with 'is sister I've 'eard."

"I'd take me chances Conk. It'd be worth it believe me. Come down the shop and 'ave a look at 'er. Actually fuckin' buy somethin' though!"

"Buy? Fuckin' 'ell Evo, why buy when yer can rob? Okay, I'll come down tomorrow. I'll get up about three o'clock an' get down there for about four."

"Yer a lazy bastard Conk!"

"Yeah I know. Great isn't it!"

"Why don't yer get up at a normal time, say, ten o'clock or somethin'?"

"Ten o'clock? In the mornin'? I didn't know there were two ten o'clocks in one day! Anyway, what's there to get up for? Me pigeons don't need feedin' 'til four o'clock."

"'Ave yer ever even *thought* about gettin' a job Conk?"

"Fuck that! I've told yer Evo - I've gorra feed me pigeons. Anyway, it'd ruin me street cred wouldn't it?"

"Okay, well get there for four. Don't let on yer know me though 'cos Gibbo'll think yer on the rob."

"Well I will be on the rob."

"I know that soft arse! We don't want Gibbo to know though do we!"

Now as you might have gathered Conk was the laziest man on the planet. To get him up at three o'clock (quite early for Conk really) and walk from Bootle to Linacre Road on the pretext of buying a small sliced Hovis must have meant that Evelyn was indeed a very special young lady, which, of course, she was.

Conk duly arrived in Tesco's just before closing (must have overslept) and walked surreptitiously round the shop for five minutes followed every second and every inch by Gibbo's beady eyes. No chance of Conk robbin' anything today! I couldn't wait to get home to hear Conk's verdict on my darling Ev.

"All right Conk. What d'yer think?"

"Fuckin' 'ell Evo, *you're* in love? *I'm* fuckin' in love! Yer weren't kiddin' mate. *She* is fuckin' gorgeous!"

"See, I told yer didn't I?"

"Fuckin' right! That's instant 'ard on material that Evo!"

"Fuckin' tell me abarr it! I'm pole-vaultin' round the shop all day!"

"Yer gonna get into 'er then or what?"

"Well obviously I'd like to but I don't think there's much chance."

"Well 'urry up Evo 'cos if *you* don't get into 'er, *I* will!"

"Fuck off Conk, I saw 'er first! Anyway, 'aven't you got enough? Yer still bonin' Carmel?"

"Yeah - and Joan!"

"Yer spawny bastard! I think I'll ask Ev to come the Empire with me on Saturday to see Gene Pitney."

"Oh yeah, she's really gonna be fuckin' dyin' to see Gene Pitney isn't she?"

"Yer've got no style Conk. By the way, did you pay for that fuckin' loaf?"

"Did I fuck!"

"Yeah, yer didn't rob anything else though did yer? Gibbo never took 'is eyes off yer."

"Yer fuckin' jokin' aren't yer!"

With that Conk produced, like rabbits from a hat, not only the Hovis but also: a tin of pilchards; a tin of salmon (red salmon too, not that pink shite - Conk didn't rob shite); a bottle of lemonade; twenty Rothmans (again, only the good stuff for Conk); three Mars bars; a packet of crisps and a Topic.

"You cheeky, robbin' twat! Fuckin' David Nixon's got nothin' on you! "What are yer gonna do with that lot?"

"I'm 'avin' the ciggies meself. The rest I'm gonna sell to you, yer fat bastard."

"Okay, I'll give yer two bob for the lot."

"Done."

"You certainly 'ave been!"

I did that much tuggin' for the rest of the week that there was only spud juice comin' out in the end! The shop was full of Andy Fairweatherlowe's dulcet tones: "If Paradise is half as nice as heaven that you take me too, who needs Paradise I'd rather have you." Very apt considering my burgeoning love for Ev. Diana Ross and The

Supremes and The Temptations were also fighting my corner: "I'm gonna do all the things for you a girl wants a man to do, oh baby. I'll sacrifice for you; I'll even do wrong for you, oh baby. Every minute, every hour, I'm gonna shower you with love and affection. Look out I'm comin' in your direction, 'cos I'm gonna make you love me, yes I will. Yes I will. I'm gonna make you love me, yes I will, you know I will." Nice one Diana and co! I loved that song! There was only one thing I loved more and that was Ev. Well, apart from Liverpool that is!

I always knew that Saturday was gonna be a big test. Rumour had it that our match at West Ham would be on Match Of The Day that night. If that were true then it followed the match would also be broadcast live on Radio 4. Also the reserves were at home to Newcastle. A young lad we'd just signed from Bury who was supposed to be a very good player was making his debut: Alec Lindsay. I could listen to the match on someone's tranny while I watched the reserves. Do you think in the face of all that I stayed in Tesco's 'til eight o'clock? No chance!

I was having my dinner (crisps, a Mars bar and a can of coke, all of which I'd just nicked off the shelves) with Ev.

"Ev, d'yer wanna come and see Gene Pitney with me at the Empire tonight?"

"Err...I can't...I'm err... goin' to a party."

Obviously making it up as she went along. She sounded as if she would rather be in Tulsa, never mind twenty-four hours from it, than to go the Empire with me. I was gonna have to hit her with the big one!

"Joe Cocker's support. You know, 'im who 'ad the Number One, 'With A Little Help From My Friends'?"

"Yeah, I know who 'e is, I just can't go. I'm goin' to a party."

Well if Joe Cocker couldn't swing it, nobody could!

"Can't yer ask somebody else to go with yer?"

"Yeah, I'll ask me mate Wocko."

Wocko, who had twatted me all over the place a couple of weeks previously, had now made friends with me for the very good reason that he was shaggin' our Pauline's mate, June, in our house every night!

"No, I mean ask another girl."

"I don't wanna take any other girl Ev - I wanted to take you. Right Ev,

I'm off."

"Yer dinner hour isn't finished yet."

"No but I 'ave. There's no way I'm workin' in 'ere when Liverpool are at 'ome."

"They're away aren't they?"

Told yer I was convertin' 'er!

"Yeah but the reserves are at 'ome. Anyway, the match is on the wireless."

"You're mad you." Oh, okay I'll see yer Monday. What are yer gonna say to Mr. Gibb? Yer sick?"

"No, yer don't get it do yer Ev? I'm goin', leavin', fuckin' off - for good!"

"Yer can't just do that!"

"Who fuckin' can't? You watch me!"

"Well what abarr yer job?"

"I'm not arsed! I'll get another one. Listen Ev, the only good thing about workin' in this fuckin' shit'ole is you! I love you."

There I'd said it - the "L" word! It was the first time I'd ever told anybody I loved them and I truly meant it.

"Don't be stupid, yer don't love me! You've only known me a week - less!"

"Look Ev, don't tell me I don't love you; I do. Right, I'm off now. I'll probably never see yer again."

With that I put my coat on and walked out, never to return to the confines of Tesco's again. Not before I'd put half a dozen Mars bars (I liked them), three packets of crisps, a can of coke, twenty Embassy and half an ounce of Golden Virginia in my pocket though! Tesco's principles of "Stack it high. Sell it cheap!" weren't quite the same as mine: "Stack the shelves and then rob as much of it as you can." So ended my brief sojourn with the retail industry. I'd also given up all aspirations of merchant banking, although I was doing plenty of the thing that rhymes with it! Factory fodder I was, so factory work I was going to do. I'd ask Auntie Ann to get me into the No-Nail Box Company.

I was going to have to wait to see whether Dad was Johnny Jekyll or Johnny Hyde before breaking the news of my unemployment to him. No matter what though I decided honesty would be the best policy: a first for me I know but that was the way I was going to approach it. Johnny Jekyll would understand that the Reds were uppermost in my thoughts and that anyway I would get another job, so no problem. Johnny Hyde on the other hand would give me a good hiding for walking out of a job. Mam would just nag me to death but I definitely wouldn't get a crack off her. Wasn't *quite* the way it turned out!

Mam and Dad rolled in steamin' as usual for a Saturday night.
"Hiya Dad. 'Ave a good time in the club?"
"We didn't got to 'Arland's son. We went the Melly."
"Gorra 'ave a few bob to go there 'aven't yer Dad?"
"Yeah, but I won a fiver on the 'orses so I treated yer Mam."
Good, he was Johnny Jekyll. I'd probably get away with it. Let's hit him with it now!
"Dad, I left me job today."
"Why son?"
"Well yer know, it was too much like, all that ten hours a day lark and twelve on a Saturday. I left at dinnertime and went to see the reserves. We won 2-1. There was fifteen thousand there!"
"Oh aye yeah, that new lad was playin' wasn't 'e?" What's 'is name? Alan Lindsay?"
"*Alec* Lindsay Dad. Yeah, 'e looked good too. Scored a cracker from thirty yards. Got a great left foot."
"Not as good as Stevo's was though eh?"
"Not yet maybe but given time it could be."
"'Ow the first team get on?"
"Drew one all Dad. Roger scored. I listened to it on a tranny. I've just watched it now on Match Of The Day."
Whack! A hand cracked right across my face with all the force of an Exocet missile. No, not my Dad - my Ma! I was at least *half* expecting a belt from me Da but *definitely not* from me Ma!
"Ee arr Mam, what was that for?"
"What was that for? What was that for?"
Yeah, what the fuck was that for? Yer fuckin' nearly broke me jaw!
"Yer know what it was it for! Yer know what it was for!"
I fuckin' don't. D'yer think if I knew what it was for I'd be wastin' me fuckin' breath askin' yer? Anyway, why the fuck are yer sayin' everythin' twice, or is there a fuckin' echo in 'ere?
"That's two jobs yer've 'ad now. Yer got sacked from one and walked out of another."
Yeah, I know! I can fuckin' count!
"Well I'll get another one. I'll ask Auntie Ann to get me in her place."

"Well yer better make sure yer keep that job then."

Too fuckin' right I would! If somebody in the family got you a job you fuckin' *had* to stick with it - or else! My Granny Martha had got our Pauline a job in the chicken factory but because she fuckin' hated it she wanted to leave and got herself a job lined up in Reid's Tin Works. Granny Martha went off 'er 'ead and threatened our Po with dark retribution should she even think of taking up the job at Reid's. Pauline stayed where she was. You didn't mess with Granny Martha!

"'Ang on, I'll get yer Granny Martha to get yer a job in the chicken factory."

FUCKIN' 'ELL, NO!

"Ah no Mam, please. I've seen the state our Pauline comes 'ome in of a night. Covered in chicken blood, guts and poo."

"Ah leave the lad alone Lily. Let 'im go to the No-Nail. 'E might get on the machines there."

*Err...excuse me! This is **my future yer decidin'** 'ere. Do I get a say in it like? Thanks for the back up anyway Dad.*

"Yeah, that's what I wanna do Dad. Ee arr, I bought yer 'alf an ounce. Ee arr Mam, I bought yer twenty Embassy."

"Ah, thanks son, yer a good lad. I'm sorry for 'ittin' yer."

Yeah, I should fuckin' think so too! I won't be able to fuckin' eat for a week!

"That's okay Mam. No problem."

"Yeah, thanks son. Yer a good Red."

So are you Dad. So are you!

My prediction that "I'm Gonna Make You Love Me" would reach Number One the following week was correct. "Half As Nice", good song though it was, went back from whence it came - down to number fifteen, adding credence to the rumours that the first computerised chart had been rigged.

Evelyn? Was that the last time I ever saw her? Certainly not! What do I mean? Keep reading!

CHAPTER TWELVE

DAYS OF DESTRUCTION

Life in the No-Nail was much more to my liking. Enough women there for my hormones to run riot. Most of them were married and quite a bit older than me. The ones that weren't were soon snapped up by the eager young bucks I worked with. Loads of lads there too, every one of whom were well into their footy: Joey Shields, Kenny Sands (who was actually a first cousin of mine but whom I'd never met previously), Terry Mac, Chris Nelson, Dave Fredson, Tony Donohue, Joey Humphreys (more about him later) and Bobby Cloney (him too). Then there were the owld arses who had seen it and done it all before: Pat, Sid and Johnny. The fact the owld arses all had fingers missing was testimony to their years of working on woodcutting machines. There seemed to be a competition to see who had least fingers. I think Pat won it; he had a total of six. The manager, Mr. Duncan was sound as a pound too. A big bluenose, we had some great banter.

Games of dinnertime footy on the field outside soon achieved almost legendary status. How we all came back into work with two lower limbs apiece is beyond me! Bobby Cloney however took the piss! He had trials with a number of clubs, including Liverpool, as a very talented schoolboy 'til he sustained a bad injury, putting paid to his career at that level. He did however go on to play at a fairly good semi-pro standard.

The morning ritual was that Mam would interrupt my dreams of Jane, Ev or whoever happened to be the object of my nocturnal lust, the sexual flavour of that particular month at seven o'clock. A quick splish-splash and then sit dozing in front of the roaring coal fire 'til my two boiled eggs and toast were ready. Then came the hard part! That dreaded ten-yard crouch and shuffle from fireside chair to table. Evo's donga would absolutely refuse to go down until I reached the comparative safety of under the table! Even Cissy Mulhall's famous bloomers were no longer doing the trick. Not that I was getting turned on by the thought of the dragon's piss-stained underwear you understand! It was just that the part of my brain (such as it was) controlling my hormonal instincts had now developed an immune system against those horrible pink monstrosities!

The dash to catch the 57A bus from Linacre Lane to Bridle Road was always hilarious. I'd leave the house at about twelve minutes to eight to catch the bus arriving at Linacre Lane two minutes later. A mad dash up the back jigger and on to Fernhill Road. Then a crazy feat of daring involving a flying leap to catch hold of the pole on the platform of the moving bus which crushed my pilchard sarnies to smithereens. I always had pilchard sarnies. The thing I did wrong was to tell Ma that I liked pilchards. I got them then every single day. The same also went for Mars bars and chocolate cup cakes. It really was a great feat to have all that lot in my hands plus a copy of the Daily Mirror and still be able to negotiate my way safely (sort of) on to the bus. Once on the bus I had to endure the constant barrage of abuse from the chicken factory girls. Our Pauline would already be on the bus having left home ten minutes or so earlier to avoid the terrible possibility of being seen alive with her mad younger brother.
"Sit downstairs will yer!" Pauline would hiss at me.
I must say I can't really blame her. I must have looked a right divvy: hair all over the place and uncombed, steel toe-capped boots with the laces untied, coat unbuttoned and flies undone showing the chickeny girls the gruesome sight of my Y-fronts! There was one very good reason though why I put up with the smoke, bad language and abuse from the chickeny girls on the top deck - Maureen Shears. Maureen was known to come across on a regular basis. Indeed quite a few of the No-Nailers had felt the welcoming embrace of Maureen's voluptuous thighs. So too had most of the lads between Dodge City and Marsh Lane. I wanted some of it! Was I going to get it? Was I fuck!

A much-postponed fifth round FA Cup-tie at Leicester had finished in a goalless draw. Leicester were struggling badly in their fight to avoid relegation while we were challenging Leeds for the title so the replay should be a fairly easy game. Andy Lochead had other ideas. The big, bruising, Scottish gorilla of a centre forward gave Leicester the lead. We were struggling to break down Leicester's, for once, resilient defensive rearguard. There was also the small matter of getting the ball past their outstanding young goalkeeper Peter Shilton. Desperate situations require desperate measures. It was time for a change. Yeah, come on; let's get the sub on. Bobby Graham was on the bench and raring to go. Yes, he's coming on! Who's coming off? Why is Sir Roger walking towards the touchline? No, Roger can't be getting brought off! Evans, Thompson, St. John or somebody but surely not our beloved Kop knight. A crescendo of booing accompanied Sir Roger's long walk to the dugout. Then, in an instant, all Sir Roger's games, all his goals, all he'd ever done for Liverpool FC, every last ounce of sweat, every off-the-ball run, every unselfish pass, every defence-assisting tackle seemed to be forgotten as the great man - my hero, everybody's hero, tore off his sacred shirt and threw it at Bill Shankly sitting in the dugout. 54,000 people stood in stunned disbelief. It was bad enough that Sir Roger had been substituted. Even worse that he had torn his shirt off. Worse still that he had thrown it towards the dugout. The fact Roger had threw it at Shankly was barely comprehensible. I cried. It wasn't Bobby Graham's fault. He hadn't asked to replace a Liverpool legend. Bobby was unmercifully and unfairly booed. The substitution made no difference. Leicester deservedly held on to their lead. Outside the ground I bought a massive poster of Sir Roger. Whether it was a mark of respect for the demise of my hero I'm not sure. All I know is that night marked the beginning of the end of Sir Roger's illustrious Liverpool career.

The cliché, "Out of the Cup. Let's concentrate on the League" stood us in good stead as we embarked on an unbeaten run of nine matches, winning five of those games. The crunch though would come in our final home match of the season against Leeds at Anfield. Leeds required only a point from this and their remaining home fixture against Nottingham Forest. We needed maximum points from this game plus our final two games of the season at Manchester City and Newcastle. Roger, having been restored to the team after his career-changing substitution, had then sustained an injury that kept him out of this and the previous three matches. Leeds were experts at going away for a draw and getting it. Sure enough, they held out under our barrage in front of nearly 54,000 people to deservedly clinch their first ever League Championship. Leeds, under Don Revie's astute management, were not always pretty to watch but were very effective. They lost only two League games all season - 1-3 at Manchester City and 1-5 at Burnley. Their unbeaten home record saw them drop only three points against Sunderland, Spurs and West Brom. The Leeds players, led by their captain, Billy Bremner, came towards the Kop at the end of the match where they were rightly saluted by the thunderous roars of, "Champions! Champions." We were disappointed but sporting enough to acknowledge a team of worthy Champions. Our own 61 points would have won us the League in most other seasons but we still ended the season six points behind Leeds' then record Championship-winning haul. Sportsmanship however was forgotten at the end of the match as hundreds of scallies set about Leeds supporter's coaches in a mission to exact revenge for the Battle of Elland Road early in the season.

Joey Humphreys it was who set me on my drinking career. I must admit to having previously had a little dabble. Dad's bottles of Mann's brown and Ma's bottles of Mackies that they kept in the pantry were always easy targets and I happily guzzled away at them 'til I got caught. I should have realised that it was bloody obvious they were going to keep count of how many were there. I learnt a painful lesson when Dad thudded a beauty of a right cross into my temple as retribution for robbing his ale! Humbug knew the score though! A walk down to the Lift Bridge and along Linacre Road where he could get served in offies with bottles of QC. Humbug was about a year older than me but actually looked about 20 with his rugged, weather-beaten kite. He could even get into alehouses and we'd sneak into the Saltbox, Kent's or the Red Lion with me keeping out of site in the doorway while we sipped our brown-mixed until the inevitable happened and I'd be lashed out by the landlord. Christ, I barely looked old enough to drink a bottle of milk never mind a bottle of ale! It was fun though getting slaughtered along Linacre Road with that warm feeling of cheap plonk inside my young body. Even more fun keeping from Mam the fact I was absolutely rat-arsed. I mean, she must have thought it very strange indeed that her eldest son had suddenly started kissing her goodnight and telling her how much he loved her. How the hell she never smelt the plonk on my breath I'll never know. Perhaps she did!

"Peter, Maureen Shears wants to go out with yer."
That's strange; I'm sure our Pauline just said, "Peter, Maureen Shears wants to go out with yer."
"Yer what?"
"You fuckin' 'eard!"
"She wants to go out with *me*?"
"Yis daft arse - *you*. Fuck knows why like! She must feel sorry for yer."

Our Pauline had perfected the stock-in language of the chickeny girls. "Fuckin' yessssss!"

"Don't get yer 'opes up. She won't let yer do anythin'."

"Why not? She lets everybody else."

"Yeah, but not you."

She had a point I suppose - I was an ugly bastard.

A date was fixed up for me to take Maureen to the Carlton to see "The Good, The Bad and The Ugly." That was my mistake. If I'd taken her to the alehouse I'd have had a chance. Getting her pissed would have probably swung it for me. In fact it was my only chance! My schoolboy looks were doing me no favours in the shagging department. "The Good, The Bad and The Ugly" was not only being enacted on the flickering silver screen of the Carlton by Clint Eastwood, Lee Van Cleef and Eli Wallach but also on the back seat of the balcony by me and Maureen. I was good for a long time - after all it was a boss film and I actually wanted to watch it. I was bad as I set upon my pathetic attempt of trying to snog Maureen. Oh, she was up for it all right but I was so fuckin' nervous I just kept covering her in spit rather than let my tongue dance around her tonsils. The ugly came right at the end of the film when Maureen's hand ever so delicately brushed against my protuberance. I absolutely shit myself and legged it for the safety of the toilet, not returning until the last strains of the National Anthem had faded. Oh well, it would be different once we were back at our house. I'd be on home territory and there'd be no stopping Evo as he rampaged through Maureen's knickers!

Back at ours, Wocko and June were adjusting their clothing as I walked in with Maureen.

"Where's our Pauline?"

"Upstairs with Joe Cooke," replied June, matter-of-factly.

"Who the fuck's Joe Cooke? I've never 'eard of 'im!"

"Some lad she met in Reece's."

"An' she's upstairs with 'im now?"

"Yeah! What the fuck's it gorra do with you?"

June was also a chickeny girl! Anyway, there was no way I was gonna argue with her. I'd made that mistake once after I'd been fighting with our Pauline. June had battered, knocked fuck out of me, all over Grogan Square. I couldn't be arsed with it. I had my own sordid pleasures to think about. Evo was gonna finally get his end away!

The sex-rampaging octopus that had been sat next to me in the Carlton had turned into a Cissy Mulhall clone on our couch. Trying to neck Maureen now was like kissing a brick. No chance of tongues now! My feeble attempt to unhook her bra ended only in me poking myself in the eye - Maureen too! Meanwhile Wocko and June were giving it large on the other couch. This Joe geezer was upstairs with my sister. 'Ang on; I fuckin' live 'ere and I'm the only fucker not getting any action! Ah, fuck it! I gave up the ghost with Maureen and offered to walk her home. She politely declined my kind offer with the words, "Fuck off!" Ah well, a virgin I was and a virgin I would remain for the rest of my days.

"Pauline, it's nearly midnight. Me Mam an' Dad'll be 'ome soon."
"Oh, okay," came the muffled reply
"All right mate," I said to this Joe geezer. Fuck me I wasn't gonna argue with him. He was about five feet four but seemingly just as wide. He looked hard as fuck and I wasn't for one minute gonna ask him if his intentions towards my sister were honourable; not that for one minute did I think he'd been playing Snakes and Ladders upstairs with Pauline!
"Are you Peter?" Joe asked almost incredulously.
"Err...yeah...why?" I managed to splutter. Fuck me, he wasn't gonna beat me up was he? I'd only just met him. I hadn't done any harm to him. Why should he wanna do me in?
"Fuckin' 'ell, I thought you were gonna be dead big and dead 'ard. Your Pauline kept sayin, "Don't touch our Peter's records. Don't touch our Peter's records!" I thought you were some big 'ardcase or somethin'."
Fact was, my records were my pride and joy and I did get a cob on if anybody started arsing around with them but this fella could have made them all into ashtrays and I wouldn't have argued with him!
"Ah, you're all right Joe. Play them if you like mate."
It wasn't just that I was shit scared of Joe but I took an instant liking to him. He looked dead cool in his Wrangler jacket and jeans. I had the same outfit myself so I saw him as one of my own. Joe was more Mod than the Skinhead I was but he'd do for me!
"Where d'yer live Joe?"
"Scotty Road."
Fuckin' 'ell! No wonder he looked hard. You had to be rock hard to live down that end! Scotty Road lads made the Marsh Lane boys look

like St. fuckin' Trinian's hockey team; that didn't stop them taking them on every so often though.

"Who the fuckin' 'ell are you?" was Dad's somewhat less than friendly welcome to this stranger in his house. Looked like Dad was Johnny Hyde tonight.

Dad, for fuck sake what are you doin'? 'E's from fuckin' Scotty! 'E'll fuckin' murder yer!

"Joe Cooke Mister Evo. I'm goin' out with Pauline."

"Oh fuckin' are yer now? Who fuckin' told yer that?"

Ah, I'm calling the bizzies. Now!

"I've been goin' out with 'er a few weeks now."

"Well she's said fuck all to me about yer!"

Well that's hardly fuckin' surprising is it Dad given yer attitude now?

"Well she thought she'd let yer meet me first."

I was impressed with Joe standing his ground.

"Yer look like a fuckin' cowboy! Yeah, Cowboy Joe!"

"Ah, leave 'im alone John," interrupted Mam, looking at her most glamorous. Seemed she'd really made the effort tonight. Cowboy Joe gave her an admiring glance.

Eh, fuckin' eyes off you Cookie! That's me Ma yer eyein' up.

"'Ello Mrs. Evo," Cowboy Joe all grace and charm.

"Ah, call me Lily."

Ma then proceeded to strip herself of all glamour. First of all, off came her glasses. They were followed by her blonde wig. When Ma's teeth joined her glasses and wig there was actually more of Lily Evo on the sideboard than off it. Joe's initial impression of Mam was totally destroyed when she hitched up her frock, removed her corsets and flung them to join the rest of her ensemble on the sideboard.

"Make us a cuppa Peter." Mam by now had a ciggy dangling out of the corner of her mouth. Joe's face was a picture - his jaw dropping helplessly to his chest. I couldn't resist a little chuckle to myself as I made the tea in the kitchen. That was Ma for you - no airs and graces! Cookie had met the real Lily Evo and good bloody luck to him!

Joe was a frequent visitor to our house, especially on a Saturday night when he used to stay. Dad's house rules were that Cookie had to sleep in my bed and top and tail. This was an arrangement, as you can imagine, that didn't meet with my full approval. It was bloody dangerous too! Joe would make a line in the middle of the bed with his hand, karate style, and say, "Move over your side of the line Evo and yer dead."

Well 'ang on - it is my fuckin' bed after all!

The couple of times I did accidentally venture into cowboy territory were severely punished by Joe slicing his big toenail, which I'm sure he used to sharpen specially, right down the inside of my upper thigh. I've still got the scars to prove it! I perfected the technique though of pretending to be asleep. Joe would then fuck off to our Pauline's room for which I was very thankful as I could then spread out and get a good night's kip in my own bed! I wished our Po would oil her bloody bedsprings though!

I was still fighting with our John. After one memorable battle he locked himself in my bedroom while I was out in the street playing football. I heard my bedroom window open and then a tearing of paper. As I looked up I could see one of my programmes floating down.

"I'll fuckin' kill yer!"

My murderous threats fell on deaf ears as John continued to rip my programmes.

"Please John don't."

My whimpering pleading also had no effect.

"'Ere's yer Inter Milan one."

"No John, not the Inter Milan one."

Rip!

"An' your Ajax one."

Rip!

I couldn't get into the house to slit his throat as the cunning bastard had also locked the front door. Nothing for it but to seek retribution. John's bike lay in the front garden.

Kick! Twang! Half a dozen spokes gone.

"Celtic."

Twang!

"Cup Final."

Crack! Twang!

I took great delight in kicking the bike to bits, spoke by spoke with my steelies. It was only sheer fatigue on both our parts that put an end to the carnage. John had an unridable bike while I had fifty or so programmes torn in half. The effort in sellotaping them together was to prove futile.

The summer of '69 was a good one. I was doing well in the No-Nail: I was never going to get on the machines but I was quite happy labouring. I was earning plenty of money so as well as tipping up to Mam I had more than enough to spend on records, clothes and the occasional bevy of which I was getting rather fond. The Beatles were on the verge of splitting up. John Lennon was going more and more his own way but together they were still producing great music. It was their last Number One, "The Ballad of John and Yoko" that I was happily singing as I walked towards the back garden of our house after finishing work one glorious June afternoon. The temperature must have been somewhere in the high eighties so it was something of a surprise to see Dad had a bonfire going in the garden. Dad often had "bommies" in the back garden to get rid of all the old shite that accumulated in the house. Surely today though was far too hot to be burning anything? Must have been something he desperately wanted to get rid of.

"Hiya Dad. What're yer burnin?"

"Your programmes."

He'd said it in such a matter-of-fact manner I thought he must have been joking. He couldn't be burning my programmes. All my spare money had gone on them when I was at school. Even since leaving school I'd spent loads of money on them. I had programmes from all over the world. I was an avid collector and had accumulated some eight hundred or so dating back to Liverpool programmes from the 1950's. Nah, he wouldn't be burning my programmes.

FUCKIN' 'ELL 'E'S BURNIN' ME PROGRAMMES!

I looked down at the heap of ash at his feet. At that precise moment I could happily have committed patricide. All that remained of my marvellous collection was a charred remnant of the Roger Hunt (or was it Peter Thompson?) lookalike that adorned the front cover of home programmes from 1962-'65.

Yer fuckin' bastard! I fuckin' hate yer! Why the fuck did yer do that?

"Why did yer burn my programmes Dad?"

"They were causin' bugs in yer bedroom."

Were they fuck causing bugs, yer fuckin' owld twat!

"Oh okay Dad."

What could I do? I couldn't argue with him, he was my Dad! Anyway to have done so would have meant certain pain for me. Dad was not a man one of his kids would have argued with. I never did get to the truth of just why he burnt them. Was it jealousy as he'd seen me growing up to be an independent young man who was able to go to any match I wanted to? Was it some kind of retribution for a supposed indiscretion of mine? I just didn't know. It took me years and many hundreds of pounds to replace just the Liverpool programmes he'd burnt. The ones from Switzerland, USA, Brazil, Denmark, Scotland, Argentina and other far-flung corners of the globe were irreplaceable. I very nearly replaced all the Liverpool programmes but some were just too rare or too expensive to ever be replaced. Maybe he'd seen our John rip my programmes and me demolish his bike and thought he'd put a stop to it once and for all. Our John wore that vengeful smile; a bike could be replaced - he'd just go out and rob another one - my programmes couldn't. I locked myself in my lonely room and cried away the rest of that blazingly hot day.

CHAPTER THIRTEEN

SHIRTS, STEALING AND SKINS

Two new words entered the English language at the start of the 1969-70 season: "Agro" and "Bovver". The first time we were to hear, or rather see, them was on a shop (lifting) expedition to town on the morning of the first game of the season against Chelsea.

Me, Timmy and Steph were going for Wrangler jeans and jacket and Jaytex shirts. Timmy met us wearing the shabbiest pair of jeans I'd ever seen and a shirt his Granddad wouldn't have worn. He looked like he was on his way to one of those Fancy Dress parties where everybody is dressed as tramps. Smart pair of shoes on though - couldn't work that out! I didn't want to say anything though, as I knew Timmy was skint. Me and Steph were okay; we were both earning good money, so could afford to splash out on clothes. Timmy, on the other hand, was waiting to go to Merchant Navy Training School so he was going to have to rob his gear.

First stop was the Army and Navy Stores on Lime Street. Me and Steph sorted ourselves out with the top of the range Wranglers and very pleased we were with our purchases too!
"Keep this divvy talkin' for five minutes," Timmy whispered to us.
The divvy in question was the beleagured assistant who had a shop full of people intent on getting as many clothes as they could for nothing!
"I'll just go an' try these on mate," Timmy said to Divvy Dave.
"Yes okay, I'll just see to these gentlemen."
Fuckin' 'ell, I'd been accused of being many things but never a gentleman!
"Yeah, ee arr mate, show us those Levi's again."
"Nah, don't get them Evo. Get Lee Cooper's. Aren't Lee Cooper's better eh mate?"
"Well, a couple of years ago maybe but I think your friend has it right in that Levi's seem to be the most popular choice of denims now, although we do still sell plenty of Lee Cooper's. Wranglers also sell very well."
Not in this fuckin' shop they don't mate!
Five minutes of banal conversation with Divvy Dave later and Timmy reappeared looking resplendent in his Wrangler finery. Gone were the lowly rags of Trampy Tim: they were left for some poor sod to throw

in the bin later on. Like Superman coming out of that phone booth Timmy looked ready to take on the world, except that SuperTim had remembered to put his skids *under* his jeans! Timmy, without turning a ginger hair or a trace of hesitancy walked calmly straight down the stairs and out of the shop! Conk might have been Prince Grocery Grabber but Timmy was definitely King Clobber Robber! Conk could go into Tesco's in the Strand, fill a trolley full of goodies and rob the fuckin' carrier bags too! Then wheel the trolley to the back jigger outside his house (didn't wanna be carrying those bags all that way) bag all the groceries up and keep the flim his Ma had given him to get the shopping. No wonder the cunt never worked! I wonder if Mrs. Colquit ever twigged on why her son was the only lad in the street who liked going for his Ma's messages? Our Price and his mates would then be made up getting rides in the trolley all day. Timmy though had just walked out of the Army and Navy with about twelve quid's worth of clobber - a far better haul!

"Err, yeah okay mate. Thanks for that. Yeah, we'll back next week for those Levi's. Thanks for the advice. See yer next week."
My arse!

Next port of call was the little Jewish shop on London Road. This was the only place in town you could get Jaytex shirts. Boss shirts were Jaytex. Mostly checked (very rarely saw a striped or plain one), front placket, back collar button, button down collar, back pleat and hanging loop. Jaytex were the sort of poor man's Ben Sherman. Quality obviously wasn't quite as good as a Benny but at two quid, about half the price, they were certainly very good value. No chance of robbing from here though - not even Timmy! The little Jewish bloke behind the counter watched our every move. The advantage Manny had over any other shop assistant was that he knew we were a robbin' shower of thievin' scally bastards and it would take a fuckin' monkey wrench to get money out of our hands - much the same as himself!

Two squids handed over for a lemon and blue Jaytex and we were off down to Skelly to get the bus home. We were just having a little walk around by the Royal Court minding our own business when we chanced on three lads spray-painting something on a wall.
"CHELSEA AGRO", "CHELSEA BOVVER BOYS, "CHELSEA SKINS", "SHED RULES OK" were the legends the three cockney sparrers had left daubed for posterity on the wall of one of Liverpool's finest theatres.
"All right lads. What does that mean, AGRO?"
We soon found out! We were genuinely asking in a nice manner and were quite prepared to talk to our Chelsea counterparts about the

forthcoming afternoon's entertainment.

"This is wot it fackin' means, you fackin' Scarse cants!"

Fuck off! Bang! My fuckin' nose again! Why me? Why me all the fuckin' time? Why does fuckin' God hate me?

Two minutes of flying fists and boots later without any real harm having been done, except for the usual Evo bust nose, and the Chelsea Bovver Boys were on their toes screaming behind them dark threats of what their "mob" were going to do after the match.

"So that's Agro is it?" Timmy said. "Right, we'll fuckin' 'ave some of that! See 'ow fuckin' 'ard they are at the coaches after the match!"

"Fuck that Timmy! I'll get twatted in the fuckin' nose again. There's only so much even my fuckin' fat schnozzle can take!"

"No yer won't Evo," said Steph, "There'll be fuckin' 'undreds of us there. They fuckin' won't get away with that!"

So it was that the term and culture of AGRO was born. It was chanted at every ground up and down the country for the rest of that season and for many more seasons after that. We though, as per usual, were the only fans to see the humorous side of it, chanting as we did in very posh voices: "A - G, A - G - R, A - G - R - O, AGRO!"

Every club in the country had their "mob" or "crew".   Even small, barely supported clubs would have their yob element. There was no escaping AGRO. Everywhere we went we were faced with howling mobs of lads, mainly outside the ground after matches, who were intent on kicking shite out of any Scouser they could. Not that they succeeded that much. You see we were no angels ourselves and there were always plenty of lads who were well up for it. Me personally? I just wanted to go away, watch the match, avoid getting my head booted in and get home! I actually think that was the case with most lads but if you went watching Liverpool away in that era you had to at least be prepared to have a go if AGRO came your way or you'd get wasted. There wasn't much point in hiding or running away if a baying mob of Geordies came running at you. Stand and fight or get kicked to fuck anyway; there wasn't much choice.

HAVING A GO

Late sixties - early seventies you had to be tough.

Give and take a dig and take the smooth with the rough.

You had to have a go when faced with a mob

Or you'd end up with a shiner and a split open gob.

Go to Anfield; hand over your money.
Enter the land of milk and honey.
"Come on you Reds. Tear 'em to pieces!"
After the match, off to Reece's.

Joe Magebe, Andy Fisher, Peter Kelly too
Taking cockneys and mancs two by two.
"Down the coaches, let's sort 'em out!"
Kopites ruled; there was no doubt.

No Road End then calling us "gobshites"
They were still in school trying to get their sums right.
Scary trips to Sunderland, West Ham and Spurs.
Man U, Forest and Wolves - they were all nightmares.

"Stay! Don't run! Stand up and fight!"
All this against the Gelderd End's might.
But did they fight five hundred Scousers just standing there?
No, they turned around and ran like a hare!

"A - G, A - G - R, A - G - R - O, AGRO!"
Was the shout against us wherever we'd go.
Arsenal thought they were hard dressed in their white coats
But when we ran at them it was like a rush for the lifeboats!

Getting off the coach, the old flutterbyes
Would be churning in your guts but you had to be wise.
Everybody knew just what it meant
If you got caught at Forest - you got thrown in the Trent!

Going to Chelsea and taking the Shed.
Dodging the missiles aimed at your head.
Waiting outside would be loads of their loonies.
Safely back on the coach we gave them the moonies!

Burnley, Huddersfield, Derby and Stoke
All thought they were hard: what a fuckin' joke!
Ten thousand to Burnley every bloody season.
Plates of mashed spuds with loads of mushy peas on.

Newcastle and Man City both had good crews.
"The Liverpool boys are in town": that was their bad news.
"Fight us if you dare 'cos we won't run away.
And don't forget you've gotta come to Anfield some other day."

You had to stand. You just couldn't run
Although getting a crack wasn't much fun
If you took to your toes you'd get caught anyway
Unless there was an escort - That'll be the day!

It's calmed down a lot now; even Old Trafford's a doddle
But not in '69 when I got hit with a bottle.
Concussed for three days or so I was told
But I had my revenge - a dish best eaten cold!

It might not have been him who hit me with a chair
But I had to get some manc: I just didn't care.
But that's how it was: it was the law of the wild
You very quickly became a man when you'd only just been a child.

The point of all this is not to glorify thugs.
Hooliganism is strictly for mugs.
But it was dog eat dog - you had to be wary.
Going away in those days was very bloody scary!

Don't get me wrong I was never really violent.
Just has to be said; no point in being silent.
If you weren't prepared to at least have a go
You'd get your head kicked in; I'm telling you, you know.

Of course by the time we got in the Kop for the game Timmy had exaggerated the three Chelsea lads into thirty of their top boys. According to Timmy we, the three mucketeers, had stood our ground and fought the baying mob off. Only my nose was testimony to his utter bollocks.

Alun Evans had been slashed across his face in an incident at a Wolverhampton nightclub during the summer. Obviously some cretin had taken great exception to Alun's heinous crime of leaving the former greats to further his career at Anfield. So it was that his injuries prevented Alun from starting the season. Bobby Graham (seemingly everybody's understudy) took his place. We won the game 4-1 with Ian St. John notching two of the goals. Steph had been right about what it would be like at the Chelsea coaches after the game. Utting Avenue and Priory Road were scenes of absolute mayhem. Bobbies on horseback and motorbikes were up and down the road trying to keep the hundreds of Liverpool scallies away from their Chelsea counterparts. I was looking for the twat who had bust my nose but the miserable, horrible, slimy bastard must have crept unnoticed on to a coach.

A cracking game against Manchester City at Anfield followed three days later. The Saint gave us an early lead but City, inspired by their triumvirate of Bell, Lee and Summerbee and also great performances by a couple of young lads, Ian Bowyer and Stan Bowles, fought back to lead 2-1 with only seven minutes remaining. The usual baying noise of, "Attack, attack, attack, attack, attack," boomed down from the Kop. Sir Roger equalised and The Saint, in great early-season form, finished the job off with two minutes left on the clock.

Plans were made after the game for the trip to Tottenham the following Saturday. The coach would be leaving Lawrenson's on Stanley Road at 11:30 on Friday night, picking up at Cherryfield Drive, Kirby and getting us to the ground at about 5:30 - 6:00 on Saturday morning. This was my first ever visit to London so I was very excited. Timmy and Steph however were old hands at it.
"What do we do when we get there Timmy?"
"Well, we just mooch around the ground for about an hour, rob some milk off the doorsteps, see if we can get any brekky somewhere and then bunk the tube at Seven Sisters to Trafalgar Square. We'll 'ave a look round Downin' Street and the 'Ouses of Parliament and then get back up the ground for about twelve o'clock or somethin' like that."
"Yeah, yer 'ave to watch out though for all the London mobs. They're always knockin' around lookin' to pick off lads in twos or threes." Steph also knew the score.

That Lawrenson's coach should have been renamed "The Scally Bus". There were some right vagabonds on there. It got even worse when we picked up at Kirkby. The feuds between Bootle and Kirkby lads were forgotten when they were all together following Liverpool. There was a common enemy up against us: Cockneys, so there was no room or time for infighting.

Timmy had this huge Union Jack which he'd robbed from the flagpole of his old school, St. George of England, the previous night. Fuckin' nutter Timmy, but what a character! He also had a tin of spray paint he'd robbed from Halford's. Not that he needed to re-spray anything; it was going to be used to mark our arrival at White Hart Lane.

Upon arrival at White Hart Lane we followed the milkman as he made his deliveries around the local houses. A lot of North London Cockneys went without their cornflakes and coffee that morning! We then set about the task of daubing the Liverpool legend in bright red paint all over the turnstile doors of the Park Lane End and the Paxton Road End.

"What end are we goin' in Timmy?" I thought it was a valid enough question.

"Are you fuckin' stupid? The same fuckin' end we go in 'ere every year. This fuckin' one of course. The Park Lane End. Their end; we're gonna take it."

Fuckin' sorry for askin' I'm sure!

"Oh right Timmy, okay."

It was quite pleasant walking around Trafalgar Square early on a lovely August morning. It turned out to be hilarious when a pigeon shit on Steph's head! Of course we used the old joke: "'Ee arr Steph, I'll get yer some bog roll."

"Fuck off, it'll be miles away by now."

We were still laughing when we got to Downing Street. This was in the days when the public could actually go on to Downing Street and stand right outside the door of Number Ten. It's such a pity that nowadays the public doesn't get a chance to see those impressive houses and part of our heritage at close quarters, having instead to peer through a set of railings trying to sneak a glance. I'm not saying I don't agree or understand why this should be so, just that it's a great pity. The exact opposite is now the case with Buckingham Palace. We could only see the Palace from a distance of hundreds of yards. Nowadays the public pay for guided tours of the inside such is commercialisation and Betty's need to recoup a few bob of the millions needed to restore one of the other of her many houses after it was fire-damaged. I don't half feel sorry for her, don't you? It must be dead hard being the Queen and having loads of money. You know, it's tough when one of your castles gets burned.

Next stop was Whitehall and the Changing of the Guard. We had loads of fun taking the piss out of the sentries. There was also a guy about ten feet tall sitting motionless on a horse as we jibed him. That's one shit job that! I think he cracked once though and mouthed, "Fuck off" at us. I'm fuckin' glad he didn't dismount though: I'd rather have fought his horse than him!

We were on The Embankment with a few other Reds we'd met when a group of about half-a-dozen lads came towards us.

"Oh, ee arr, fuckin' look out 'ere's trouble," said Steph.

"Awoit mate. Wot time is it?"

Well I wasn't to know was I? I was new to all this. I just thought this Cockney lad genuinely wanted to know what time it was on this glorious summer morn. I mean, it might have been the case that him and his mates were members of the Royal Horticultural Society and were planning a trip to a flower display at Kew Gardens having to be there for, say, a twelve o'clock start. I didn't know they were six of Millwall's finest sussing out Scousers.

"It's 'alf eleven mate," I said a second before I got the Millwall knuckle. Where did I get it? Yes, you've guessed, right in the fuckin' nose! Fuck me, did I have a target on it or what? Or was there a sign on it saying, "I'm a Scouser. I'm fuckin' stupid. Please twat me as hard as you possibly can on the nose"? Whatever it was I was in deep pain while the rest of the lads fought off the pseudo-RHS who then went in search of more gullible twats like me. I'd liked my first experience of London up 'til then, but fuck me the Millwall boys had given me a sharp, painful and bloody introduction on to what was to turn out to be a steep learning curve.

The mile or so walk from Seven Sisters tube to White Hart Lane was an opportunity for Timmy, me and Steph to indulge in one of our favourite pastimes: robbing. I was good, Steph was better but Timmy was fuckin' marvellous. The stock check at Woolworths, Seven Sisters Road for the month ending August 1969 must have realised a huge deficit. Timmy didn't care what he robbed; if it wasn't nailed down he'd have it!

"Why are we goin' in this end Timmy - the Paxton Road End? I thought we were gonna take their end?"
"We are soft arse! We don't just go straight in their end; there'd be fuckin' murder. We go in this end and then walk round to their end." I was going to have to get a bit more clued up here.
The Park Lane End was full of evil looking bastards. Christ, I thought our lot looked hard and ugly but these Tottenham Skins looked like they meant business. The battling started about two o'clock. Guess who was stuck right on the edge of two thousand or so Scousers faced with the same screaming amount of hard case Cockneys? Yes, once more you've guessed it (you're getting good at this aren't you?), me! Only this time my nose was spared further injury. This time my arse would get it. I've never been kicked so hard and so many times up the arse. All the bastards were wearing steelies too (not that we weren't similarly attired in the footwear department) so it felt at one stage as if my arse was going to come out through my head. It got worse only two minutes into the game when Emlyn Hughes scored, and right in front of us too! So what does soft arse Crazy Horse do? Shake hands

politely with his team mates, go back to his own half and take up his position so not antagonising the Spurs faithful into kicking seven kinds of shite out of their Liverpool foes? Like fuck! He went fuckin' ballistic (God love him) right in front of us.

For fuck sake Emlyn, fuck off will yer. I'm getting kicked to shit 'ere because of you.

Of course Emlyn didn't know any other way. It was always the same when he scored. His enthusiasm for LFC knew no bounds so his reaction after scoring a goal was like mine would have been if Bill Shankly had told me to come down to Melwood for a trial. Not that Bill Shankly was ever going to invite me to Melwood for a trial you understand seeing as I was the worst player ever to disgrace a football pitch! Emlyn's goal celebrations were all very well at Anfield you see but not away at Spurs!

Chris Lawler had the right idea. He doubled our lead eight minutes before half-time but not for Chris Emlyn's impression of a whirling dervish. The Silent Knight just ghosted back to his full back position before anybody could get anywhere near him. Yeah, I still got a good arse - kicking for it but nowhere near as badly as when Crazy Horse had done his victory dance. I tell you if there was ever a national arse-kicking contest those Tottenham lads would definitely have won it!

Half-time came and Steph reappeared white-faced from the Park Lane End toilets.

"Fuckin' 'ell Steph, what's the matter with you? Yer look like yer've seen a ghost."

"Don't go down there Evo, it's fuckin' mad! All the Tottenham 'ave got fuckin' knives. Someone's gonna get killed down there. I nearly got fuckin' stabbed meself."

"Fuckin' 'ell, this is scary!" said Timmy, shittin' himself

"Well you fuckin' told us to come in 'ere!" said I about to poo my pants after failure of the arse.

The battle continued in the second half but thankfully we didn't score any more goals. A 2-0 victory would do me but the hard part was to come. Getting back to our coach through the maze of tenement blocks was nightmare enough but once on there we were bombarded with all kind of shite being thrown at us; bricks, bottles, pieces of wood, iron bars, even, believe it or not, a pair of crutches! Once on the safety of the M1 we were able to laugh about the day's events but I was still nursing a battered nose and definitely wouldn't be able to sit properly, or shit properly for that matter, for a week! I'd enjoyed my first visit to London even though it had been very scary. I'd learned lessons though; never tell anybody the time, try not to stand right next to the opposition's loonies, if Emlyn Hughes scores leave the ground immediately and put a piece of concrete down the back of my Shell-Mex!

My sixteenth birthday arrived on the day we were to play Sheffield Wednesday at Hillsborough. I was in the kitchen making a cuppa before I set off. Jane walked through our open back door to join me in the kitchen.

"Where's yer Mam and Dad Peter?"

God, she looked even better than usual! A white blouse with a red bra underneath (how sexy is that?), short black skirt, black stockings and black shoes. As usual her Tommy Smith's footy studs were on prominent display; I nearly hung the teacups on them rather than the mug tree!

"They've gone to town Jane. Not sure why; they never normally go."

"I'm gonna give you a birthday present Peter."

"Oh, are yer Jane, that's nice what is it?"

"This!"

With that, Jane began slowly, deliciously, temptingly unbuttoning her blouse. After what seemed to be three hours Jane's buttons were all undone to reveal the bright red lacy material of her bra. Slowly, effortlessly my beautiful woman slipped off her blouse. Jane's arms went behind her back and I heard the snap as she unclipped her bra. Very sensuously she let the bra slide gracefully down her arms and on to the floor. Revealed before me were those beautiful globes. Stuck right in the middle of each one was what looked like a chocolate digestive, topped off of course by those marvellous, extra-long TSFS.

" J-J-Jane, what are you doin'?"

"Peter, I've seen the way you look at me with those eyes. You're sixteen today. Today's the day I'm gonna make you a man."

As Jane drew me close to her for me to bury my head in amongst those marvellous mounds my donga burst through my jeans.

"Come on Peter, let's go upstairs and make a man of…………………….."

"Peter. Peter! Peter! Come on, wake up! Yer gonna be late for yer match. Yer mates are at the door waitin' for yer."

FUCK OFF MAM! FUCK OFF TIMMY! FUCK OFF STEPH! FUCK OFF DREAM MASTER!

Fuckin' 'ell! All been a fuckin' dream! Bastard! Not again!

"Uh, yeah, yeah Mam. I'm getting' up now."

Just let me see to this first!

Travelling to Sheffield in those pre-M62 days was a nightmare, as you would inevitably have to go through Manchester. Waiting to greet us in Manchester of course were those wonderful rivals of ours. Nice chaps of course, always ready to give us a cheery wave, wish us a safe journey and speed us on our way.

My arse!

Crash! A window in the middle of the coach was smashed to smithereens as a brick came hurtling through it.

Oh, fuckin' thanks yer manc twats! Good job it was a late summer's day and not a freezin' fuckin' cold winter's day! The driver did a sterling job in getting us to fuck out of there without any further damage being done to one of Lawrenson's super-dooper coaches.

Once inside the ground at Sheffield we could tell trouble was brewing. We were stood on the high triangular piece of terracing in the top left-hand corner of the Leppings Lane end. The Wednesday fans in the West Stand next to us were goading us from the moment we walked in. This got steadily worse until Wednesday scored after about twenty minutes. Then all hell broke loose! The trouble seemed mostly to be going on a lot further back from where I was standing but it was gradually spreading downwards. Okay, I'm not gonna say I did nothing! I was shouting down a copper's ear. Not a brilliant thing to do but hardly the crime of the century either! I was grabbed from behind around the throat and was then half pushed, half kicked down steps at the back of the terrace and thrown into an arrest room. I was charged with obscene language. I know you're not gonna believe this but I honestly DID NOT swear. Taking the piss out of a bizzy by shouting down his ear, thinking I was dead big, showing off in front of my mates and just generally being a prick I certainly was but I didn't use a single F word whilst doing it! According to the arresting officer PC Shaw (never forget his name) I was (and I'll never forget this word either as I've never heard it before or since) MIMIWAUKING another policeman. MIMIWAUKING? What the fuck's MIMIWAUKING? The prick knew I hadn't sworn but I suppose I deserved arresting just for being a twat alone! The roar I heard coming from our fans about twenty minutes later told me that we'd equalised. I didn't think it would be a good idea to do an Emlyn Hughes while I was being fingerprinted so I just gave it a Chris Lawler, who, as it turned out incidentally, had scored!

After the nice policemen had taken my photograph (aren't they kind?), officially charged me and phoned Bootle police to inform my Mam and Dad that I'd been arrested I thought they would at least kick me out on to the street there and then. That way at least I could either try and get back in the ground or at the very least wait at the coach for the others to get back after the match. Not a bit of it! The wonderful South Yorkshire Police seemed intent on keeping me in that arrest room as long as humanly possible.

"I'm gonna miss me coach!"

"That's your fault Sunny Jim!"

Look, I'm not feelin' particularly Sunny and my name certainly isn't fuckin' Jim! Give us a fuckin' break will yer an' let me go!

"Come on please, me Ma's gonna kill me anyway."

"Well you shouldn't have been mimiwauking a policeman should you?"

Fuck off with that bastard word will yer!

It was futile trying to argue with them. They were going to let me go when *they* wanted to - when they knew the coach had fucked off that is. PC Shaw then turned hero.

"I'll walk with you down to the train station. There's some nasty characters hang around here after the game."

He wasn't fuckin' kiddin' either! Loads of evil-looking bastards all over the place who looked as if they would willingly kick my head in had it not been for the presence of that single policeman. Then I spotted it! The Holy Grail of the coach was parked up a side street away from the Yorkie mobs who would surely have finished off the job the mancs started had they seen it.

"There's me coach! Thanks officer. Sorry for that before!"

"Fuck off!"

Tut, tut! Obscene language from a policeman! What's the world coming to? But at least he hadn't mimiwauked anybody!

Jammily for me the driver of the coach had been waiting for ages for a local repair centre to come out and sort us a new window for the coach. Nice one! There was Mam and Dad still to negotiate though. It didn't turn out too bad though. I think sixteen was the benchmark beyond which it was pointless beating me up to try instil some discipline into me. I received an official caution by post from the Chief Constable of South Yorkshire Police for my misdemeanour. I was getting good at these cautions wasn't I? I was collecting them! Once again Evo was the butt of the scallies jokes on the way home but that's only to be expected. I joined in with the merry-making and of course exaggerated the incident out of all proportion. The next time I was to have dealings with South Yorkshire Police though, nearly twenty years later, was to be no laughing matter.

CHAPTER FOURTEEN

MOANS, MANCS AND MIMIWAUKING

We went to Old Trafford on a roasting hot September day having won seven of our first nine matches, drawing the other two. Confidence was running high. The Saint, Sir Roger and Bobby Graham were scoring regularly. Lawler, Hughes and Geoff Strong were also chipping in with goals so thing were looking rosy. Old Trafford was still a daunting place to go though and not just on the pitch. The lads on the coach were full of stories of how dodgy it was at Old Trafford. The days when Scousers would take the Stretford End were well gone. It was time to keep your wits about you.

I know we shouldn't have been drinking and going into any pub in Manchester was decidedly unsafe, let alone the Dog and Partridge, but as I say it was boiling hot and we were very thirsty. We'd decided that if we kept our mouths shut we'd be okay. WRONG! We'd ordered our ale in a weird sort of sign language that involved a lot of head nodding, winking and pointing. We'd got away with the first round so must have let our guard down when we were enjoying our second pint. BIG MISTAKE! The now familiar, "What time is it mate," came drawling our way in that horrible Manchester accent. Fuck, we'd been sussed! No chance of getting away with this so Steph just lamped the man without a watch. As I say, we shouldn't have been drinking and were very stupid to be in that pub but I didn't deserve what happened next. We were attacked from all angles and not just by young lads either. Grown men were hitting us with chairs, tables, ashtrays and anything they could lay their hands on. I got well and truly battered! Getting hit over the head with pub furniture is no laughing matter I can tell you. We finally managed to escape and get inside the ground where we proceeded to clean ourselves up.

The three of us were in a terrible mess: me being by far the worst. All I remember of that match was it being absolutely red hot standing in the Scoreboard End and Alan Gowling scoring the only goal of the game for them in the Stretford End. Gowling was an amateur player (wouldn't get them playing for nothing nowadays) studying for a degree. I'm not sure what he was studying but he'd have had a million letters after his name had he decided to devote a career to being the ugliest man on the planet. I kid you not; he was gruesome. He made Luke Chadwick (Mister Ed to his friends) look like George Clooney or one of those other Hollywood stars who are supposed to be dead handsome.

I was helped back to the coach whereupon I collapsed just as I was about to get on. I woke up in a strange bed, surrounded by strange walls and lots of even stranger people!

"Hello Peter."

Eh, you're a bit of all right! Why are yer wearin' a nurse's uniform?

"Where am I?"

"You're in Wythenshawe Hospital. You've had an accident."

'Ang on, I'm sore all over, achin' in places I didn't know could ache, me 'ead feels like it's goin' to burst an' me lips are the size of Mick Jagger's! I don't think I've 'ad an "accident"!

"You're concussed Peter. We're going to keep you here for a while to keep an eye on you. Your Mum has been informed and will be here shortly

Oh, that's all I fuckin' need, me Ma givin' me grief when I've got a fuckin' 'ead like an October cabbage.

"Thank you Nurse."

'Ang on. It's all startin' to come back to me now! I 'aven' 'ad an accident. I was fuckin' battered senseless by a load of manc bastards!

"I got beat up didn't I nurse?"

"Yes, I'm afraid you did Peter. Now just lie down and get some rest."

I left Wythenshawe Hospital on the Tuesday. Ma came to see me on the Monday. Said she couldn't come at the weekend as there were good acts on at Harland's on Saturday and Sunday. That was me Ma for you - never let me down! Three bastard days in that fuckin' hellhole! No fuckin' wonder I hate mancs!

I declared myself fit (although Ma wasn't too happy) to attend our first European match of the season the day after I left hospital. We beat Dundalk 10-0 to register what was, at the time, a record victory for us. We won the second leg 4-0. Dundalk's manager Liam Tuohy came out with the cracking comment of, "Well, we improved by six goals. If we play them again we should win two nil." Only the Irish…!

The next away game was at West Brom - not the scariest place to go, but there were loads of ructions outside the ground with incensed Throstles fans. I can't say I blame them though. We were heading for a 1-2 defeat when Roger equalised in, I kid you not, about the 98th minute. I don't think the referee's watch had stopped as much as he didn't have one in the first place and was keeping time with little stones in his pocket or something!

We drew our next two matches, both at home to Forest and Spurs before going to Newcastle. Now that was a proper scary place! A young lad playing only his third game for us, Phil Boersma, had a brilliant game but was eclipsed by Newcastle's equally young winger Alan Foggon. Foggon scored the only goal of the match and was tipped for a very bright future but weight problems meant he rather lost his way in the game.

Next stop was Portman Road. What a horrible journey that was. We left Stanley Road at 11:30 the night before, but Ipswich was no London! It took us the best part of twelve hours to get there. We were about to get our heads booted in by about ten Ipswich skins when Joe Magebe and a few of the other Kirkdale lads came to our rescue. The taking of their end was seen to be an easy proposition but it was far from it as the yokels we thought they were turned into a snarling pack of meatheads! Bobby Graham gave us an early lead but Ipswich fought back and looked to have the game wrapped up until Alec Lindsay, making his debut as substitute in place of Alun Evans, gave us a face-saving equaliser. The journey home was even worse than that going there and was made more difficult by the whole coach being arrested until we returned everything that had been stolen from a garage. Sure, I didn't mind a bit of robbing myself but all I wanted to do was get home. We eventually arrived home at six o'clock on Sunday morning. I wouldn't be going there again for a while! The highlight of that trip had been seeing the players doing a bit of shopping in Ipswich town centre before the match. Again, something that wouldn't happen now.

The next home game against Southampton was heading for a stultefyingly boring 1-1 draw when up stepped Sir Roger from the substitute's bench. Two late goals from Roger and an own goal from their defender Byrne gave us a flattering 4-1 win. Funniest part of that game was Tommy Lawrence saving a penalty with his bollocks! I swear to you the BBC commentator, Alan Weeks described it thus, "Lawrence has saved it with his jocks!" Must have been fuckin' painful for The Flying Pig but we were glad of his squealings!

A crowd of nearly 41,000 at the Baseball Ground the following week saw newly promoted Derby County absolutely hammer us 4-0. The taking of their end though, the Leyside, was like taking sweets from a kid. Having said that - have you ever tried taking sweets off kids? They don't half cry!

The 2-0 home win over West Ham was notable, as it was the first Match of the Day to be broadcast in colour. Quite an honour for us as

139

the first ever Match of the Day was our home match against Arsenal on the first day of the '64-'65 season. The usual scenario "down the coaches" was a bit quieter than usual. There were some big lads followed West Ham, and not all of them that young either! All as big and hard as fuck! No wonder they were called The Irons!

The match at Leeds was to be no "Battle of Elland Road" as it had been the season before. About 500 of us went into the Gelderd End while the rest opted for the safety of the Cowshed. Strangely enough, although faced with only one tenth of the number as the previous season, the Leeds boys backed off. Sure, they tried to start something but when we showed no fear they went back from whence they came. It must have been a good day - Big Rowdy scored!
We'd lost the first leg of our Second Round Fairs Cup tie in Portugal against Vitoria Setubal 0-1. We were trailing in the second leg 0-2 when Tommy Smith pulled one back from the penalty spot. In desperation Shanks threw on both permitted substitutes, Alun Evans and Sir Roger, just minutes from the end. Alun scored with two minutes remaining. Roger then scored a screamer from about thirty-five yards shortly after. The referee blew his whistle. This was the first season that away goals counted double in the event of the scores being equal over two legs, replacing the farcical "drawing of lots" as it was called: "the toss of a coin" to me and you. Nobody quite knew if this meant extra time was to be played or not. An anxious ten minutes or so ended when the stadium announcer informed us that we had indeed lost the tie. This game was to prove Sir Roger's swan song. After 489 games and 285 goals for us my hero was off to Bolton. A sad day not only for me and I'm sure Roger but for Liverpudlians everywhere. Shanks was beginning to dissemble the great mid-sixties team; others would follow shortly after.

The Old Trafford defeat had signalled not only the end of our marvellous early-season form but also the start of a very patchy run, winning only three of our next thirteen League games. The short trip to Goodison then was going to be an awesome proposition. Everton were riding high at the top of the League losing only two of their twenty-one games and had in fact won all ten of their home games. Evertonians were quick to tell us there was nothing down for us, how they were gonna stuff us, how Everton were not only the superior team but also the superior club and how it wouldn't be worth our while turning up. We did well to hold out against this team of "Supermen" for forty-five minutes but of course the Evertonians knew it was only a matter of time before the silky-skilled, school-of-science ones would triumph.

ENTER CRAZY HORSE AND SANDY!

Emlyn scored with a towering header two minutes after the restart. Right in front of us as well. This wasn't White Hart Lane - the Park End was full of 6,000 Reds with many more thousands in other parts of the ground. Emlyn went fuckin' crazy (no pun intended) and so did we! GREATER JOY THOUGH WAS TO COME.

The Saint won the ball in midfield and played the ball to Bobby Graham. Bobby played a peach of a ball to Peter Thompson out on the left wing. Thommo, for one glorious time, instead of beating 98 defenders crossed the ball high and deep into the Everton penalty area. I can still see it, being as I was, right behind the goal and just about halfway down the small terrace that was the Park End - in he came, leaping like a salmon, throwing his head at the ball, straining every sinew and every muscle in that broad neck. The ball arrowed towards the top corner. A perfect header - hard, strong, powerful, wonderful direction, back the way it was coming from. Poor old Gordon West never stood a chance of getting anywhere near it. The net bulged! There he was, kneeling behind the goal line and looking at his tumultuous effort. Six thousand Reds in the Park End were ready to acclaim their new hero. Who was he? Who was this man that would rank alongside all time great headers of a ball such as Tommy Lawton, Dixie Dean, Alex Young, Andy Lochead, John Charles, Frank Large, Frank Lord, Alan Gilzean and Tony Hateley? None other than Sandy Brown - Everton fullback. Thank you Sandy! Thank you so very much! We couldn't celebrate properly for laughing. None more so than me. I swear Sandy, lying like a beached whale in the net, floundering, was looking straight at me as my face was contorted in paroxysms of laughter! Marvellous Sandy! Thank you for making a sixteen-year-old boy very, very happy. MORE TO COME!

This couldn't be happening to our blue brethren could it? 0-2 down at home to a "shite" side? Surely their greater class would tell in the end. They were top of the League! They had won all their home games so far!

As they chased the game in sheer desperation they gave Viva Bobby Graham all the room he needed on the right flank. Bobby got the ball on the halfway line and just kept running. Westy, traumatised as he had been by Sandy's wonder effort, was unsure whether to stay on his line or come out to try to take the ball off Bobby. Bobby made his mind up for him by calmly taking the ball round the handbag-carrier (or should that be "took the piss out of him"? Yes, took the piss!) and slid it into the empty net so gloriously occupied by Sandy twenty minutes earlier. Three-nil against the blues. Heaven! Much singing and dancing ensued in the Park End. It was a bit painful afterwards though; I spent all night picking splinters out of my feet from the wooden terraces. Could life get better than this? A 3-0 win at the ground made of wood!

From Cloud Nine we were brought down to Cloud 0.9 the following week. Manchester United thumped us 4-1. Bobby Charlton ran the show scoring two of his specials, one of which won the BBC's Goal of the Season award. George Best was also in one of his great piss-taking moods. It was horrible to watch Besty crucify our defenders but you couldn't help but admire, if not enjoy, his play. The post-match "Battle of Stanley Park" was payback time for the terrible battering I'd received three months earlier. The cold, sweet dish of revenge was mine.

It was around this time it was announced that we would have an addition to the family. I thought our Pauline, normally Skinny Malink with sterry bottle legs, was getting fat! It was hardly bloody surprising though as Cookie was still sneaking out of my room every Saturday night. I'd also caught them at it on more than one occasion so news of Pauline's pregnancy came as no great shock to me. In the then time-honoured tradition it was decided, by the respective parents of course, that Pauline and Joe would get married. Pauline and Joe didn't actually get a say in this of course. The wedding was set for June when both miscreants had turned eighteen but the baby was due in April. A child born out of wedlock? Eternal damnation to you pair of heathens! You're both supposed to be good Catholics and yet here you are not only fornicating but also compounding your mortal sin by bringing a bastard child into the world! It really was still like that then. Christ, they were only eighteen! I hoped that never happened to me.

News of their impending Grandchild though was enough excuse for Mam and Dad to throw a big jars out party after Harland's on Saturday night. Not that an excuse was needed! There seemed to be a party going on every weekend either in our house or Auntie Eileen's two doors away. I swear there was a party one weekend 'cos somebody had paid the rent!

Half of the 23,000 crowd at Burnley on Boxing Day was made up of Reds. We'd got there early and had been introduced, in one of the many cafés around Turf Moor, to the delights of a plate of mashed spuds and mushy peas. Nothing else, no pie or anything, just mashed spuds and mushy peas. What was that all about? We won the match 5-1. One of our songs at the time was:

I'm a bandy-legged chicken; I'm a knock-kneed hen.
I haven't been so happy since I don't know when.
I walk with a wiggle and a woggle and a squawk.
Doin' the Liverpool Bootwalk!

That was our last match of the 1960's. The sixties were a golden era
for British football. Great players and great characters abounded.

SIXTIES FOOTY

Match of the Day, World of Soccer, all the rest.
Sixties footy was the best.

Kenneth Wolstenholme, Hugh Johns, Brian Moore.
Black and white pictures, days of yore.

Long winter freeze-ups, braziers on the pitch
All over the country from Carlisle to Norwich.

A fairy story for Ipswich Town
Came up, won the League and went back down!

Watching Georgie on the telly.
"Chopper" Harris trying to give him the welly.
"Chopper" on his bum, Besty down the wing
Crossing the ball for Dennis the King.

Colin Bell, Neil Young, Frannie Lee
Scoring from crosses by Summerbee.

Peter Lorimer, shoot on sight.
Hit a ball like dynamite.

Roy Vernon was the penalty king.
"Chico" Scott flying down Everton's wing.

Ian Callaghan, Peter Thompson
Put the balls where Sir Roger wants them.

Bobby Charlton's hair all wisped and swirled
But one of the best players in the World!

Charlie Hurley, hard and NOT fair
Made Vinnie Jones look like Lionel Blair.

Bremner, Hunter, Johnny Giles
Made the most of the Giraffe's guiles.

Tommy Smith, what a nark!
Loved kickin' lumps off "Sniffer" Clarke.

Brian Labone: on the outside all calm
But inside ferocious, although he'd kill you with charm!

What about our "Colossus" Rowdy Yeats?
As big and wide as the Shankly Gates!

These men were hard; didn't have to throw a punch
Many a winger felt Gerry's "Crunch, crunch!"

"Perpetual Motion" Alan Ball
One of the greatest of them all.

Terry Hennesey, Trevor Hockey.
Derek Dougan so great and so cocky.

Willie Morgan bobs and weaves.
Loads of goals from Jimmy Greaves.
Rodney Marsh at Third Division QPR
Lit up Wembley like a shining star.

Goalkeeping heroes thrilled the crowds
Ron Springett, Noel Dwyer, Harry Dowd.

Tony Waiters, Peter Bonetti and Gordon Banks
Made brilliant saves and wanted no thanks.

West Ham's trio knew the score
Hurst, Peters and Bobby Moore.

Sixties footy was really ace.
Great players performed with a smile on their face.

Nobby Stiles so full of mirth
Smile as wide as Dave Mackay's girth.

"Who's the one who's got the most?
Sandy Brown and beans on toast!"

"Bobby Moore OBE
Other Bugger's Energy."

At Chelsea's number nine we chanted "No good"
But he knocked us out the Cup: Peter Osgood.

"Tra la la la la la la la la, Trevor Hockey is a fairy!"
But he made Roy Keane look like Julian Clary.

But it was all in fun, only a jest
"You're a bigger tart than Gordon West."

Jimmy Armfield's bandy legs
Always kept them closed though, never any "'megs".

Johnny Haynes kept Fulham up every year
A hundred pound a week? Worth every penny, no bloody fear!

Bobby Tambling's five at Villa.
As a goalscorer he was a killer.

Besty's six against Kim Book
All our breath away he took.
Giant centre-forwards gave defences the shivers
Ray Crawford, Ray Pointer, Martin Chivers.

Andy Lochead: Burnley, Leicester and Villa
Had a forehead like a gorilla!

But they didn't have to be big; just look at Alex Young
"He's our Golden Vision" the Evertonians sung.

Alan Woodward, Cyril Podd
Alan Hodgkinson, what a God!

Jimmy Robertson and Alan Gilzean
Mike England at the back; all dark and mean.

Jim Baxter had us all in a fix
Doing all his party tricks.

And what about Northampton Town?
All the way up! And then all the way back down!

145

Frank was Lord and Frank was Large
Joe Baker's bum was as wide as a barge!

West Brom had Kaye, Clarke and Tony Brown
And Jeff Astle before he became a clown.

Jim McCalliog and David Ford
Roars from the Owls when Wednesday scored.

Forest had Grummitt and Ian Storey-Moore
Arsenal had Geordie Armstrong and Ian Ure.

A lad at Wolves scored loads of goals
But then found God: Peter Knowles.

Derby County: lots of grit and no little flair
Had Dave Mackay, Kevin Hector and John O'Hare

Tommy Lawrence was as wide as he was big
No wonder we called him the "Flying Pig".

Shrewsbury at Gay Meadow, Halifax at The Shay
I knew all of the grounds. I lived for footy by night and by day

Sixties footy, great memories I treasure
Gave me and millions of others so much pleasure.

Our Third Round FA Cup tie at Coventry on the first Saturday of
January had been postponed so a hastily arranged friendly was played
at Southport's Haig Avenue. That was a big mistake on somebody's
part! Southport didn't know what had hit it. Fancy letting 10,000 or
so Scousers loose on Southport on one day! Ian St. John scored the
only goal of the match. I'm sure that was of no concern to Southport
Retail Society, or whatever it was called, as they were left counting
the cost of somebody's kind invitation to a robbing spree.

The game at Coventry was played four days later. Coventry's West
End was taken with thousands more Reds on the open terrace at the
other end. On a freezing cold night we amused ourselves by constantly
singing the Number One of the time - Rolf Harris's, "Two Little Boys".
Quite why, I'm not sure but I think Rolf would have been pleased!
Bobby Graham scored the goal that was enough to give us a 1-1 draw.

The taking of the Boothen End at Stoke was the biggest piece of piss ever in the memory of man. It was just too easy. The Stoke boys didn't even put up a fight. The best they could offer was some mad song about a chicken. Never did work that one out! Bobby and Thommo scored our goals in an easy 2-0 win.

We won the replay against Coventry 3-0 in front of 51,000 people with goals from Ian Ross, Bobby and Thommo. We were hitting form, and seemingly at the right time. The League might have been beyond us as Everton and Leeds were way out in front but our current form suggested there was no reason why we couldn't do well in the Cup.

Then there was Forest. Fuck me, the Trent End Riot Squad to contend with! It was well known throughout football that if you got caught by the TERS you got threw in the Trent, no question! I was not looking forward to this match. Yeah, sure, I could have stayed at home and been completely safe but that would have been chickening out. Besides, I would have missed the buzz that going to an away match and placing myself in that position brought. There was no way of concentrating on the match (which was just as well really as it was shite and we lost 0-1) as we were bombarded all through the game, and this was in our part of the ground, never mind the loonies in the Trent End! First thing that hit me was a sharpened penny. I had my hand on a crush barrier when the penny thudded against the back of my hand with such force that a swelling the size of a golf ball soon appeared. A couple of minutes later and a light bulb hit me on the head. I ask you - what kind of fuckin' loony does it take to bring a twattin' light bulb into a football ground? The swelling on my head was twice that of the one on my hand. Coming out of the ground and we'd managed to avoid getting thrown into the murky waters of the Trent. We were just about to round a corner to get to where our coaches were parked when we were confronted by a load of our lads running back towards where we'd come from. One of the lads was Matty Griffiths, a half-caste lad whose face had turned nearly white.
"It's fuckin' mad down there. There's fuckin' thousands of them!"
The next thing we knew the Forest hordes were upon us. I was thrown against a shop window given a couple of digs and had my scarf robbed off me. Bastard! I'd only bought that scarf the day before. Still, there was no time to think about that now as me, Joey Mumford and Steve Greenhalgh gave it toes towards the sanctuary of a couple of coppers on the bridge over the River Trent (perhaps they'd make a film of this one day). Good enough on the coppers they escorted us safely back to our coach.

That scarf-robbing phenomenon was a strange thing. Other club's scarves were seen as trophies of war. The claret and blue of Burnley was very popular on the Kop as was the gold and black of Wolves. Manchester City's sky blue with maroon and black bands was much sought after. By far the most popular though were Leeds United's scarves. They were big, thick, chunky efforts. If you had one of their white with blue and gold bands scarves then you were much respected and admired on the Kop. When my Dad asked me where my scarf was I told him the truth.

"Well, I've always told yer not to wear colours to the match. Colours make yer a target. I never wore colours an' I never got into any trouble." Dad did have a point there. He had told me that hooliganism and fighting before, during and after matches was no new thing. He had recounted to me tales of fighting at train stations at Wolverhampton, Bolton and Huddersfield in the forties and fifties. Even of trouble at far-flung outposts such as Norwich, Gateshead and Worcester when we played them in the Cup. The funniest one he told me was of a match at Portsmouth just after the war. Most of Pompey's supporters were, unsurprisingly, sailors while most Reds were still in Army uniform. A mass brawl between the King's respective fighting forces had taken place inside the station after the match. Dad and his brother-in-law, Jimmy Boyle, were still signed up to the Navy and so looked for all the world as if they were Pompey supporters. The police in an effort to get rid of the Liverpool supporters as quickly as possible packed them all on to a train heading for London. Dad and Jimmy stood quietly by as they awaited the arrival of the train to Lime Street, which duly turned up five minutes later.

I took Dad's advice and never wore colours to the match again. That is, not until the advent of replica shirts. I loved it when Dad regaled me with tales of his match-going days, which sadly, because he wasn't in the best of health, were now all but over. He told me of a Cup match at Goodison in our first Second Division season, Everton having passed us on their way back to the First Division. We were going to get hammered - or so he was told by a bluenose brother-in-law Jimmy Greenlea. Dad had stood at the front against the wall of the Gwladys Street for two hours before the match so he could get a good spec and had been subjected to non-stop ridicule from Jimmy and co. Dad had the last laugh though as we stuffed the bluenoses 4-0 in one of the biggest Cup upsets for years. He told me of a ferocious Cup encounter at Maine Road. We never used to get many problems from United supporters he told me but those of Manchester City were entirely different. The game had ended in a draw and in those pre-floodlight days the kick off was scheduled for the following Wednesday afternoon.

Dad was threatened with the sack from Mersey Cables should he take the afternoon off to attend the replay. His response to his foreman was thus, "If yer think for one minute I'm gonna go to Manchester an' put up with all that shit then not go to the replay yer've got another fuckin' thing comin'!"

Dad did indeed go to the replay but escaped the sack somehow!

Having disposed of Wrexham quite comfortably in the Fourth Round, Leicester were our opponents in Round Five of the FA Cup. A sterling performance by Leicester's young 'keeper, Peter Shilton, did much to hold us to a 0-0 draw. The replay would be a tough proposition as Leicester were riding high in the Second Division. They had a very good winger in Len Glover and the fearsome Andy Lochead leading their attack. Shanks though was to play a tactical masterstroke. Everybody knew that Peter Thompson was nowhere near fit so it seemed strange that Shanks should play him in the number nine shirt. Sure enough Thommo didn't make the end of the first half and was replaced by Alun Evans, giving the Leicester defence something entirely new to think about. Alun came up with the goods scoring a classic opportunist goal twenty minutes into the second half. Lochead and co put us under incessant pressure for the next twenty-five minutes but our defence held firm superbly. Alun sealed the win, scoring another excellent goal with virtually the last kick of the game. The celebrations went on long and loud in our end after the match. Watford were next up and nobody could foresee a struggling Second Division club stopping our seemingly inexorable march to Wembley. We had to battle with Leicester supporters after the match who were intent on throwing us over a bridge and into a canal next to where our coaches were parked. What was it with these Midlands clubs fans and their penchant for water? The papers the following morning were full of headlines about Alun Evans, spawning a new footballing term: SUPERSUB!

We got all the way to the King's Road, Chelsea the following Saturday before hearing on the radio that the match at Stamford Bridge was off. I can't say I was disappointed either, as the Chelsea boys lining the streets looked a mean shower of bastards. Perhaps it would be best to leave this for another day! Suggestions were made as to possible matches we could go to that afternoon. Mine was a madcap one.
"Bolton are playin' at Millwall. Let's go to that an' see Sir Roger."
People looked at me like I had two heads. Then I remembered my encounter with the Millwall RHS on the morning of the Spurs match six months earlier and decided that it wasn't such a good idea after all. We eventually decided to go on a spying mission to Vicarage Road

where Watford were playing Bristol City. In a dire match, Watford beat Bristol City 2-0: we deffo wouldn't have a problem with these next week! The Watford lads didn't take too kindly to 40-odd Scousers invading their end and were waiting for us when we came out. The fact that we stood together and held our ground though soon made the Watford hoolies back off.

Barry Endean. That name will haunt me forever. He it was who scored the only goal of the match that gave Watford victory over us. I felt humiliated. How could we possibly have lost to a club at the bottom of the Second Division? Answer was because we were shite on the day and Watford deserved it. What was more important was that Shanks knew it too. The slow dissembling of the team that had been going on for some months was now accelerated. The great man had seen enough. It was time now for great servants of the club such as Rowdy, Tommy Lawrence and The Saint to be replaced by younger, brighter blood.

Shanks new policy didn't pay immediate dividends as we lost at home 0-2 to Derby County. This match saw, if not the birth, then certainly the embryonic Anny Road End, as loads of scallies, fed up of seeing us turned over by Terry Hennessy and co, decided to leave the Kop early and go down to the Anny Road to do battle with the Rams supporters. Oh dear, oh dear, oh dear - if they'd only realised the monster they were creating!

On the day Watford were playing Chelsea in the FA Cup semi-final at White Hart Lane (the semi-final WE should have been in) we were actually engaged in a match just up the road at Highbury. I didn't really want to go into the North Bank; a few lads on the coach talked me into it. Once inside there though it was clearly a wise move to get straight back out. The Arsenal lads looked in no mood for their end to be invaded, as it had been a couple of years previously. Luckily we weren't sussed and were able to ask a copper to escort us out so we could go and pay again in the Clock End. A load of Arsenal boys in the Clock end ensured that a shitty game, played on a shitty day, with a shitty 1-2 defeat for us would be thoroughly unenjoyable for us.

The BBC were running a competition called I think, "King of the Kops" or "Top Kop", something like that. The idea was that they would film a number of "Kops" throughout the country with the winners being determined by such means as noise made per ratio of people, enthusiasm, originality of songs etc. The winner was obviously going to be us wasn't it? Some of the other entrants were West Ham, Wolves,

Rotherham (yes Rotherham) and just for a laugh, Newport County (ha ha). We had been recorded prior to our match against Sheffield Wednesday and, as to be expected, gave an excellent account of ourselves. Wolves effort was to be recorded on their North Bank prior to their game against us. Brilliant! Plans were made not only to take the North Bank, so sabotaging their entry, but also to exact revenge for the cowardly attack on Alun Evans the previous summer. Things were going to plan when, having been met by a reception committee of about 50 Wolves fans throwing sterry bottles at our coaches, we gave chase. The shithouses ran away but we soon caught them, acquiring some of the prized gold and black scarves and hats in the process. Taking the North Bank was going to be easy. About 40 of us managed to get in with hundreds more queuing up outside. We might just have got away with it but some numbskull started up the chant of, "LIV-ER-POOL" and so gave our position away. The Wolves supporters piled down the North Bank towards us. As soon as I saw the glint of a knife I was away. Up and over the wall and on to the pitch with the other 40 or so Scousers I was and mighty relieved when I reached the safety of the South Bank. That had been a close call. This end-taking business was getting a bit hairy now. Time methinks to pack it in. Who won the "Kings of the Kop" competition? Yes, you've guessed it - Newport County!

The scariest game of that season was to be saved 'til the last. The rearranged match at Stamford Bridge was played a week after Chelsea drew their FA Cup Final 2-2 with Leeds. Wishing the Chelsea fans good luck for the replay three days later at Old Trafford cut no ice with then whatsoever as the 500 or so Scousers who had made the trip were battered all over the place, and this in OUR end - the end OPPOSITE the Shed! Getting out was going to be even harder than actually being in the ground. As I was virtually on my own (my mates deciding that this was not the ideal match to go to) I decided to take the snidey little shit's way out. Luckily I had my Wolves "war trophy" on so was able with careful placement to make the gold and black look like Chelsea's gold and blue scarf. Yeah, okay I was a big scaredy-cat but at least I was an in-one-piece big scaredy-cat! To that Wolves supporter wherever and whoever you are - thank you - you might well have saved my life that day. Oh, yeah and sorry! You shouldn't have thrown a sterry bottle at me though! We lost the match 1-2; I dread to think what would have happened had we won it!

So that's the story of football's first season of AGRO. I pride myself on missing only five domestic matches that season, all away and all in midweek at Watford (League Cup) and the League matches at Crystal

Palace, Coventry, Southampton and Sunderland. In spite of finishing only fifth and winning nothing I really enjoyed that season. It was a season where I grew up so much in terms of going the match. I had learned to look after myself, and by God you had to know how to do that in those days! The buzz I got from going to away matches was unbelievable! The excitement of it all more than made up for the butterflies and the sick feeling I often used to get in the pit of my stomach when faced with a mob of opposition supporters hell-bent on detaching my head from my body! As I say, this was not meant to be a celebration of hooliganism - just telling it how it was. Anybody who says it wasn't so is either deluded or a liar. Yes, all in all, a very good season.

CHAPTER FIFTEEN

NUTS AND NUPTIALS

Charlie Clarke was going to pay for our Pauline's wedding. Charlie didn't know that at the time but he definitely was! Who was Charlie Clarke? He was now Mam's regular, number one moneylender. What an honour! Cissy Mulhall had either hung up her piss-stained bloomers or taken her handbag and fucked off to the great counting house in the sky. Charlie's undoing as Ma's moneylender was not only, like Mrs. Roberts before him, that he was far too kindly to be suited to the task but also that he was as deaf as a door-post! Charlie also doubled as the local coal merchant. All in all, everything was set for Ma once again to kid the arse off Charlie. Negotiations went on in the inner sanctum of the outhouse. Strange places were outhouses of the houses in Grogan Square. The outhouse was separated from the kitchen (called the back kitchen in those days) by a dividing door (if you were really posh like Jane you would have those plassy strips or maybe even one of those wood effect sliding doors). The living room was called the kitchen (I hope you're following all this; I'll be asking questions later!). Back to the outhouse: it also housed the coal hole, the lecky cupboard and the gas cupboard. The lecky cupboard wasn't too bad; just basically a metal door covering the lecky meter and wiring. The coal hole though was horrible being as it was so dark and damp that the cockroaches infesting it were relatively tame! The worst place by far though was the gas cupboard. I dreaded it every time the gas went out, which it frequently did seeing as Ma would have a pot of tea stewing on a low light all day. It was not only, like the coal hole, dark and damp but, worse than the coal hole's infestation of cockroaches, was absolutely crawling with fleas! We were never quite sure whether our dog, Cindy, had fleas or the fleas had her! Cindy lived in the gas cupboard and very rarely ventured out. Should she dare make an appearance in the living room Dad would scream at her, "Get out Twinkletoes!" Dad also called Uncle Jimmy Greenlea Twinkletoes. I'm not at all sure what inferences, if any, to draw from that. Cindy's heat season was the signal for every horny dog in the neighbourhood, and there were plenty of them, to make a beeline for our side-door. Cindy was, in dog terms, the local bike! She did have one particular favourite though: Spike Morris. She always let Spike pump her up first and then she was fair game for every dog from Marsh Lane to Aintree Road. She must have been quite attractive in the canine world for dogs to come from that far and wide to get stuck together to her. Spike always seemed quite happy with the arrangement; after all he'd been the first, so the little puppies would all be his. During the last days of her pregnancy Cindy would be moved to the relative luxury of the tank-cupboard in the back-kitchen to give birth to her litter of little Spikes. I know this all sounds very cruel and were it to happen today would have the RSPCA quite rightly screaming blue murder, but as with so many things of those days it was just the way things were then. Anyway, back to the negotiations. I was in the back-kitchen listening to every word of the Great Wedding Scam.

"Hiya Charlie. Our Pauline's gettin' married today."

"Who, your Maureen? Your Maureen's been married for years to that John McKeown 'asn't she?"

"No, not our Maureen Charlie, our Pauline - me daughter!"

"Yeah, I'll 'ave a drink of water Lily. Roastin' out there isn't it?"

"Ee arr Charlie, 'ave a bottle of Mackies."

Charlie's hearing aid temporarily fired up once ale was mentioned!

"Don't mind if I do Lily!"

"Charlie, can yer lend's a tenner?"

"Okay Lily. 'Ave yer got another bottle of Mackies?"

"Yeah, ee arr Charlie. I tell yer what, I'll give yer a fiver back outa that tenner an' that'll pay for the two pound I borrored off yer last week plus the interest an' the coal I owe yer for."

"Whassyersay Lily?"

"Ee arr Charlie, 'ave another Mackies. 'Ere's a whisky as well."

"Ta Lily. So 'ow much d'yer wanna borrer?"

"Give me that fiver back an' we'll call it quits. I only owe yer for the coal then don't I Charlie."

"Yeah, sright Lily. Just the coal."

"Okay Charlie, well let me 'ave another tenner an' that'll be a tenner I owe yer plus the interest."

"Yeah, ee arr Lily. Gorranother whisky?"

"I tell yer what Charlie, John wants to borrer a tenner as well so I'll give 'im that okay?"

"Okay Lil! You wanna a tenner as well don't yer?"

"Yeah. Give me that an' that'll just be a fiver John owes yer won't it Charlie? Ee arr, 'ave another whisky."

"Ta Lily. Someone getting' buried yer say?"

"Yeah, that's right Charlie. Instead of John owin' yer that fiver I'll pay the coal with it next week. Okay Charlie?"

"Okay Lil. I'm goin' now. Tell John I was askin' abarr' 'im."

That was it. Ma had ripped Charlie off for thirty quid. Charlie went home very happily pissed and quite oblivious to what had gone on. I wished Mam could have ripped Pissy Cissy off like that but the old bat was far too shrewd to be getting pissed and forgetting about money.

The wedding was a simple enough ceremony; a few people at St. Elizabeth's, a nice frock for our Pauline and then back to ours for the reception in the manner of how we did things then. The do lasted for two days though!

Me and Conk were walking along Linacre Road having been to an offy and polished off a bottle of plonk. We saw a couple of girls in the distance walking along Knowsley Road.

"Eh Evo, isn't that Evelyn Hughes?"

"Don't know Conk. Can't tell from 'ere. Come on let's 'urry up an' catch them up."

As we drew closer it became apparent that we had indeed spotted the lovely Evelyn and friend.

"Fuckin' 'ell Conk, come on 'urry up for fuck sake or they'll be gone!"

Our breakneck run slowed to a casual saunter as we neared the lovely twosome.

"All right Ev. Didn't see ya there. Still workin' in Tesco's?"

"Yeah, hiya. Err...I've forgot yer name. What is it?"

Made a big impression then.

"Peter. Remember I worked in Tesco's last year."

"Oh aye yeah. This is me mate Lillian."

Conk instantly paired off with Lillian. I was absolutely made up about that as it allowed me to explore possibilities (and more) with Ev. I walked her the short distance to her house in Hinton Street. When she kissed me full on, right on the mouth and then started playing that delicious tongue all around the inside of my mouth I knew that I was indeed truly, hopelessly, totally in love with this girl. I took Ev out a few times and did all the kissy, gropey, fumbly stuff I'd never done before. We were baby-sitting for a neighbour one night when it happened. That glorious moment when Evo lost his cherry was undoubtedly the greatest moment of my near seventeen-year old life. It was better than Liverpool winning the League, Cup and European

Cup all rolled into one. Heavenly moments like these arrive not very often in a lifetime. Yes, the Earth moved, so did a lot of other things! It truly was a beautiful moment that I shall cherish forever. **THANK YOU EVELYN.**

Conk's tales of "Mad" John Hughes were greatly exaggerated as I got on very well with him as I did with Ev's Ma, Kitty. She could be a fearsome old battle-axe when she had a drink in her to be sure but most of the time she was very charming and funny.

That summer of 1970 was deffo "Evo's Summer of Love". I just couldn't wait to get home from work to see my beautiful girlfriend. The music of that summer was brilliant and most of it seemed to reflect my mood: Norman Greenbaum's, "Spirit In The Sky"; "Groovin' with Mr. Bloe", unsurprisingly by Mr. Bloe; "Lola", by The Kinks; "Wide World", by Jimmy Cliff, which was the first record I bought Ev; "All In The Game" by The Four Tops; Freda Payne's, "Band Of Gold"; The greatest summer record ever, "In The Summertime", by Mungo Jerry and last but not least that timeless classic, "Back Home" by The 1970 England World Cup Squad. I was also heavily into Tamla Motown, Atlantic and Stax records. They seemed to be churned out at the rate of a dozen per week but to me they were all brilliant and typified that marvellous, red-hot summer.

Our first two games of the season were away at Burnley and Blackpool so a big Reds presence at both matches was evident. One of our new songs, given it's first airing at Turf Moor was adapted from Bobby Bloom's "Montego Bay"; the simple enough, "Oh oh oh oh Liv-er-pool!" The taking of Burnley's Belvedere side was the usual piece of piss but newly promoted Blackpool's Kop proved slightly more troublesome. Quite what Nottingham Forest had done to upset Blackpool's supporters I'm not sure but this is where I first heard the following song which we were to copy and eventually every club's fans in the country would follow suit:

We hate Nottingham Forest. We hate Burnley too.
We hate Man United but Blackpool we love you.

Blackpool's Bloomfield Road didn't seem quite the setting for Elgar's Pomp and Circumstance March somehow. It certainly was no Albert

Hall! But then again Blackpool's mob (which seemed to consist entirely of Hell's Angels) and a few thousand of our scallies were certainly no "Last Night of the Prom Promenaders" either!

A win and a draw respectively from those two games set us up nicely for our first home game against the other promoted side, Huddersfield Town. A young, scrawny kid called John McLaughlin was making his mark in the first team and scored two cracking goals in our 4-0 win. Alun Evans scored the other two goals so things were looking good for Shankly's young side. The next three games at home to Palace and United and away at West Brom were all drawn 1-1. Alun Evans was again on the mark twice, the other goal being scored by Bobby Graham who was forging quite a useful partnership with Alun.

The scary trip to St. James' Park was next. An uneventful 0-0 draw left us totally unprepared for the scene we were to face when trying to get out of the Gallowgate End. I'm not exaggerating when I say there must have been 3,000 Geordies outside all baying for our blood. I'm sure they must have demolished a housing estate for their ammunition judging by the number of bricks that came hurtling into us. By some miracle nobody was seriously hurt. Even me, the unluckiest bastard on God's good Earth, had managed to avoid being struck. It was a long walk back to the Cattle Market where our coaches were parked though so we were going to have to be very careful. We were just approaching the Cattle Market where, as far as the eye could see, there were hundreds of Geordies waiting for us.
"What are we gonna do Evo?" Joey Mumford wasn't good in these situations. He was certainly no Steph!
"Keep yer fuckin' mouth shut for a start. That'd fuckin' 'elp!"
"Come on, let's just keep walkin'. We'll try and bluff it out." I liked Steve Greenhalgh's idea better but as far as I could see we were still fucked. The Geordies had the entrance blocked. No way round it; we were gonna get fuckin' battered!
The Geordies made our minds up for us by sussing us and charging at us. Odds weren't good - about 100-1 against us. Nothing for it but for us three to fuckin' leg it! That was 'til one of the Geordies jumped on Steve's back who then performed an amazing judo throw to launch Jimmy Geordie over his back and on to the cobbled road knocking him out cold. Fuckin' go 'ead! I couldn't believe what I'd just seen and stood transfixed at the sight of the unconscious Geordie. I was

stirred from my reverie by Steve screaming, "For fuck sake Evo! Come on fuckin' run!"
We legged it down a few jiggers but nobody seemed to be chasing us. Maybe Steve's martial arts skills had frightened the Geordie hordes off. Shithouses! When we returned to the Cattle Market twenty minutes later it was deserted save for our coaches, with a few windows missing, so we were able to board safely.

The burgeoning Evans/Graham partnership was cruelly broken when Bobby snapped an ankle in the home match against Chelsea. The substitution gave many people the first sight of the long-legged, bony, all knees and elbows Steve Heighway. Steve's gangly gait made him look anything but a footballer. Stevie had played in Gerry Byrne's testimonial match at the end of the previous season. While not exactly looking the part Steve, signed from non-League Skelmersdale United, certainly could dribble. His other main attribute, his speed, had to be seen to be believed. The Kop at first didn't know whether to laugh at Stevie or to cheer him so settled instead for chanting "Beep-Beep" every time he got up a head of steam down the wing. We also adapted Deep Purple's "Black Night" song to, "Stevie - Heighway".

Bobby had only been brought into the side initially that season because the close season signing from Sheffield Wednesday, Jack Whitham was injured. Jack was still injured so Shanks wasted little time in going out and securing the services of Cardiff's lanky centre forward, John Toshack, who was apparently mustard in the air. Tosh made an inauspicious debut in the 0-0 home draw against Coventry. Big Tosh and Beep-Beep were to make big impressions the following week though.

An integral part of Shanks' bright young team was Brian Hall who, at various times, was keeping Cally and Thommo out of the side. Brian, because of his academic qualifications was known as Little Bamber. Stevie Heighway because he was similarly qualified was Big Bamber. Bamber? After Bamber Gascoine (or Bamber Shilling as my Dad called him. Shilling - gas coin? Get it? No? Oh, never mind!) the host of University Challenge. Wake up at the back there! Back to the plot ("And about time too Evo!" I hear you say). Everton, while reaching nowhere near the form they had during their marvellous League Championship triumph of the previous season were still a force to be reckoned with. Neither I nor anybody else could quite put their finger on why such a great team, brimful of good, exciting players, could lose their way so much the following season. It was like they were one-season wonders but the players and management team were still in place so there should have been no reason why they couldn't have built on that fine title win. Anyway, this was a Derby and Derbies were always fraught, with the form book going out of the window. The first half was typical Merseyside Derby fare; fast, frenetic, two hyped-up sets of supporters and not much football being played at all. All that changed in the second half. Everton quickly established a two goal lead and looked like the League Champions they were. Everton though had been troubled by Stevie's pace all game and Big Bamber it was who turned the game. A piece of "trickery" (actually Steve was never quite sure what he was going to do next so how could anybody else) on the left touchline and Steve was left with an acute angle to squeeze the ball in at the near post. Right, twenty minutes to go: "Come on you Reds!" Seven minutes later and Stevie once again skipped past John Hurst for what seemed the 200th time in the match. Stevie crossed the ball deep to the far post where Tosh climbed as high as a house to bullet home his first goal for the Reds.

Stevie Heighway's always runnin'
John Toshack is always scorin'
Then you'll hear the Kopites roarin'
Toshack is our King!

Men of Anfield here's our story
We have gone from great to glory
Then you'll hear the Kopites roarin'
Toshack is our King!

The Kop were screaming for the winner! Such was the noise level that when Joe Royle came down to defend a corner he had to put his fingers in his ears. This might also have had something to do with the fact that having missed a sitter earlier on we were baiting him with this tuneful little ditty:

He shot. He missed.
He must be fuckin' pissed.
Joey Royle. Joey Royle!

Everton could have still won the game were it not for a stupendous save by Ray Clemence from Henry Newton.
Six minutes left. A free-kick came in from the left. Tosh headed it on. The Silent Knight was lurking at the far post. Goal! 3-2! Yes!!!!!!!! We'd done it! A remarkable comeback was complete. There was a brilliant picture in the following Monday's Daily Express of a lad I knew from school, "Ned" Cahill, standing on a crush barrier in the middle of the Kop after that third goal.

This photo just seemed to epitomise what the atmosphere was like in the Kop that day. "Ned" was playing for England Schoolboys at the time and looked to have a big future in the game but said in an interview with the Express that this was the greatest moment of his life. That was how much it meant, not only to "Ned" but also to everybody in the Kop that day who had screamed us to a famous victory. I spoke to "Ned" a couple of years later after he had played for Coventry City in a 2-0 win for them at Anfield in the FA Youth Cup. Not even that, he told me, matched the excitement of that comeback victory over Everton. I always wanted "Ned" to make it big in the game because of that. It never quite happened for him though, although his cousin, Paul, who had also played in that victory at Anfield fared better making over 100 appearances for Portsmouth before a handful of games for Aldershot, Tranmere and Stockport.

January 2nd 1971 was to prove a momentous day. We beat Aldershot 1-0 at home in the Third Round of the FA Cup. John McLaughlin scored the goal but I can't tell you much more about the game, as I didn't see most of it being as it was played in thick fog! The big Cup upset of the day was Blackpool's 4-0 win over West Ham. The big news story surrounding the game was of West Ham dropping and sending home four of their players including England captain, Bobby "Golden Bollocks" Moore after a late night drinking spree.

News was also coming through on the TV of a terrible tragedy at Ibrox Park after the Old Firm match between Rangers and Celtic. 66 people had lost their lives after being crushed on exit steps at the back of the terrace. The black-and-white still photographs of people lying dead at a football ground were truly horrific. The steps were virtually an exact replica of those at the back of the Kop. I wondered then why there had never been a similar disaster at Anfield as it was truly frightening going down those steps after a match. I thanked God that there hadn't been and prayed to the same God that there never would be.

We were baby-sitting that night for Eddie and June Physick who lived opposite Ev. Eddie was a Red too and had been the match but most of the talk before he and June left for their night out was of the Ibrox disaster. Having established that baby Helen was fast asleep in her cot and given a respectable half-hour just in case Eddie and June came back me and Ev then settled down to out favourite past-time - shagging! We honestly never stopped. We were at it at every possible opportunity. You know when it's happened don't you? You just know! We certainly knew. Not only did I fail to get off at Edge Hill; I went right on through Lime Street, careered on and ended up in fuckin' Southport somewhere! Oh fuckin' deep shit! Fuckin' 'ell no!

It came as no great bombshell when Ev announced a few weeks later that she had missed her period and was off to the doctor's for a Gravindex pregnancy test (no home pregnancy testing kits in those days)!

Confirmation of the forthcoming little Evo was inevitable. My Mam and Dad would fuckin' murder me! How the fuck was I gonna tell them? Cookie had the answer.

By this time I was on my sixth job, working in Edwin Butterworth's Waste Paper Company in Lightbody Street off Vauxhall Road. Every Friday after work a gang of us would go drinking in the pubs on Scotty Road. Cookie had always told me about this lethal Cornbrook Bitter that was sold in the Honky Tonk. Apparently you got beaten up if you were to even *ask* for a brown-bitter as that was seen as watering down the potent brew. Cookie's idea was for me to get fuckin' lashed on the Cornbrook, which would give me the courage to break the news to Mam and Dad.

Fuck me, it only worked! Four pints of the loony juice and I was offering out the 57a that Cookie had poured me on to in order to get me home. I was spewing my ring up in the back garden.
"Peter, what's the matter?"
"Oh Mam, I'm dead sick with worry."
"Why, what're yer worried about son?"

"Evelyn's pregnant."

There, I said it, no problem! Hurrah for Cornbrook Loony Juice!

"Well yer'd better get inside, clean yerself up and tell yer Dad."

"But Mam, 'e'll kill me."

"'E won't. 'E'll be all right."

I had to be honest he was a lot more Johnny Jekyll than Johnny Hyde these days.

"Peter, tell yer Dad what yer just told me."

"Evelyn's pregnant."

"Well yer've made yer bed - yer'll just 'ave to lie in it."

Classic parent's saying from me Dad! Piece of piss that! Have to try some more of that Cornbrook gear - good stuff that!

Going to Leeds was a hairy deal at the best of times but with a big, fat, pounding head it was no fuckin' joke at all. Luckily, for once, we didn't get much agro from them. Tosh scored in the second minute and that was virtually that. A 1-0 win and no agro: perhaps *they'd* all been on the Cornbrook bitter. I bet they hadn't all got their birds up the duff though!

In the grand manner of these things it was decided that at 17 years of age - still a boy - I would do the decent thing and marry my pregnant girlfriend. Not that I'm saying we wouldn't have got married eventually; after all we were very much in love with each other. It was just that I felt I was being cheated of my youth and that I had no say in whether or not I got married - it had been decided for me.

It was decided also that my Mam and Dad should meet Ev's Ma and we would all sit round to discuss the forthcoming nuptials. Seeing as neither family had two halfpennies to rub together I didn't see there would be that much to discuss! We'd go to see Father Taylor at St. Elizabeth's. The Reverend Taylor would have no problem in agreeing to marry us. The Catholic Church was funny like that - told you not to fornicate but then couldn't wait to make sure you got hitched, even if you were pregnant, to make sure you'd bring many more good Catholics into the world. Charlie Clarke would be stung, this time by my Dad, in the Great Wedding Scam II. Ev would have a new frock. I'd have a new suit. We'd use Joey McKeown's nice Zephyr for a wedding car. Everybody else could do the short walk to the church. A few people would have cameras and let us have the photos. We'd come back to

Ev's for a drink and something to eat, then go to ours for the same. All down to Harland's later on. Then finish the day off with jars out back at ours! Simple! What was there to discuss? No problem the respective parents meeting - I was all in favour of that - it was just that I didn't see the need for me to be there.

"Tell yer Mam an' Dad to come an' meet me Mum next Wednesday. We'll 'ave a drink."

"Well tell me what it was like 'cos I won't be there."

"What d'yer mean yer won't be there? Yer've gorra be there!"

"No I 'aven't and I won't!"

"Why not?"

"I'm goin' the match."

"This is more important than the match."

"Ev, let's get this right, *nothin's* more important than the match. I've always gone the match an' I always *will* go the match. Let's get this straight before we get married - nothin's ever gonna stop me!"

"Nothin'?"

"Only when they put me in a wooden overcoat an' bury me six foot under!"

"Who are they playin' anyway?"

"Bayern Munich."

"Who are Bayern Munich?"

"Who are Bayern Munich? Who are Bayern Munich? Only one of West Germany's best teams that's all! In fact, one of the best teams in Europe."

"Well why are Liverpool playin' them?"

"'Cos it's the quarter-final of the Inter Cities Fairs Cup."

That was a mistake. I might as well have been telling Ev that we were playing Spacedust City from Venus in the Inter-Planetary Cup. To be honest though we could have been playing Hartlepool United in the League Cup at Anfield and I would still have gone. I wasn't going to miss a home match for anything, no matter who it was against - even Spacedust City!

"Come on Peter, you've gorra come."

"Make it Tuesday or Thursday and I'll come but not Wednesday."

"Can't. It's got to be Wednesday - it's been decided."

"Oh well, pardon me for 'avin' no say in that decision. I'm not goin' an' that's final. I'm goin' the match - end of!"

I got the same shit from my Ma and her Ma - Dad was a bit more understanding, but I was determined - I was going the match!

Having disposed of three good sides in the earlier rounds; Ferencvaros, Dinamo Bucharest and Hibernian I was quite confident of our chances against Bayern. Yes, they had a reputation as a very good, up and coming side with class players such as Gerd "Der Bomber" Muller, who had destroyed England and finished as leading score at the previous summer's World Cup in Mexico, and Franz "Kaiser" Beckenbauer but we were also a very good young side. Alun Evans, after his superb early season goal-scoring form had been injured for nearly five months and was making his comeback in this match. Alun eclipsed even Muller, scoring all the goals in our 3-0 win; his third goal, an acrobatic volley, being reminiscent of "Der Bomber's" winning goal for West Germany against England in that World Cup match.

I was soon brought down from my euphoric state by my Mam when I got home.
"You and Ev are gettin' married on May 8TH."
"No we're not!"
"What d'yer mean, no yer not? Why not?"
"'Cos it's Cup Final day an' I'm not gettin' married on Cup Final day."
"Well, it's been decided. You an' Evelyn are gonna see Father Taylor next Wednesday."
"Oh, an' who decided that Ma? Don't I get a say in it?"
This was doin' my fuckin' 'ead in. Here I was, an adult in all but name, soon to be a father and still getting treated like fuckin' shit by adults!
"Well that seemed like the best date. Yer can't leave it much longer than that. Evelyn'll be four months pregnant by then."
"Don't yer think I know that Mam. It was me who got 'er pregnant after all! Remember?"
"Well you should've been there tonight shouldn't yer?"
No fuckin' way!
"A fortnight after that'd be good Mam."
My thinking was all the footy would be over then. The Home Internationals would have been finished so there would be nothing in the way.
"Who are Liverpool playin' in the Cup Final?"
"We might not be playin' anybody Mam. We've got the quarter-final replay against Spurs next week. We might be in the Cup Final - then again, we might not"

"Well there's nothin' stoppin' yer then is there?"

"Mam, it doesn't matter who's playin' **I - AM - NOT - GETTING - MARRIED - ON - CUP - FINAL - DAY!**"

I would have told Mam that Scunthorpe United could have been playing Accrington Stanley in the Cup Final and I would still have watched it but the irony would have been lost on her I'm sure!

"Oh, you sort it out with Evelyn then!"

Hooray! The fuckin' penny's dropped!

"Okay Mam, I'm goin' to bed now. Goodnight."

My head was banging far more than it had been when I'd been drinking Cornbrook. It hurts when you bang your head against a brick wall!

I got my own way in the end - by a bit of a fluke as it happened. St. Elizabeth's was fully booked up for weddings until May 22ND! Thank you God: you saved me from eternal grief! I fuckin' hated this Catholic Church! It always did things arseways bastard round! One day it might all make sense, but I doubted it.

We beat Tottenham in the replay at White Hart Lane to advance to the FA Cup semi-final. We would play our lovely blue neighbours at our other pal's ground - Old Trafford.

We were given the Stretford End for the game. While not as high as the Kop it did sort of sweep round a bit more and had funny triangular bits up the sides. For some reason these bits were called "Paddocks". Paddocks as I knew them were, like ours at Anfield on the side of the ground. For all that the Stretford End was impressive. Like the Kop it generated massive noise because of the roof.

Alan Ball gave Everton an early lead, which they just about deservedly held on to 'til half time. We were looking tired after our exertions in Munich three days earlier, having drawn 1-1 to give us a 4-1 aggregate victory. The spirit of that young side though was showing through as we battled back. Alun Evans, now firmly restored to the side, equalised on the hour mark. The roar nearly took the roof of our temporary "Kop". There were over 62,000 inside Old Trafford, split, as you can imagine, fairly evenly between Blue and Red producing a crackling atmosphere. Alun it was who set up the winning goal. He crossed the ball from the left. Who should be stood in the middle of the Everton penalty-area - John Toshack? No - the diminutive (in size but not stature) Brian Hall. Howard Kendall was in close attendance but Little Bamber managed to get his foot almost as high as his head to hook the ball home.

He shot, he scored
And all the Kopites roared
Brian Hall! Brian Hall!

At the end of the game the Stretford Kop (there's one for you!) reverberated as about 20,000 bandy-legged chickens and knock-kneed hens sang:

Oh, I've got joy, joy, joy, joy down in my heart, down in my heart, down in my heart.
Oh, I've got joy, joy, joy, joy down in my heart, down in my heart today!

I had greater joy in my heart when I got home.
"Peter, yer Dad's in the Corry. 'E said to follow 'im over."
"What?"
"Yeah, go and 'ave a drink with 'im."
I couldn't believe this! My Dad wanted me to have a bevy with him! I didn't need any second asking. My arse was on fire as I legged it up the jigger towards the Corry. I'd actually dreamt this scenario many times.
Dad was standing at the bar, bottle of Manns Brown in one hand and a glass of rum by the other.
"Hiya son. Great win today eh? We'll 'ave to see if we can get yer a ticket for the Final. What are yer 'avin'?"
"Brown mixed please Dad."
I wanted to throw my arms around the little fat fella and tell him this was what I'd wanted for ages, but he was me Dad. I couldn't be doing stuff like that to me Dad could I? We had four or five pints together and a couple of rums before Dad left to meet Mam in Harland's and I toddled off quite drunk but very happy to Ev's. By the time me and Ev fell out of the Saltbox at half-ten we were both absolutely bladdered and singing, "I'm gettin' married in the mornin'!" I was actually beginning to warm to the idea. There was much bandy-legged chickening and knock-kneed henning along Linacre Road that night!

Billy Bremner broke my heart on April 14th. As I've said earlier Bremner was a great player, narky little bastard but still one of the game's greats nonetheless. I swear it was me he was laughing at as he lay prone in the Kop goal-mouth after scoring with a superb diving header to give Leeds a 1-0 victory in the first leg of the Fairs Cup semi-final. I would definitely have strangled the little twat if I could have got hold of him that night. What fuckin' right did the freckly-faced fucker have to laugh at me? Maybe the Great God of Football was getting me back for laughing at poor old Sandy. Whatever it was, that photo of Bremner remains one of the all-time great football photographs.

We drew the return at Leeds 0-0. They went on to win the trophy and good luck to them as they deserved it.

"Evo, can yer gerrus a start in your place?"
Christ almighty, what's the world coming to when Conk, confirmed Doleite, wants a job?
"Are yer jokin' Conk?"
"No. Me Ma said I've gorra gerra job or she's lashin' me out."
"Not before time either yer lazy twat!"
"Fuck off Evo. I wouldn't be fuckin' bothered but she said if I go - the pigeons go. There'd be no fucker to look after them so I'll 'ave to get a job! Anyway when are yer gettin' married soft arse?"
"About six weeks time. Lasted longer than your week with Lillian didn't it?"
"'Ad to fuck 'er off Evo. She was interferin' with me pigeons."
"What, Lillian was sexually abusin' yer pigeons? No wonder yer fucked 'er off!"
"Don't be fuckin' stupid! Yer know what I mean! I wasn't looking after me pigeons properly when I was with 'er. They 'ave to be fed an' watered at all the right times yer know. The shed 'as to be cleaned out regular and everythin'. Yer can't just keep them an' leave them. I don't know what I'm gonna do when I gerra job."
"Okay, I'll ask Jimmy Taggart for yer."
Jimmy Taggart was the foreman in Butterworth's and a right bastard he was too:

The working class can kiss my arse!
I've got Jimmy Taggart's job at last!

I did a lot of creeping round Jimmy T and got Conk a start for the following Monday.

"Fuck me Conk! 'Ow long d'yer think yer 'ere for? Got plans to work overtime 'ave yer?"
Conk had arrived with a bag of sarnies that could have fed the Third World for a month - or me for a day!
"Yeah, me Ma said I'll need them. Roast beef, cheese, ham an' salmon."
Well that just about put the pilchard sarnies Ma was still making for me to shame!
"Right, first break's at ten o'clock. Come on, there's the buzzer."
From the moment Conk stepped on to the wagon unloading it with me I knew, just knew, he wasn't cut out for work. Think it had something to do with the fact the lazy twat only took his hands out of his pockets to have a ciggy! An hour passed during which time he hadn't so much as lifted a scrap of paper, had smoked five ciggies and asked what time break was 437 times.
"I'm just goin' for a piss Evo."
I knew. I just knew!

Five minutes passed. Then ten. After fifteen minutes JT arrived.
"Where's yer fuckin' mate?"
"'E went for a piss five minutes ago Jimmy," I lied.
"Like fuck! I've seen yer on 'ere on yer own for at least a quarter-of-an-hour. Now go an' fuckin' find 'im! If yer not back 'ere with 'im in five minutes the fuckin' pair of yer bone idle twats are sacked!"
"Oh, I was gonna ask yer for a rise as well Jimmy."
"A fuckin' rise? I was thinkin' more of fuckin' sackin' yer!"
"Ah, go on Jimmy. I'm gettin' married soon an' we've got a baby on the way; I'll need the money. I'll be going on full money when I'm eighteen anyway so just put me money up now."
"Get to fuck. Now go and find fuckin' dead legs!"
It was pointless searching for Conk. The lazy prick would be at home now warming his bollocks in front of his Ma's coal fire while I was sweating mine off getting grief, and probably the sack, from Jimmy Taggart because of him! I went the bog and read the Daily Mirror for five minutes while I was supposed to be on the Great Conk Hunt.
"Can't find 'im Jimmy. I've looked everywhere. 'E must've fucked off."

"Right, well get back on that fuckin' wagon and get it unloaded before break or yer *definitely* fuckin' sacked!"

Fuckin' 'ell! **HALF AN HOUR TO UNLOAD THIS FUCKIN' LOT!** In normal circumstances it would have taken two men an hour to unload the rest of the wagon but I didn't want the sack so I gave it all I had and got it finished just in time. I fuckin' hated Conk - the twat! His butties were fuckin' lovely though!

"What the fuck 'appened to you Conk?"

"Ah, I fucked off Evo. I couldn't 'andle it. It was 'ard fuckin' work."

"'Ard work? Yer didn't lift a fuckin' finger yer lazy prick!"

"I know. I meant 'ard work just bein' there."

"Yer lazy fucker. So that's it is it? One hour's fuckin' work in yer life an' yer've 'ad enough? What about yer Ma anyway? Thought she was gonna binbag yer?"

"I threw a load of pepper over meself when I got 'ome an' scratched meself to fuck. Told 'er I was allergic to the paper an' came out in a rash so they sent me 'ome."

"An' she believed yer?"

"Yeah, she's fuckin' thick isn't she? Anyway, who walloped me sarnies?"

"Who the fuck d'yer think? Me, of course! Tell yer Ma thanks!"

I got my rise. I even had a bevy once with Jimmy Taggart in the A1 at Lloyd's. He wasn't such a bad old stick after all!

There was never much chance of me going to the Final. Each club's allocation was still a miserly 16,000. Even Season Ticket Holders were missing out and seeing as I didn't have one I was basically fucked! My Dad and Uncles put the feelers out for me but I'd resigned myself to watching it at home on our black-and-white telly hoping for a repeat of the victorious scenes at 21 Grogan Square six years earlier.

Dad fell asleep during normal time. There wasn't much happening in the match and he'd had a skinful in the Corry so sleep seemed the best option for him. The team of Clemence, Lawler, Lindsay, Smith, Lloyd, Hughes, Callaghan, Evans, Heighway, Toshack and Hall virtually picked itself except for a slight injury and form doubt about Alun Evans. Those fears proved founded as Alun hardly got a kick of the ball and was rightly substituted for Peter Thompson. This proved an astute substitution as Thommo, looking very sharp, played the ball out to

Stevie Heighway. Stevie cut in and drilled his shot into the net through the gap left by Bob Wilson at his near post. Dad had woken up by this time and was jumping all over my back as I was hugging Ma. Little Price, like Collette six years before him, was left aghast at the behaviour of these loonies! Our celebrations lasted but minutes as a combination of Eddie Kelly and George Graham netted Arsenal's equaliser. Nobody has ever been quite sure who got the last touch on that goal but I think George Graham has since claimed it as his own (not like him that is it?). The superior fitness of the Arsenal players was beginning to tell as our youngsters wilted in the intense heat. It should have been the other way around as Arsenal too had just finished a gruelling programme. They had clinched the League by defeating arch-rivals Spurs 1-0 at White Hart Lane the week before and now looked on course to complete the second part of the double so emulating Tottenham's efforts of ten years earlier. Sure enough the goal arrived. Charlie George's shot thundered past Clemence and in one of the most sickening moments of my life George lay supine on the Wembley turf, his long, stupid, straight hair flapping all over the place as he waited for the rest of his team-mates to jump on him. I really did feel like puking up. It was the saddest, most disappointing day of my seven-year career following Liverpool Football Club. Of course Ma summed it all up perfectly didn't she?

"I bet yer glad yer didn't get a ticket now aren't yer? Wouldn't 'ave been worth goin' would it? Yer could've got married today couldn't yer? It wouldn't 'ave mattered now would it?"

In that order Ma: No. Yes. No. Yes. Now fuck off you stupid woman!

"Yeah, suppose so Mam," I managed to lie through blubbering, quivering lips. My red, swollen eyes and the salty wetness on my cheeks told the truth of it. It wasn't Ma's fault though. She was a woman. We all know women say the most fuckin' ridiculous things at the most fuckin' ridiculous times!

It was tough on our players. They'd given everything, not just in the Final, but in every match that season. Arsenal had proven the better team on the day and were quite rightly acclaimed as the best team in the country. They deserved their double; just a pity it had to be at our expense. It was no mean feat for our young, transitional side to finish fifth in the League, reach the final of the FA Cup and the semi-final of the Fairs Cup. We had a problem in that we didn't score enough goals, only 42 in the League, but the defence, conceding only 24 League goals, was sound enough so just a little fine tuning should see success at Anfield in the not too distant future.

I really suffered that night as we listened to Radio Luxembourg in Ev's. That fuckin', bastard, stupid, "Good Old Arsenal" song, written by soft twattin' arse, Jimmy "Fuckin' Wanker" Hill, was played about 958 times. If the tranny hadn't have belonged to John Hughes I would have threw it as far as bloody Luxembourg! Of course if I had have done, it belonging to "Mad John", I would have ended up in Luxembourg with the tranny stuck up my arse (ooh err missus!).

My stag night started off in the Jester on Scotty where we watched Chelsea playing Real Madrid in a replayed European Cup-Winners-Cup Final. We then moved on to the Seven Stars before going into town. Yatesy's, The American Bar and the She Club were all visited by the four dudes: me, Cookie, Tony Lomax (Ev's sister's husband) and "Mad John" later meeting up with Alec Dolan and Jimmy Maloney before catching the last 57a to Bootle. Not much of a stag night? Maybe not, but that's how it was then. Not in those times stag weekends in Amsterdam, London or Dublin. It was a few bevvies in town and home in time for the chippy. By the way this all took place the night before the wedding too not three months before as is the case now!

The nuptials, such as they were, went quite well. Ev did look funny, and bloody lovely too I might add, walking down the aisle with her little pot-belly being given away by her brother-in-law Tony who was about four feet taller than her! There was only one small snag: I'd miscalculated the dates of the Home Internationals so England were kicking off against Scotland at Wembley just as Ev was walking down the aisle. I had thought about asking the FA to delay the kick off to avoid clashing with this year's Evo wedding but I didn't think Sir Alf would have been too happy about that. Neither, I'm sure, would 70,000 or so Jocks; I didn't want them on my case! Anyway, I got to watch the second half and England won 3-1! Everything else went just the way I said it would and we all lived happily ever after...or did we?

CHAPTER SIXTEEN

JUNIOR EVO

Fine tuning, and more goals, arrived in the shape of Kevin Keegan. Signed on Cup Final eve for £35,000 from Scunthorpe, and instantly dubbed Mighty Mouse, Kevin was an immediate sensation. He was a little coiled spring of explosive energy. He scored three goals in his first five games and was linking up very well with Tosh. One of those games was the now annual Scarefest at St. James'. It was Malcolm MacDonald's home debut and Tyneside was "Supermac" nuts. Emlyn Hughes gave us an early lead but two goals before half-time by the Geordie hero soon wiped that out. When the bandy-legged one completed his hat-trick in the second half the place went crazy! Kevin pulled one back but It was Supermac's day. There were some very happy Geordies around as was evidenced by the fact I arrived back at our coach with my thundercrackers unsoiled! Not a hint of trouble. Nice one! We'd got away with that!

September produced one win, one draw and three defeats. The 0-1 defeat at Leeds in that month was their first home game of the season as they had to play their first four scheduled home games away from Elland Road after crowd trouble the season before. The Leeds lads let us know they were back too. Me and Joey Mumford had hitched it to Leeds and arrived early being dropped off near the train station. Bad Leeds lads were everywhere. I was scared but Joey was touching cloth 'til we reached the apparent safety of the ground. We joined up with a few other Reds 'til we were sussed by about ten of their lads. Not much point in legging it on this one so we just got stuck in when they charged us. We didn't come out of it too badly and for once my nose was intact!

Little Evo was due on October 2nd - a Saturday, but not too bad as we were away at Stoke. I sacrificed that so I could be with my darling when she produced my offspring. We waited, and waited, and waited some more. By the following Friday morning I was bricking it as we were at home to Chelsea the following day and it looked like I was going to miss it. Relief came in these little words; "My water's broke."

An ambulance was summoned and we awaited the birth of our child in Fazackerley Hospital. At 3:30 I was ushered out of the delivery ward by a battle-axe of a midwife. No staying to watch the birth of your child for fathers in those days! We were seen as having done our bit and looked upon as an annoyance at childbirth. It was nothing to do with us of course was it? Twenty minutes later a tiny but sharp cry indicated that Little Evo was in the world. I'll never forget Ev's words as I walked in to the room, "What've I 'ad?"
I looked down and saw a little Evo donga.

"A boy," I croaked, struggling to hold back tears. I couldn't have been seen to be crying at the mere birth of my beautiful little son. "'Ow d'yer know?" Ev was crying enough for two of us.
"Err…'cos there's a little willy there Ev," which was a bit of a lie as it was actually quite a big one. Didn't know who the little fella took after; certainly not me! We'd already chosen names: if we had a girl she would have been called Evelyn, after her Mum obviously. I didn't want a boy named after me. Our little boy was to be called after my football and music heroes: Messrs Heighway and Wonder - **STEVIE**! Of course we had to officially christen him Steven but to us he was our little Stevie.

Little Stevie, so sweet and small
You're the loveliest little baby of them all.
Your mop of blonde hair and cute little curls
When you grow up you'll break the hearts of all the girls.

You look so beautiful in your Mum's arms
Lying there asleep and so calm.
Resting awhile after you've been fed
As your Mum lay down her weary head.

You both look so lovely fast asleep
My love for you both goes very deep.
As deep as an ocean and as beautiful too
My love is so powerful for both of you.

The proud father took his place in the Kop the following day for the visit of our Cockney friends. The Kop were being recorded in this match and the following match against Bayern Munich (again) in the first leg of the second round European Cup Winners Cup tie. The Kop were in top form for both matches even though they were both goalless.

Scousers rule and don't you forget it Chelsea!

The Dambusters March, picked up from Elland Road where for some unknown reason it had been played prior to our match against them, was belted out against the West Germans. I'm sure Eric Coates never envisaged the tune he wrote being sung by 20,000 + Scousers in the Spion Kop! Bayern had obviously learned their lesson from the previous season and put eleven men behind the ball at every opportunity to the point that they played Gerd Muller, Europe's and possibly the world's best striker, as sweeper. They won the second leg convincingly 3-1 to end our European hopes for that season.
We went into the Goodison derby on a run of form having won three and drawn the other four of our previous seven League games. Everton's young debutant, David Johnson, gave them a 1-0 win.

Our return to form the following week coincided with what I'm sure was the wettest day ever in the memory of wetness. We stood on that lovely open end at Highfield Road and it rained, and rained, rained again and then rained some more. How the referee didn't abandon the game I'll never know but we were glad he didn't as Jack "The Flipper" Whitham scored both late goals in our 2-0 win.

Jack Whitham had the greatest moment of his injury blighted Liverpool career a fortnight later when he scored a superb hat-trick in a great game against Derby County at Anfield, which we won 3-2.

The three games just after Christmas were catastrophic for us as we lost all three: 0-1 at West Brom, 0-2 at home to Leeds and 0-1 at Leicester. After that game I was hoping that a Leicester fan *would* throw me in that canal!

That run certainly looked as if it had put paid to our League chances so time to concentrate on the Cup! Me, John Dever, Corky, Mick and a few others were getting the special from Lime Street to Oxford. We arrived at Platform 9 (where the specials, no matter where they were going to, always left) in plenty of time and a good job too! Just twenty minutes before the train was due to leave I realised I'd left my match ticket at home. All ticket games were still something of a rarity in those days so if I didn't get home pronto and get it I was fucked. I literally dived in a fast black, told the driver not to spare the horses and he would be bringing me back. Good on him, he made Jackie Stewart look like Reginald Molehusband! Ticket in pocket and dived (yes, dived again) back into the cab. I made Platform 9 with but seconds to spare but at least I made it. That was it though - every penny of my spare money for ale, food, a programme and the bus home had been given to Jackie Stewart. This is where your mates come in and John Dever was certainly one of them. John paid for everything, good lad that he was. Only problem with John was that he absolutely shit himself going to any away match, even the "safe" ones like Stoke and Burnley. I really don't know why he bothered going! He made Joey Mumford look confident! You can guess then how he was when for some unaccountable reason we had tickets for Oxford's London Road End. Most of the Reds were on the open terrace at the Beech Road end but Oxford United in their wisdom had given us 100 or so tickets for the home end. We spent most of the match fighting off the Oxford hooligs, and believe me, for a small club, there were plenty of them! That was until Kevin Keegan scored his second goal of the match 10 minutes from time to virtually seal the match. That was the signal for a mass pitch invasion from the Beech Road based Reds who legged it across the pitch to where we were about to engage in battle for the 200th time that day. Seeing the Scouse hordes charging towards them the dead 'ard Oxford hooligs did what all big shithouses do - fucked off! Not before they got sent on their way though with a few vengeful cracks from us, fed up as we were with putting up with their shite all game. By the time Alec Lindsay definitely wrapped things up with our third goal three minutes later there wasn't a blue and yellow scarf to be seen in that end - well not on an Oxford fan anyway!

The turning point in our league season came the following week when we achieved a Bayern Munichesque goalless draw at Wolves. That game saw another link with the great Sixties side broken when Peter Thompson made his last appearance for us, later taking his silky skills to Bolton. Rowdy had also departed and was doing reasonably well as player-manager at Tranmere. The Flying Pig had also flown to Tranmere but I don't think Prenton Park ever saw him save a penalty with his plums as we had!

A 0-0 draw at home to Leeds the following week meant that we would replay at Elland Road the following Wednesday afternoon. The early kick-off was due to a floodlight ban imposed during the national miner's strike. No problem getting time off work as I didn't have any work being as me and Edwin Butterworth Waste Paper Company had parted on less than amicable terms a few weeks previously. Wasn't too bad as I was actually getting more money on the dole than I was taking home from the rat-infested paper warehouse. Fuckin' 'ell, if I thought me Ma could nag me about being out of work she had nothing on Ev! Anyway, back to the plot. Having had blue murder with the Leeds fans at Anfield we were guaranteed to get it back in spades on their home patch. The Leeds lads didn't let us down. A massive pitched battle in the road outside the Cowshed End lasted for what seemed twenty minutes or so until the bizzies turned up. Me and Joey used this as our diversionary tactic to bunk in by climbing on top of a conveniently placed TV van and dropping down into the bogs in the Cowshed. Nice one! Leeds won 2-0 so that was our season over in February...or so we thought.

Jack Whitham scored the seventh and last goal of his Liverpool career a week later in a 1-0 win at Huddersfield. Huddersfield too had a Cowshed End, which we were in and about to take until the bizzies got wind of it and herded (no pun intended) us round to the terrace at the side of the ground. I was quite glad they did when I saw the kip of their loonies after the game.

Whoever thought it might be a good idea to have Liverpool, Everton, Manchester City and Tottenham fans all in the same city on the same day must have been cracked! We comfortably beat City 3-0 while across the park Spurs were burying Everton's season by knocking them out of the FA Cup. The scenes in Stanley Park after the games and in town afterwards had to be seen to be believed. Suffice to say it was not a pretty sight.

Well this was good wasn't it? We were getting up a good head of steam with four successive League wins as we faced another Merseyside Derby. I don't know what Everton's full-back, and a good one at that, Tommy Wright had done to upset the big man in the sky but a week after scoring a first minute own-goal at Maine Road the soft twat went and did it again! This was all right wasn't it - getting Everton to score our goals. Fuck me, if it didn't happen again. The dick'ead this time was their other full back, John McLoughlin, who planted a brilliant header off his shiny pate high into the Kop net.

Wasn't as good as Sandy's mind but it was a cracker. Well anything their fullbacks could do so could ours! The Silent Knight though scored his at the right end. 3-0 up and cruising against the Blues: time to take the piss!

So bye bye Mr. Catterick bye bye
You're goin' to the Second Division bye bye
Them good old Kopites drinkin' whisky and rye
Sayin' this'll be the day that you die,
This'll be the day that you die!

Emlyn, who loved scoring against the Toffees more than anybody else crashed home a fourth before running that far round the ground someone had to give him the bus fare to get back!

Easter Monday arrived with us incredibly having dropped only one point in our last ten League matches. Old Trafford's Scoreboard End had been revamped and now housed a posh new stand above a smart new terrace. That terrace was chocker block with Reds as we demolished United 3-0 with goals from Lawler, Tosh and Hughes. There wasn't even any trouble from the normally nasty mancs. That didn't stop Joey from "turtle's heading" it again though. I think he felt just about safe when we got to the Rocket!

Keegan, Toshack and Smith goals in a 3-1 win at home to Coventry kept the amazing run going.

Anfield's biggest crowd of the season, 56,000 and thousands more locked out, assembled on a cold, wet Tuesday night on April 11th - for a testimonial! But this was no ordinary testimonial for no ordinary player. This was a testimonial for **SIR ROGER HUNT!** Under the prevailing Liverpool Football Club rules a player could only have a testimonial match if he was either retired or about to. Halfway through the season Bolton's manager, Jimmy Armfield, had told Roger that he was no longer part of his plans - a decision that hastened Roger to retirement at the end of the season and the consequent taking of his testimonial. Armfield later changed his mind and offered Roger a two-year contract but by then it was too late - Roger's plans for his testimonial were well advanced - there was no going back. Had Liverpool Football Club relaxed their rules then, as they subsequently did with Tommy Smith, then Roger could have carried on playing for another two years. As it was football was deprived of at least two years of a great talent.

Back to League action and our amazing run continued with a 2-0 victory at West Ham. We'd got not one iota of the expected trouble at Upton Park.

Another two goals from Tosh, his fifth in four consecutive games, gave us a home win over Ipswich.

We were now in with an outside chance of the League Championship after our amazing run of form but Leeds were still the favourites with Derby being the other team in the hunt. It was to the Baseball Ground we would go on May Day, not then a Bank Holiday, so it was skiving a day off work for Evo. I was now working with John Hughes at Walter Holme's Builders. We neither expected nor got trouble at Derby, but then again "me ducks" weren't gonna mess with ten thousand Scousers were they? The atmosphere created by us and also the Derby fans who sang all around the ground was booming. The Baseball Ground might have been a shithole but it was an atmospheric shithole. Soft arse Brian Clough was the butt of most of our acidic humour:

HR Brian Clough
Don't yer know that 'e's a puff?
HR Brian Clough
He only gets a little 'cos 'e can't get enough!

Old Whiskyhead had the last laugh though as John McGovern scored to give them a 1-0 win. We should have won the game though as Tosh missed a sitter from a yard out after Keegan had done brilliantly and taken the piss out of Colin Todd on the touchline.

I was going to have to skive another day off work the following Monday for our last game of the season at Highbury on the night when the title would be decided a year to the day after Charlie George had broke my heart. Would I eat the sweet, cold dish of revenge at the table of the floppy-haired fucker?

I travelled down to Highbury on the "footy special" with Noel Kelly and John Patterson, a couple of lads who drank in The Saltbox.

If we won and Leeds lost at Wolves then we would pip Derby County, who had finished all their games, for the League on goal average. We arrived in Euston at about five o'clock; that was the easy part over. The hard part would be trying to avoid the Arsenal hooligans for the next two hours or so. They wouldn't be in a very good mood as their team had lost to Leeds in the FA Cup final two days earlier. I did think it was a bit unfair on Arsenal and Leeds to play just two days after the Cup final, especially on Leeds who were going for the League. But that was the way it was then, nobody moaned about fixture congestion, they just got on with it. Can you imagine it happening now? No chance!

The journey from Euston to Finsbury Park was negotiated safely enough and we took our places in the Clock end about an hour before kick off. There were thousands of Reds present and we all got absolutely soaked as it pissed down all night! Our team did us proud that night as they battered away at the Arsenal defence seeking the win that would give us our first trophy for six years.

The game was goalless with a couple of minutes to go when news came through that Leeds were losing 1-2. We started singing; "We only need a goal to win the League." John Toshack put the ball in the net at our end from a Kevin Keegan cross. We all went berserk until we realised that the referee, Roger Kirkpatrick, had disallowed the goal for offside. The bastard! I never did like him! He was fat, had this big pair of bushy sideburns and revelled in the "Mister Pickwick" tag he had been given. I thought he was just a sad tosser.

The final whistle signalled that Derby County had won the League as Leeds had indeed lost at Wolves. One disallowed goal off winning the League! Thousands of hugely disappointed but loyal Reds stayed for ten minutes after the game singing, "Shankly, Shankly, Shankly" to the tune of the number one record of the time: Amazing Grace. There was a photograph in the following morning's Daily Mirror (believe it or not but it was a half-decent paper then) of Emlyn Hughes covered in mud from head to toe, socks round his ankles, absolutely knackered and in a severe state of distress. I thought to myself then, "We've got to win it next season, if only for him." Apparently Shanks said to the players after the game, "Don't worry lads, we'll win it next season." We'd come so close this time and with an ever-improving team nobody doubted the great man.

We went to Arsenal station instead of Finsbury Park to get the tube back to Euston. This turned out to be a bad mistake! As soon as we sat down a load of "White Coats" got on. Oh shit! The "White Coats" were a notorious Arsenal hooligan firm, so called because they wore white coats of the type doctors etc., wore. All told there must have been about fifty Arsenal scallies in our carriage, but the noise from other carriages as we passed through stations suggested to me that there must have been two or three hundred all told on the train. Most of our lads would have got on at Finsbury Park, so basically we were fucked!

"Scarsers where are you?" sang the Arsenal rabble.

Er, there's three of us 'ere shittin' ourselves. 'Ang on, we'll identify ourselves to you so you can kick the shit out of us. Just give us a minute. Is that all right?

"If you all 'ate Scarsers clap your 'ands."

Yeah, well we fuckin' 'ate you too, yer slimy Cockney bastards.

What could we do? We had to mumble the words and clap our hands. Not to do so would have meant certain identification followed by the equally certain pasting.

"We all fackin' 'ate Scarse."

Well actually, I love it; a tasty combination of meat, spuds an' as much veg as you can throw into it. Yum, yum! Much better than that jellied eels shite you lot eat. An' what's that pie and mash lark all about? With green gravy as well an' vinegar on your mashed spuds. Oh yeah, that's normal isn't it? Yeah, dead normal!

"What's the time mate?" one of the "White Coats" asked Patto. Oh no, this was it. Kickin' time.

Patto looked at his watch.

Patto, what the fuckin' 'ell are you doin'? Let's just run - now! If yer open yer mouth we're fucked!

"Quarter to ten mate," Patto answered in the best Cockney accent I'd ever heard.

Go 'ead Patto lad! Yer've done us proud there mate!

"Sorry mate, I thought you were a Scarse cant."

"Nah, fack that. I fackin' 'ate 'em."

Patto shut the fuck up will yer! Yer've done well so far, but yer gonna get us killed. Let's just get the fuck outta 'ere.

The doors opened to let us out at King's Cross. This was going to be the big test. We were going to have to get on another tube to Euston, with consequently more chance of getting sussed. What jeans did we have on? They were dead give-aways. I had Wrangler's on; they were okay. A quick glance at Patto's revealed he was wearing Levi's - no problem there. I looked at Noel's and quite literally nearly pooed my pants! There, on the back of his jeans, was a big fat Fleming's sign. You know, the one with the Union Jack and the address underneath: County Road, Walton, Liverpool. Fleming's were top quality jeans at half the price of the leading designer brands. The only place in the country that sold them was a little shop on County Road. They were rightly proud of this and made sure the world knew it by putting their address on the label, but they were no good for wearing to away matches, you just didn't do it, especially in London. To be fair to them, they didn't ask numbskulls like Noel to wear them outside of Liverpool.

"Scarsers!" came the shout from two hundred or so wailing banshees disguised as Arsenal hooligans. We bounded up the stairs hoping to reach the sanctuary of the platform, but we had no chance. The chasing pack was soon upon us and proceeded to give us a fearful kicking. We sought refuge in a guard's room and locked ourselves in there.

The Arsenal loonies were hammering on the door, screaming for us to come out. Oh yeah, I can't wait to get my head kicked in again! After the mob had dispersed we were escorted by British Transport police for the rest of the short journey to Euston.

We got to Euston at ten o'clock with just seconds to spare before the special departed. The scallies had relieved the newsagents, without payment of course, of their copies of the men's magazines of the day: Penthouse, Mayfair, Knave, Rustler and Forum and these were freely distributed round the train. The song all the way home was, "We were robbed at Highbury" and indeed we were as TV replays later proved: Toshack wasn't offside. The train, it seemed, broke down every five minutes and it didn't help that some knob'eads kept pulling the communication cord. The journey was only made bearable by the aforementioned magazines. The pictures of naked ladies and reading the salacious stories made me yearn even more to be at home in the ample bosom of my beautiful wife. We'd been married just under a year and were still at it like knives! Come on, I *was* only eighteen!

We arrived back in Lime Street at three o'clock. Nobody had the taxi fare home, so it was an hour-long walk in the pissin' down rain home to Litherland. We had a laugh though.

"Noel, what the fuck were yer doin' wearin' Fleming's at Highbury?"
"Fuck off Evo! Who are you, the fashion police?
"'E's right though," said Patto, "why didn't yer wear yer dodgy Lee Cooper's or yer even dodgier Falmer's?"
"Get to fuck, Alf Garnett!"
"I thought 'e sounded more like Sid James."
At this the three of us just fell in to a heap laughin'. We didn't stop laughin' 'til we reached Stanley Road, when we broke into a chorus of, "We were robbed at Highbury."
By the time we reached Linacre Road this had changed to, "We got fucked at Highbury."
"Do you lot know what time it is?" a woman shouted.
We couldn't help it. It had to be done. She asked for it.
"It's four in the mornin' and once more the dawnin' has woke up the wantin' in me," we all sang in unison. Faron Young had nothing on us!
"You lot! Shut up or I'll have me fella down to yer!" shouted another woman from an upstairs window.
"Ah get yer 'ead in missus. Yer'd think it was a bleedin' cattle market," bellowed Noel at the top of his considerably loud voice.
We beat a hasty retreat when we heard said fella running down the stairs.

I was cold, wet, hungry, tired, battered, bruised and feeling extremely sorry for myself. All I wanted was to get home in front of our nice warm coal fire, fill my belly full of food and fall into the arms of my beloved.

I entered the house as quietly as possible, so as not to wake anybody up. There wouldn't have been much of a problem if I woke Ev, their John or our little Stevie. But if I woke my mother-in-law, Kitty! Kitty was four foot-nothing, weighed about six stone and was the nicest, sweetest, gentlest person you could ever wish to meet; when she was in a good mood. When she was in a bad mood she was, as I said, a fearsome old battle-axe!

The fire was nearly out, so I crept out to the backyard, got a shovelful of coal and deposited it on the fire. While the fire was re-lighting I made myself a wagonload of chips, two eggs, five slices of bread with lashings of butter and a big fat mug of tea. A feast fit for a King! When I returned to the living room the hearth was a blazing, crackling, roaring inferno of bright orange and red flames. Within seconds I could feel the chill leaving my bones. I was well stuck in to my marvellous repast when I heard the wooden stairs creak under the weight of footsteps. Fear, trepidation, call it what you will but whatever it was it stopped me eating, which was really quite something. The door handle turned.

Oh no please, not Kitty! The door then opened fully to reveal, standing there before me, a vision in a black negligee!

No, of course it wasn't Kitty! It was my darling Evelyn.

"Are you comin' to bed or what? I've been waitin' for yer!" she screeched Kitty style.

"'Ang on, just let me finish this."

"Look at all that, yer fat get!" still in Kitty mode

"Give us a break will yer Ev. I'm starvin'. I've 'ad nothin' to eat all day."

"Well, yer shouldn't go off gallivantin' to Arsenal then, should yer?"

"Yeah, yeah, whatever."

"Where've yer been?" screaming now.

"I've been to London to see the Queen. Where d'yer think? Yer know where I've been."

"Well 'ow come you've only just got 'ome now then?"

"'Ow long do you think it takes to get 'ome from London?"

"Yer 'aven't been to London. Yer've been to Arsenal!"

"God give me strength," I muttered through clenched teeth, nearly choking on a particularly large chip. "Anyway, calm down an' be quiet will yer. Yer gonna wake everybody up."

"Well if I do it'll be you're fault."

"Oh right, yeah. I thought it'd be my fault. You're shoutin' an' screamin', I'm whisperin', but it'll be my fault if you wake everybody up. Yeah, I can see the logic in that."

"'Ow did they get on anyway?" her voice slightly quieter now.

"We drew nil-nil."

"Does that mean they won the League?"

"No, Derby won the League."

"Who were they playin'?"

"They weren't playin' anybody."

"Well 'ow come they won the League?"

"Oh, I'm too tired for this."

"Yer won't be too tired when we get to bed though will yer?"

"I'm never too tired for that!"

"Well yer can just sod off!"

"We'll see."

"What's that cut on yer 'ead?"

"Er, it's a cut."

"I know that smart arse. I meant 'ow did it happen?"

"I got done over by a load of Arsenal fans."

"Right, that's it. Yer not going to any more away games if that's the trouble yer gonna get into."

"Yeah, okay. Try stoppin' me."

"Who comes first, me or Liverpool?"

"Liverpool"

"See, yer love Liverpool more than yer love me!"

"I love Everton more than I love you."

"Oh, very bloody funny! Well I'm not playin' second fiddle to any football team!"

"Listen girl, with a gob like that yer lucky to be in the band."

"I hate you sometimes," her voice slowly dropping in pitch.

"I know yeah, but only sometimes. Yer love me most of the time though don't yer Ev?"

"Yeah, yer know I do. Come on let's go to bed. This better be bloody good," her lilting voice now barely audible.

"Oh, it will be. Don't worry, it will be." I whispered softly in her ear as I carried her gently upstairs to bed.

CHAPTER SEVENTEEN

SCRATCHING THE SEVEN YEAR ITCH

The proposed summer transfer of Huddersfield's Frank Worthington fell through after Frank failed a medical suffering from "high blood pressure". My arse! Rumour had it that Frankie boy had been dabbling somewhere he shouldn't have been and had caught a nasty little something. Great pity for Frank and us because he was a good player. Shanks, not being one to dwell on a disappointment, wasted no time in going out and spending the money elsewhere. Alec Lindsay, signed as a midfielder, had been moved, with great success to left-back; indeed Shanks said that Alec's left foot was that good he could open a tin of beans with it! John McLaughlin's emergence as a top-flight midfielder had failed to materialise. John was just a little too lightweight for the hurly-burly of First Division and European football. Shanks and the staff had decided young John needed building up. To this end Shanks had secured a deal with a local butcher to provide John with steaks daily. John went to see Shanks one day to break the news that he had got his girlfriend pregnant and would have to commit the cardinal sin (according to the great God Shankly) of getting married during the football season. Shanks called all his staff into the office, "Quick lads, come in here and see this! We've created a monster!"
All this meant that the midfield had been left ever so slightly under strength so Shanks used the Worthy money on acquiring the massive talents of Forest's Peter Cormack.

We started the season in much the same vein as we'd left the previous one. Two 2-0 home wins against our darling Manchester neighbours were followed by a 1-1 draw at Crystal Palace. A baking hot day stood on Selhurst Park's Whitehorse Lane end produced not only a bad case of sunburn for me but also a 1-1 draw into the bargain. I'd never been to Palace but Timmy had said the South Londoner's were a right nasty bunch (or words to that effect). I had absolutely no problem with them though.

A catastrophe was about to hit Evo: I was going to have to miss a home match! Money was very tight. Bringing up a family was hard. I knew now how Ma and Da had felt for all those years. Some weeks I would have plenty of money and others virtually nothing to spare. I didn't mind if the skint weeks fell when we were away - it wasn't the end of the world to miss an away match but it was unthinkable to miss a home match. The Saturday morning of the West Ham game found me with either enough money to go the match or buy baby food for little Stevie. There obviously was no contest. Then an idea hit me! Not the most original or even the greatest idea I'd ever had but needs must.

So there I was standing outside the Kop bewailing passers-by, "Lenzyerodz! Any odds lads? Spare any odds mate so I can get in?" I gratefully accepted the odd few coppers that were thrust into my hand but I felt like shit doing it. I'd seen plenty of lads outside the ground doing this but in most cases they hadn't wanted the money to get in; I'd see them go in and pocket the money they'd scrounged. I was genuine but I wasn't getting very far. Dad's words then came to haunt me; "You follow them all over the country but if you went to the gate with a tanner short they wouldn't let you in!"

Well I was a bit more than a tanner short but it was worth a try.

"Ee arr mate I'm ten pence short, lerrus in."
"Fuck off!"
"Go on la. Keep the money an' I'll jump over!"
"Fuck off!"

Plans A and B were fucked so go to Plan C. I wasn't bad at bunking in to grounds so I gave it a go - three times! I was like a boomerang as the same copper collared me on each occasion! "If yer try an' bunk in again I'll fuckin' twat yer an' nick yer!"

Fuck that - wasn't gonna argue with PC Plod!

There was nothing else for it: Plan D was going to have to be put into effect. I had nowhere near enough money to get in the Kop but I did, just about, to get in the Boy's Pen. Fuckin' 'ell no - not the monkey cage again! The fact that the age limit for the Pen was 15 and I was four days short of my nineteenth birthday was against me. In my favour was that I was a fresh-faced youngster: my boyish looks belying my age. Only the week before I'd been refused a pint in Kent's because I looked under age. Not only was it worth a try, I had no Plan E! Fuckin' 'ell this was sad! Here I was, nearly nineteen years of age, married with a kid and I was trying to get in the Boy's fuckin Pen!

"Fuck off lad before I call a bizzy!"

Bastard!

It was ten to three. I must have cut a miserable figure as I stood outside
the Kop, tears streaming down my face, and I'm not ashamed to admit
that! I was fucked, well and truly! One last desperate, "Lenzyerodz!"
I was about to start the long walk home when the great God McKenna
smiled down on me.

"Ee arr lad yer can 'ave this."

An old fella, probably in his seventies, thrust a season ticket voucher
in to my hand.

"'Ow much d'yer want for it mate? I 'aven't got enough."

"Nothin', yer can 'ave it lad. Me lad couldn't make it. I saw yer doin'
yer bezzy there to get in."

"Ah, ta mate. Thanks a lot. Tell yer lad thanks too!"

I could have kissed that old fella! He would have to put his teeth in
though - it's horrible necking gummies!

That old geezer surely couldn't have realised how happy he'd made a
young lad. Mind you I wasn't feeling totally happy seeing as we were
two goals down to the Hammers! Tosh pulled one back just before
half-time, which put us in with a chance. An own goal just after an
hour's play put us level. Here we were on another of our famous
comebacks! Emlyn completed it two minutes later and was eventually
caught by his team-mates somewhere on Priory Road! No wonder
they called him Crazy!

Four days later and the tables were turned on us at Leicester. Tosh put
us two goals ahead but Keith Weller had brought the Foxes level by
half time. Weller's winner was as inevitable as it was sickening.

We were getting good at losing leads as after going a goal up at Derby
(Tosh again) we eventually lost 1-2.

Salvation for me arrived in the shape of a national football quiz
competition, sponsored by tobacco firm John Player, which I won.
The prize was a season ticket for three years for the club of your choice.
Waaahhhaayyy! There were though a couple of snags (aren't there
always): the season ticket was actually only for one year - the difference
between one and three years was made up by a cash amount (well
actually a cheque) to renew it for two years. The other was that the
season ticket was for the Anfield Road end. I was a confirmed Kopite
even though some of the more famous "faces" had migrated to the
Road End to form the fledgling "Barmy Anny Road Army". I didn't

have much trouble getting rid of the individual vouchers and using the money to go in the Kop but I always had to put a bit of money to it - the Anny Road scallies would always insist that I sold it for slightly less than face value. I learned early not to mess with the Road End! The money to renew for two years? I saved it 'til the appropriate time to renew for those two years? My arse! Ev had my windfall well and truly spent before I had the chance to feel the crispness of the fivers! I didn't really mind though as a lot of it went on little Stevie and we also had a few good nights out - Ev was always very randy when she was pissed! Method in my madness!

Old Trafford on a wet, cold, miserable November Saturday afternoon was not a nice place to be if you were a Scouser. Me and Patto had got there very early and decided rather than risk getting twatted outside we'd go for the safety of standing in the Scoreboard end for two hours. As the terrace started filling up it became apparent that the Scoreboard End was going through an Anny Road type metamorphosis in that a lot of the Stretford End hoolies had decided to make this their new home for the express purpose of having a battle with the away lads. We moved over to a corner of the terrace where we thought we'd be safe as there was no apparent presence of Scousers. The Scousers that were in there were doing what me and Patto were doing - keeping it well and truly fuckin' shut.

At ten to three; "LIV-ER-POOL!" The crew had arrived in force thank fuck and were making their way to the corner where we were stood. The mancs must have had it all planned as they immediately left their stations in the middle of the terrace to go round the back, come up through the entrance close to us and attack us from behind. The mayhem, with people on the running track and on the pitch, was still going on when the players came out. Our already perilous position was worsened when hundreds ran across the pitch from the Stretford End to join in the caning of the Scousers.

There was blood and snot everywhere as we were getting whacked all over the place. I had flashbacks of my stay in Wythenshawe Hospital just over three years earlier. There was nothing else for it but to climb over the fence and into the paddock. As we were getting over the fence the mancs were trying to drag us back into the steaming cauldron.

"Get back yer fuckin' Scouse twats!"
I'd rather not if you don't mind. Thank you however for your very kind offer. Thank you also for your excellent hospitality but I would like to make it to my twentieth birthday if that's okay with you.
"Fuck off!"
One of my lovely Mancunian hosts had hold of my left leg and was succeeding in dragging me back to receive my kicking. I kicked back as hard as I could with my right heel. Mine host relaxed his grip as my boot connected with his nose. I had been totally shitting myself and would definitely have come to serious harm had I not lashed out so I feel no shame in saying that the noise of his nose bone splintering beneath my boot was one of the most welcome, satisfying sounds I have ever heard!

It was a good ten minutes into the game before the bizzies were able to restore order. They allowed the rest of the Scousers left in that mosh pit to climb over the fence to join the others already in the Paddock. There were some hard lads in that Paddock with seriously worried looks on their faces. It had been a nightmare experience so I was glad that there were lads much harder than me who had felt the same fear I had. I wasn't such a big tart after all!

Considering all this it was no surprise that bottom-of-the-table United beat top-of-the-League Liverpool by two goals to nil. United were fielding their new £200,000 signing from Bournemouth, Ted MacDougal (a former Liverpool player whom Shankly had released as he was never going to be a first-team regular). SuperTed it was who did most of the damage, the other goal being scored by Wyn Davies. Davies had played for Manchester City in the first match of the season at Anfield and had been sent off along with Larry Lloyd. Larry reckoned his sending off was because he had hit Davies' fist with his throat! So, all in all, a bit of a twat was Mr. Davies wasn't he? Eleven days after the "Battle of Old Trafford" we were faced with more of the same at Elland Road. It was strange at Leeds - sometimes, if you were lucky, you'd get no bother (after the League match which we'd won 2-1 there earlier in the season we'd even managed to have a chat with Jack Charlton) but most times we expected, and got, a battle royal. This was to be one of those occassions. Things weren't too bad before and during the match but afterwards was a different story. A tannoy announcement was made halfway through the second half that a national rail strike had been called with effect from midnight and that anybody who had travelled from Liverpool by train should leave now to catch the specials which would leave at 9 o'clock to ensure being back at Lime Street before midnight. Yeah okay! The Gelderd End loonies started making their way out to get their action. The League Cup replay was finely balanced at 0-0 with extra-time looking a distinct possibility so none of our lot were going. The lads on the specials would just pile on to the coaches. The gates were opened early to allow anybody wanting to leave to do so, although, as I say, none of ours did. This allowed the Leeds hoolies to infiltrate our Cowshed End only to see them royally booted back out. The punishment of extra-time on a freezing cold night was averted when Keegan won the match for us with a last gasp goal. The Leeds lads had put two and two together (they were clever like that) and deduced, Sherlock Holmes style, that it wasn't worth making their way for agro at the station as there would be no fucker there to have agro with! Instead, using their powers of intuition, they made their way to where the coaches were parked - fuckin' hundreds of them. I'd seen some big Leeds mobs before but never this big! The best thing we could do was to stick together and fight our way through them and on to the coaches, which we did.

I wouldn't have liked to see the repair bills for coaches the following day as every single one of them got bricked to fuck! Ours had three windows put in. There was glass everywhere. Some lads on the coach had been cut by flying glass; one quite badly having a massive gash on his head. Still, we'd won, hadn't shit out and backed off from the Leeds mob when we could easily have done, and all arrived home virtually in one piece, even if there were sixty-odd people on each coach designed to hold forty-two, so we were all quite proud of ourselves. Tales of that night have been told, retold, and yes exaggerated, for years but that's a truthful account of how it was. It was fuckin' freezing coming home over those Pennines!

Our penchant for not making things easy for ourselves was never more evident than in the home game against Birmingham. Birmingham, in their first season in the top division since 1964-65, were something of an unknown quantity but did have some good players: Bob Hatton; the Latchford brothers, centre-forward Bob and goalkeeper Dave; a bright young lad, Trevor Francis; centre-half Roger Hynd who was Bill Shankly's cousin and a flying winger in Gordon Taylor. When

Taylor hit a 30 yard screamer which flew in off the shoulder of the injured Tommy Smith's deputy, Trevor "Stan" Storton, to give Birmingham a 3-0 lead halfway through the first-half the game looked dead and buried. Our fighting spirit came shining through like a beacon piercing the early December gloom. Alec Lindsay pulled a goal back after 32 minutes and just before half-time Peter Cormack netted to give us a fighting chance in the second-half. Cormack was proving an astute Shankly buy, not only linking up well to set up the Keegan/Toshack partnership for many goals but also chipping in with the odd strike himself, most notably the only goal of the Anfield derby in October. Lindsay levelled the scores with a superb shot ten minutes into the second-half. Tosh won the game for us after 77 minutes with a brave goal, injuring himself in the process, after again being brilliantly set up by Cormack and Keegan.

A punishing schedule saw us draw 1-1 with Tottenham at home in the League Cup fifth round just two days after the hard-fought Birmingham game. The replay, played another two days later at White Hart Lane, saw us bow out of the competition 1-3. There were never any complaints from our players though about playing too many games. In fact I think the likes of Smith, Hughes, Cormack and Keegan relished it. Whilst they always looked knackered at the end of every game, having given their all for the cause of LFC, I'm sure they would all have quite willingly played another game immediately afterwards if Bill had asked them to.

"I'll be your long-haired lover from Liverpool."
God, what a shite song that was! The Christmas number one by the fuckin' irritating little twat, Little Jimmy Osmond was being belted out by us on the away terrace at Sheffield United's Bramall Lane. Okay, yeah, I'll admit it - I started it! Christmas prezzies were much in evidence, mostly the brand-new, new-fangled invention: Liquid Crystal Display timepieces, or digital watches to me and you!

Whist the "telepathic" partnership of Keegan and Toshack was working wonderfully well in home games Shanks decided on a "horses for courses" policy when playing away. This meant that the speedier Phil Boersma could use his electric pace in counter-attacking tactics. Shanks tactics proved spot on when Phil gave us the lead after 27 minutes. Second-half goals by Lawler and Heighway sealed the win. Whilst

I'm sure Chris Lawler loved playing for Liverpool, and enjoyed scoring even more, The Silent Knight did have a gob on him that suggested either he owed loads of money to somebody dead hard or he was an undertaker suffering from an acute case of Plymouth Argyles!

My two previous trouble-free visits to Upton Park had lulled me into a false sense of security. In a reversal of the vogue of a few years earlier supposed "away" ends were now being infiltrated by the hooligan element of home clubs. It was bad news in the South Bank that day. The West Ham hooligan song of, "We wore our boots and braces in the West Ham Cavalry," was much to the fore. West Ham supporters were always portrayed on telly, especially by Motson and Moore, as real family type chirpy cockney sparrer supporters. They backed this up with endless shots of old dears with small kids in their arms stood at the front of the terracing. Those 'Appy 'Ammers!

MY FUCKIN' BIG FAT ARSE!

Why didn't they show the nutters intent on knifing us to death in the South Bank? Why didn't they show hundreds of them making Zulu noises at us before charging down the terrace and kicking fuck out of us? Unlike Old Trafford a couple of months earlier there was no easy escape route over a fence and on to another terrace; we just had to put up with it and try to defend ourselves as best we could. West Ham supporters now, and I've met quite a lot of them, are sound as a pound, but that day they were a thoroughly evil bunch of horrible bastards! It didn't really help that I was with John Dever who wanted to just fuck off out of there as early as possible and get back to Euston.

"John, what fuckin' use is it fuckin' off now? We'll probably only get fucked outside so we might as well stay an' battle it out."

The lovely Metropolitan Police were no fuckin' help either.

"Ee arr, are yer gonna stop this or what? We're getting' fucked 'ere."

"That's your fackin' fault for comin' 'ere! If you don't fackin' like it you should fackin' stay at 'ome!"

The great British Bobby eh? Ever so helpful! My fuckin' arse!

Apart from the fact that Keegan scored to give us a 1-0 win it just wasn't our fuckin' day. We'd just about got to Euston safely save for a few skirmishes at the tube station and on the tube itself. We were coming up the escalator from the underground into the main line station when we were ambushed by a load of the QPR Bushwhackers. I didn't know QPR had that many supporters never mind loonies! Ever tried running down an escalator that's moving up? Not easy but that was the only way of not getting my head kicked in so I did it. I just jumped on the nearest tube, went one stop and came back, by which time it had all calmed down. Where was John? Sitting in the café at Euston having a coffee while I was risking life and limb trying to fight off these London Loonies. He hadn't really shit out it was just that he somehow got split from me when it was going off at Euston and sidled his way out of trouble and into the safety of the café.

I was glad that the following away game was at the "safe" Burnley. Again, there were about ten thousand Reds at Turf Moor for the FA Cup Third Round tie. Where were all these fuckers when I needed them last week at West Ham? Still, they made plenty of noise:

Here comes Stevie Heighway runnin' down the wing
He crosses the ball to Toshack who is the Kopites King
He heads the ball to Keegan who scores a glorious goal
And as for Joey Royle you can shove 'im up your 'ole!

Liverpool's got Keegan in the middle,
Keegan in the middle,
Keegan in the middle.
Liverpool's got Keegan in the middle,
That's why it's called supreme.

We'd take tunes from anywhere and put our own words to them. The first of the above songs was "Circles" by The New Seekers. The second was a tune used to advertise Lyon's Supreme cakes - dead nice they were, full of cream - yummy! The match finished goalless.

Sitting in the Main Stand at the 3-0 win in the replay was Celtic's Lou Macari whom Shankly had invited to the match, as he was about to sign for us. Sitting next to Macari was Manchester United manager, Tommy Docherty. Docherty had wangled himself a seat next to Macari in order to talk him out of signing for the potential League Champions and instead join the Old Trafford battle against relegation. The fact that Docherty succeeded says much for his powers of persuasion. Shithouse!

We continued our topsy-turvy ways by contriving to lose at Wolves after leading 1-0. I was with my next-door neighbour David Jones for that match. No chance of ever getting into any trouble with David around - he was much too quiet for all that. I loved going to away games with David in his marvellous old 1954 Ford Popular. The little Pop didn't, I don't think, go much above the pace of a milk float or Paddy Crerand on speed but it was a lovely old car and was very reliable, always getting us there in one piece. You did have to do an overnight journey to Burnley though!

Malcolm Allison's boasts that Manchester City were gonna stuff us at Anfield in the Fourth Round of the FA Cup wound us all up no end. Worse was to come though when City's flamboyant manager came on to the pitch before kick-off to be greeted by, "Allison, Allison, shut your mouth! Allison, shut your mouth!"
Allison lapped it up - absolutely loved it! He loved it even more as his team battled their way to a scoreless draw.

A match at Maine Road was a hairy enough prospect at the best of times (not that there was ever going to be a best of times) but a midweek match in the dark surroundings of Moss Side was "poo yer pants" time. Even more so as City had demolished the old open terrace and while the now covered end was terraced the previous season it had since been seated. The smart new stand was renamed, "The North Stand". All of this meant that the only standing accommodation now was in City's home end (or side to be exact) the Kippax Street. To make matters worse (if they could get any worse) was the fact that there seemed to be as many United loons as City intent on doing us as much damage as possible. What the fuck it had to do with those cunts I don't know! It was bad enough having to deal with the City hordes, and there were loads of them, without having the other half of Manchester on our case too! It was, quite firmly, "keep yer gob shut". We lost 0-2. Me and John managed, with the aid of a Fast Black, to get back to Victoria before all hell broke loose at the station.

The 0-2 defeat at home to Arsenal the following week had the newspapers screaming, "CRISIS AT ANFIELD!" It was like that then - two successive League defeats (even though we were still top of the League) and elimination from the FA Cup spelled disaster. It was clear however that something was going wrong and needed changing. Shanks' solution was to take the captaincy from Tommy Smith and hand it to Emlyn Hughes. To say this didn't go down too well with

"The Anfield Iron" is like saying the Incredible Hulk was a little peeved when people upset him!

David cranked up his old jalopy (he really did crank it up, honest, with a proper starting handle!) for the trip to Maine Road for the League game against City. Sensible David had the perfectly sound idea that it might not be too safe to go on the Kippax and that a seat in the Platt Lane Stand might be our best bet of not getting our blocks knocked off.

Sitting at a match was an alien concept to me. Ev had given me some terrible grief about the state of my skids after the Cup match at City though so I decided that, for the first time ever, I would sit down at a match. We were 0-1 down and played bloody awful. Tommy Smith was conducting a running verbal battle with referee, Clive Thomas. As the teams were leaving the pitch at half-time Tommy and Emlyn Hughes were involved in a heated exchange. We then saw the incredible sight of Tommy flooring Emlyn right there on the pitch and right under the nose of Mr. Thomas. Tommy should have been quite rightly sent off for that. He didn't have to wait very long for his early bath though. Mr. Thomas's patience was tried beyond the point of endurance and Tommy was on his way. Phil Boersma gave us a barely deserved point with a late equaliser. The flaw in David's plan soon became evident when the Platt Lane stand was invaded by the Kippax crew looking for the Scousers they had spotted from their vantage point on the terrace. Time for sealed lips and no eye contact. We were lucky to get away with that one.

In my opinion Tommy's hatred of Emlyn was born out of jealousy because of the captaincy situation. This hatred still festers 28 years later. But why? I didn't hear Rowdy bleating when Tommy took the captaincy off him. Neither did I hear Emlyn bleating when his captaincy was handed to Phil Thompson. Tommy has gone very public on his thoughts about Emlyn. Emlyn, on the other hand, has always maintained a dignified silence. Tommy's assertion that Emlyn thought more of England than he did of Liverpool doesn't hold water as there was no more committed player to the Liverpool cause than Crazy Horse. This showed up vividly whenever he scored a goal. Even the quickest of players couldn't catch Emlyn once he was off on one of his goal celebrations. Again, Tommy's feelings could have been born of the jealousy that Emlyn was capped 59 times while at Anfield. Tommy's sole England cap belied his ability; he should have won many more but that wasn't Emlyn's fault. I just feel it's such a shame that such a Liverpool great as Tommy should have those feelings about another Liverpool stalwart. The two player's career statistics are almost identical: they were Liverpool players for almost exactly the same length of time; appearance records were, to within a few matches (Emlyn just shading it), the same; even on goals scored Emlyn was just ahead, the fact that he played further forward than Tommy for much of his career being counterbalanced by Tommy scoring a lot of his goals from the penalty spot. Let's just hope that one day it all sorts itself out.

Having got back on track with the fortunate point at Maine Road we stayed there with a 2-1 win at Ipswich.

The improvement was maintained with a convincing 2-0 win in the Goodison derby. Emlyn's two goals were celebrated in the Park End almost as much as Sandy's monumental header a few years earlier.

A 3-2 home win over Southampton, another late winner from Keegan doing the trick, was followed by what I will always remember as the Stoke Glamfest.

Believe this or believe this not: LFC fans have been known to wear make-up. "Nothing unusual about that," you might think, "loads of women wear make-up." Yes, but these LFC fans were men! Well to be more precise, young lads really. You know, scallies, 15-25 age group. It was back in the days when Glam Rock ruled the world: circa 1971-'75.

David Bowie, Alice Cooper, Gary Glitter, Wizzard, Sweet, Slade, T-Rex, Mud etc were doing more for make-up sales than even the gorgeous blonde on the cosmetics counter at TJ Hughes in Bootle Strand. Football fans, being the dedicated followers of fashion they were, soon followed their idols. Fans of LFC were no exception. The phenomenon, strangely enough, was mostly confined to away games. Maybe the Alice Cooper lookalikes didn't fancy a right hook from the docker standing next to them in the Kop! Maybe it was for a similar reason that the "make-up boys" were more in evidence at "safer" away games such as Stoke, Burnley, Derby, West Brom etc rather than the "shit-yer-kecks" venues of Old Trafford, White Hart Lane, Stamford Bridge, St. James' Park etc. I mean, it wouldn't really have been a pretty sight to see a David Bowie lookalike with his mascara spoiled by a load of blood running into it! The height of all this was the game at Stoke; Christ, it was like a bloody Glam Rock convention!

It was funny on the way home on the coach or special trying to wash the make-up off. The more clued-up lads though had not only robbed their bird's (or their Ma's depending on whether you had a bird or not) make-up but also their make-up remover.

Matching the garishness of face decoration were the truly most awful clothes in the memory of fashion. Okay, we didn't think they were terrible then, but believe me, when I look back at photos of that era, they were. Yeah, we must have looked daft, but I tell you what - we had fun, and isn't that what life's all about?

Early to mid-seventies: Glam Rock was cool
So was supporting Liverpool.
Goin' away games, yer face caked with glitter.
If yer did that now yer'd get one up the shitter!

Robbin' yer bird's make-up to blacken yer eyes.
If she ever found out - what a surprise!
Thick red lippy and rouge for yer cheeks.
We must 'ave looked right bloody geeks!

Rupert the Bear kecks and platform shoes
Stacked heels or wedges, whatever yer'd choose.
Wear yer colours? Yer 'avin' a joke!
I'm wearin' me tart's make-up for the trip to Stoke!

Feather cuts and penny round collars were all the rage.
We would have looked daft in any other age.
Forty-inch Lionel's: T-shirt - "Fruit of the Loom"
I think of it now enshrouded in gloom.

Budgie jackets, velvet ones too
Were the height of fashion for the "Max Factor Crew"
Stripey tank tops with dayglow shirts
All the owld fellas sayin', "Look at those blurts!"

Falmer's jeans with a tartan trim.
'Earin' the owld ones, "Just look at 'im!"
Sprayin' yer Air-Wair silver or gold
Wearin' yer tank top even when it was cold.

Washin' away the make-up on the way back.
If yer tart found out she'd give yer a crack!
Who were these loonies, these right nutcases?
I'll tell yer two of them: Evo and Braces!

We won an eminently forgettable game 1-0 thanks to an own goal by Stoke's John Mahoney - John Toshack's cousin. Nice one John - keep it in the family!

A 3-1 home win against Norwich gave us five on the bounce. Things were looking good again.

Tottenham came to Anfield on Grand National morning having not won at Anfield since the year the Titanic sank - 1912. They nearly did it this time though thanks to the finest display of goalkeeping I've ever seen at Anfield. Tottenham scored early and then defended as if their lives depended on it as we laid siege to their goal. Stopping everything that got through was Pat Jennings. HE WAS INCREDIBLE! Pat was stopping shots and headers from all angles. HE EVEN SAVED NOT ONE PENALTY BUT TWO. Visiting goalkeepers had, for years, a reputation of saving their best for Anfield. This might have been because they were always warmly welcomed by the Kop. Even the annual presentation of the handbag to Westy was done in a light-hearted manner - the big man was one of the best. Gordon Banks had become one of the Kop's favourite players even to the point of us chanting his name despite him breaking our hearts on many occassions. Cologne's Schumacher had survived a barrage at Anfield in 1965, leaving the Kop with his reputation enhanced. None of these though had anything on Pat Jennings' superb display in this match. It was going to take either a very good effort or a fluke to beat him. It turned out to be the latter as a bobbly shot from Keegan evaded him. If Kevin had hit the shot properly Pat would probably have read it correctly and made a save. Spurs probably just about deserved their draw for the way they defended but Pat Jennings that day deserved a knighthood!

Nobody quite knew what to expect when we went to Birmingham. They hadn't been in the First Division for ages so consequently hardly anybody had been before and nothing was known about which end to go in. We soon found out!

I was walking along the back of a big covered end with John who was his usual sweaty-palmed self!
"I don't like the feel of this Peter. It's a bad atmosphere in 'ere."
For once I had to agree with him. There was a sinister air about St. Andrew's that didn't bode well for us getting out of there in one piece
"Come on then, let's go over to that big side."

Having got to the top of the big terrace at the side of the pitch above the corner flag we had an unrivalled view of what happened next. There were plenty of Reds in the end we had just walked out of but they were scattered all around the terrace. The next thing there was an almighty kick off right behind the goal where a big knot of Reds were. The Brummies booted them out of that end and on to the pitch were they were joined by hundreds of other Reds from the different parts of that terrace. The other end soon filled up with Scousers being booted out of that end. We stayed where we were - to have made a move then would have meant an inevitable kicking as we were the only Scousers up there. A Brummie voice behind me said, "You're Scousers aren't yow?"
Fuckin' 'ell this cunt didn't even have the decency to ask me the time! No point in denying our birthplace - we'd been well and truly sussed!
"Yeah."
"Well I don't loike Scousers so yow'd better fuck off hadn't yow?"
Poo touched cloth as I saw the glint of his knife!
We couldn't get down the terrace fast enough and eventually found a safe place next to two old ladies. We lost the match 1-2 but that was almost an irrelevance compared to being about two seconds away from being knifed in the back!

Pat Jennings received a tumultuous reception from the Kop when he returned with Tottenham for the first leg of the UEFA Cup semi-final. He had another brilliant game as he kept out all but the Alec Lindsay effort which gave us a slender lead to take to the cauldron of White Hart Lane for the return leg.

West Brom were beaten 1-0 at Anfield before we went to Coventry.

The run-in to the Championship was looking very interesting. Arsenal and Leeds were well in contention but we were favourites. The disappointment of Highbury the previous season was, it seemed, spurring on not only the players but also the supporters. We'd even taken the tune of Cliff's Eurovision Song Contest entry, "Power To All Our Friends," to rally the lads at Coventry:

Power to LFC
They're the Champions you must agree
It's the Champions we've come to see
Singing Power to LFC.

A bit naff I know (okay VERY naff) but I liked that one! Pity not many more people thought so as it didn't get much of an airing after that. Shanks was sticking mainly to playing Tosh at home and Boersma away. It was working a treat and worked once again as Phil scored both goals in our 2-1 win. The Coventry West End Crew came into our end ten minutes before time trying to spoil our party but after an initial scare we soon fought them off. It was still a long, scary walk back to the station though.

Other results had been going for us, which meant that a combination of further good results could see us win the Championship if we triumphed at St. James' Park on Easter Saturday. The mood at Newcastle was once again ugly as Reds were getting launched all over the place outside the ground. We'd been told that The Strawberry, right outside the Gallowgate End, was a good pub to go in where we'd get no hassle. To be fair there were a few Geordies in there who were willing to engage in conversation with us. Overall though I think we'd been set up. A big mob of Geordies came and twatted anybody they even thought was Scouse. They ran amok through the pub. I don't know what it was that made me and John look Geordielike but whatever it was I was glad of it. We never got touched but once the battle had died down we went into the ground.

The Gallowgate was supposed to be our end but it became apparent long before kick off that the Geordies in that end had come for a fight. We were grouped at the top of the terrace with the Geordies below us but that all changed as soon as we started singing. The Mad Magpies charged at us and there was no stopping them - too many for us to do anything about it. They then took the position above us. It was hard work dodging the Newcy Brown bottles that were raining down aimed at our heads.

The sight at the other end, the Leezes, was something to behold as everybody in there seemed to have a Newcastle team shirt on - this, remember, some fifteen years or so before replica football shirts were marketed and became a fashion item. Keegan gave us the lead. Oh shit! The Geordies waded into us from above cracking all before them. John Tudor equalised shortly after and the Geordies charged us again. Fuckin' 'ell, getting charged at when we score we'd come to expect now everywhere but these fuckin' nutters charging us when **THEY** scored was a bit fuckin' much! Fuckin' 'ell lads, come on, play the game!
Malcolm MacDonald netted their winner in the second half played in driving rain. "SuperMac" always seemed to revel in the rain!
The usual scenes of mayhem were going on outside and all the way back to the station. As the train was pulling out it was bombarded by a hail of bricks, which put in about a dozen windows, including the one I was sitting next to.

The Newcastle result meant that we couldn't now DEFINITELY win the League at home to Leeds two days later. It would take an almighty mathematical miracle to stop us though if we did beat our Yorkshire rivals. Our constant assault on the Leeds goal was fruitless in the first half. Leeds' David Harvey was having another one of those inspired days we were so used to seeing from opposing goalkeepers. It took a great goal from Peter Cormack to break the deadlock and beat the resilient Harvey.
A mistake by the otherwise impeccable Harvey gave Keegan the opportunity to seal the match, and almost inevitably our Championship triumph, in the 85th minute. The chant of, "Champions. Champions," might have been a little premature but only if we lost our last match at home to Leicester 58-0 or something! Not even Leicester were that much of a bogey team to us! But first there was the little matter of our UEFA Cup semi-final second leg at White Hart Lane. I'm sure those nice Lilywhites supporters would welcome their Scouse counterparts with open arms!

We expected, and got, a heap of trouble at Tottenham. There was no "taking" the Park Lane End anymore. We'd be in the Paxton Road End and knew there would be a load of Tottenham boys in there with us. We weren't prepared for how many though. The first half was a constant battle trying to keep the Spurs mob at bay while on the pitch our lads were doing their bit by keeping the Tottenham players similarly at bay. We managed, just about, to stay at the side of the Spurs loonies. If we had let them get above us as we had the Geordies we would have got well and truly fucked!

Spurs scored early in the second-half to level the scores on aggregate. There was pandemonium in the Paxton Road End when Steve Heighway gave us back our aggregate lead, and more importantly a vital away goal, shortly after. The Tottenham hordes didn't take kindly to the fact that their darlings now needed to score another two goals to win the tie. Two lone bizzies tried to keep order but we were virtually left to our own devices to protect ourselves. Martin Peters scored to make the aggregate score 2-2 but we had the crucial away goal and as it stayed that way we had reached our first ever European Final. We would be playing West Germany's Borussia Moenchengladbach, again over two legs.
I'd decided, **EVO WAS ON HIS WAY TO GERMANY!** Well fuckin' look out the Germans! That was if I managed to get home in one piece.

The walk from White Hart Lane to Seven Sisters tube station is a twat at the best of times but when you're getting pummelled all the way by Spurs supporters it's fuckin' horrendous! There wasn't so much as a bobby on a bike to escort us so we had to fend for ourselves. Having managed to get to Seven Sisters and being on my own I thought I was safe. Think again Evo. I got sussed as I was getting off the down escalator leading to the platform. Having perfected the technique of running down an up escalator at Euston after the West Ham game I thought I'd try my hand in the opposite direction. I was getting quite good at all this now! I made good my escape on to the next tube and would get off at the next stop to return safely to Seven Sisters, completing my journey by tube to Euston. This ploy had worked when escaping the Bushwhackers so there was no reason why it shouldn't now. Luck was against me this night. The tube was chocker block with Spurs loons. The situation was made even worse by Tommy

Ticket the Ticket Inspector. Oh for fuck sake!

"Tickets please."

What the fuck was I gonna do? I didn't have a ticket - who the fuck ever did? I mean it wasn't the first thing on my mind when the Spurs hardcases were after my blood to go to the fuckin' ticket office and buy a bastard ticket!

"Tickets please!"

I'm afraid what I did next wasn't very PC but the term hardly existed then so I was okay. I pretended to be a deaf mute!

"Mmmm hhhhh nnnn."

I should have got a fuckin' Oscar for that as Tommy left me alone and even the Spurs boys didn't get on to it! After looking initially as if I'd fucked everything up it all turned out a treat. I arrived safely at Euston and joined in with all the songs and horror stories on the train home. There were plenty of lads who had taken a bit of a hiding but overall everybody was okay. I arrived back at Lime Street at about four o'clock a bit battered and bruised, tired, but extremely happy. This football club of mine could make me forget almost anything. I was certainly prepared to put up with anything for them!

Leicester didn't beat us 58-0 but did manage to scrape a goalless draw. That was enough to give us the title. The celebrations went on for ages with Shankly joining in the lap of honour. Scarves were being thrown to the players from all angles. One from the Kop landed on the pitch and was thrown on to the dirt of the running track by a bizzy. Shanks apparently went spare at Plod saying something like, "That's somebody's life and you're just trampling it in the dirt!" Shanks picked the scarf up and wrapped it round his neck. **HE MUST HAVE FELT AS PROUD AS US!** The young team he had started assembling some three years ago was maturing and with more youngsters, such as Phil Thompson, coming through the future looked **RED**. Time to conquer Europe!

I booked my flight to Moenchengladbach with Town's Travel well before even the first leg had been played. £30 including match ticket was a week's wages (with overtime!) but it would be worth it for my first European trip. Only snag was Mrs. Evo wasn't too happy about it seeing as by now, due to certain frictions within the Hughes/Etherington household, I was back living at my Ma's. Not an ideal situation I know but it was agreed that the only way we could get back together was by getting a place of our own. Litherland Council (or whatever it was called then) had singularly failed to find accommodation for us even though we had been on their housing list for two years and had the bonus points of little Stevie. The places we had been sent to look at by Flat Agencies and Housing Associations weren't even fit to put our fuckin' Cindy in and she'd been dead two years! So Mrs. Evo came up with the suggestion that we should move to SKELMERSDALE NEW TOWN. Skem was an overspill town and we actually knew a few people who had moved there. One in particular, Ev's mate and Conk's old flame, Lillian, had been there for a while and quite liked it. Okay, anything to get back together, we were on our way to Skem.

The first leg of the UEFA Cup Final kicked off in driving rain on an already sodden pitch. Pools of water were rapidly forming on the pitch turning the game into nothing more than a lottery. After half-an-hour of these shenanigans the Austrian referee, Mr. Linemayer had seen enough and abandoned the match. Shankly had also seen enough. Enough to know that Tosh, who had been left out of the starting line-up, should play in the replayed game the following night. Borussia were very weak in the air and the downpour had given Shanks the chance to exploit this. It was tough on the man left out, Brian Hall, but it was imperative that Tosh should play. Although not scoring Tosh was a constant thorn in the side of the Borussia defence. While the Germans were watching Tosh, Keegan scored twice, one of them a header and Larry Lloyd also netted, again from a header, to give us the massive cushion of a three-goal lead to take to Moenchengladbach.

Only three weeks after going on the housing list in Skem they came up with the goods for us. We went to look at a three-bedroomed house. This was our chance to get back together and seeing as I was missing little Stevie so much we jumped at it. There's always a snag. This one was that we would have to move in on May 21st - just two days before I was due to fly to West Germany for the second leg of the Final. Of course I had to put my wife and child first so there was no way I could go. It was with heavy heart I went to Town's to cancel the flight. They kept my five pounds deposit for my trouble - which was nice of them!

Borussia soon set about their task of wiping out our lead with two goals from their brilliant striker Jupp Heynkkes. Our defence was made of solid stuff however and held out for Emlyn Hughes to lift our first ever European trophy. I watched the highlights later on telly after having my nerves shot to pieces by the BBC radio commentary. I was sad that I wasn't where I should be - cheering the team on in Moenchengladbach, and seeing us win the trophy. I reckoned I deserved it after the traumatic season I'd had following the Reds away. All those scary trips would have been worth it to see us lift the trophy. Not that those trips weren't worth it. I wouldn't have changed one kecks-shitting minute of it! I was a Liverpudlian and these were things you just had to put up with then - it went with the territory. We'd be back in the big competition of the European Cup next season and we had visions of much more domestic and European glory ahead of us.